THE SIKHS AND GURDWARA SYSTEM

THE SIKHS AND GURDWARA SYSTEM

V. K. GUPTA

ANMOL PUBLICATIONS PVT. LTD.
NEW DELHI-110 002 (INDIA)

ANMOL PUBLICATIONS PVT. LTD.
4374/4B, Ansari Road, Daryaganj
New Delhi-110 002

The Sikhs and Gurdwara System

First Edition 1998
ISBN 81-261-0049-4

PRINTED IN INDIA

Published by J.L. Kumar for Anmol Publications Pvt. Ltd., New Delhi-110 002 and Printed at Mehra Offset Press, Delhi.

Contents

PREFACE

The present study is concerned with the Process of Institutionalisation of Sikh Shrines—with special reference to prominent Sikh Shrines in Delhi. The separate identity and entity of the Sikhs cannot be estimated without examining and analysing the institutional aspects of these shrines. A diverse set of circumstances spanning more than a decade have developed the shrines as an estate. As the study relates to an almost uncharatered area hence leaving aside some working hypotheses the study may, in strict sense, not claim well-defined hypotheses for testing the validity and reliability of data. To emphasise further the exercise attempts to highlight the process of crystallisation of norms and standardisation of behaviour patterns among the Sikhs through the instrumentality of these shrines.

The study covers fifty Sikhs Shrines in Delhi in which sixteen shrines (ten prominent historical shrines and six those surrendered by the disputes managing body of Sri Guru Singh Sabha) were managed by the Delhi Sikh Gurudwara Management Committee and rest thirty four by other separate body of Sri Guru Singh Sabha. The Chapter scheme of the study and the various aspects and dimensions thereof have been dealt with in the 'Introductory chapter".

First of all, it is my sacred duty to express my profound gratitude to my learned teacher and supervisor, Dr. J.K. Misra, Head of the Dept. of Sociology, Hindu College, Moradabad. In fact, I am deeply indebted to him for the pains he has taken to help me at all stages. I had regular sittings with him for weeks on end, and he never felt tired of going into the minutest details of the study and settling my endless doubts and questions. But for his guidance and involvement, it would not have been possible for me to cope with the problem and to conduct the study in a crucial and sensitive area as it is.

My grateful thanks are to Dr. R.N. Gupta, former Principal of Hindu College, Moradabad later Vice-Chancellor of Poorvanchal University, Jaunpur, for his always evincing keen interest in my work and his spontaneous inspiration. Also I owe my heartiest gratitude to my Principal, Dr. V.A. Jemini, for his cooperation and help. I am also grateful to my former teachers, Dr. S.D. Singh now Reader in Sociology, Kashi Vidyapeeth, Varanasi, and Dr. (Mrs.) S.P. Jain, Dept. of Sociology, Hindu College, Moradabad, who not only encouraged me but also gave valuable suggestions. Also I put on record my appreciation and compliments for my cousin, Dr. Satish Kumar, Principal, Govt. Degree College, Noida (Ghaziabad), for his ever boosting up my morale and kind encouragement. Further a deep appreciation is due to my colleagues and friends, Dr. P. Johari, Dr. S. Vashistha, Dr. A.K. Rastogi, Dr. B.R. Saran, Dr. M. Srivastava, Dr. (Smt.) M.B. Saxena and Dr. Girijesh Kumar, Dept. of Education, Hindu College, Moradabad, who were of help and cooperation to me in more than one way. I am equally grateful to Dr. S.P. Agarwal, Vice-Principal, Maharaja Agrasain Inter College, Moradabad, and Sri K.K. Gupta, Asst. Manager, Regional Office, P.N.B., Moradabad, for their great help in preparing the maps and graphs. I would also like to acknowledge the kind hospitality and homely atmosphere extended to me by my friend, Mr. Piyush Kumar Gupta serving in Vijaya Bank, Kamala Nagar, New Delhi, and my relative, Sri Rajendra Kumar, Pashchim Vihar, New Delhi, during my stay in Delhi for data collection.

My research work afforded me a chance to get into touch with a large number of Sikh scholars who offered their ungrudging suggestions and shared their encyclopaedic views with me. To mention a few I would like to offer my special thanks to Sri Khushwant Singh, 49E, Sujan Singh Park, New Delhi, Prof. Harbans Singh—Editor-in-Chief, Encyclopaedia of Sikhism, Punjabi University, Patiala, Dr. Mohinder Singh—Director, Guru Nanak Foundation, New Delhi, Dr. Jitinder Kaur, Khalsa College, Delhi University campus, Delhi and Prof. Devendra Swaroop, D.A.V. College, Delhi, who appreciated and valued my research work and did me good turn by thrashing out various issues and sorting out problems cropped up in the course of investigations.

I shall be failing in my duty if do not offer my compliments to the authorities of National Archives of India, Delhi Archives of Delhi Administration, Central Secretariat Library, I.I.T. Library and J.N.U. Library for providing access to their valuable reports and rare books. I am equally appreciative of and thankful to Sri H.O. Gupta, Librarian and Sri S.K. Agarwal, Library Asstt., Hindu College, Moradabad, for their providing me all the facilities and help given to me in going through this exercise. Besides this, I must register my profound obligation to all the subjects of enquiry, authorities of the shrines and their managing bodies, who bore with me in replying the typical questions and providing me with necessary facilities for collection of data.

There is much revered place in my heart for respect Smt. Vimal Mishra and sister Meera Mishra, who always encouraged me and never felt bothered during my endless sittings with my beloved Guru, Dr. J.K. Misra. Especially, I am beholden to my parents for their untold patience and unreserved inspiration. I am thankful to my wife Sushma who not only contributed her share in reading and checking the draft of my work but also was a constant source of inspiration and provided congenial environment by making me free from all family worries through the years of seemingly endless research activity and of writing.

V.K. Gupta

Glossary

Adi Granth, Previous name of Sri Guru Granth Saheb.

Akal, Deathless or Timeless one, the God.

Akal Takht, The throne of the Almighty; the highest religio-political seat of the Sikhs.

Akali, The name used for the orthodox Sikh devotees or a devotee of Akal.

Akhand Path, Non stop recitation of the Sri Guru Granth Saheb performing by a team of priests or granthis.

Akhara, Missionary sect of the Sikhs such as Udasis and Nirmalas.

Amrit, Nectar of Immortality.

Amritdhari, A baptised Sikh.

Ardas, The Sikh Mode of Worship.

Arti Sohilla, Night prayer of the Sikhs.

Asa-Di-Var, Morning prayer of the Sikhs.

Ashwari, The procession of Sri Guru Granth Saheb.

Baisakhi, The first day of Baisakh.

Banda, A human being, the name of the Bairagi disciple of Guru Gobind Singh and the military leader of the Sikhs.

Bani, Devotional poetry recorded in the Adi Granth.

Bhai, A title of sanctity and respectability among the Sikhs.

Bhakta, A devotee of God.

Bhakti, Belief in and adoration of a personal God.

Charat, Offering.

Chela, A disciple.

Dal Khalsa, The united army of the Khalsa.

Darbar, It is generally applied to the Court of the Guru.

Dera, A troop of Sikh army or a camp of Sikh fundamentalists.

Dharamsala, Previous name of Sikh historical prominent place of worship or Gurdwara.

Dharam Prachar, Propagation of religion.

Fateh, Victory or success.

Giani, A reputed Sikh scholar.

Golak, A secret receptor for money offerings.

Granth, The Sikh scripture.

Granthi, Reciter of the Holy Granth and the functionary incharge of a Sikh shrine.

Gurbani, The sacred hymns of the Sikh scriptures.

Gurgaddi, Succession to the spiritual throne of the Sikhs.

Gurmatta, A decision made by a representative assembly of the Sikhs.

Gurmukh, A pious man.

Gurmukhi, The script used for writing Punjabi.

Gurpurab, A Sikh festival celebrated on the birth or death day of a Guru.

Guru, A religious teacher.

Gurdwara, Guru's abode or a Sikh Temple.

Sri Guru Granth Saheb, The Bible of the Sikhs.

Guru-Ka-Langer, Free mass meal attached to the Gurdwaras.

Hari mandir, The Central shrine in Amritsar commonly known as Golden Temple.

Japji, The opening part of the Sri Guru Granth Saheb.

Jatha, A group of volunteers.

Jathedar, Leader of a group. Now this title designates a leader or a Akali Dal.

Kirtan, Singing of hymns from Sri Guru Granth Saheb.

Kiwar, Entrance doors of the Shrine.

Mahant, Head of a religious centre.
Manji, Head man or holding a rank of authority.
Masnad, An agent of the Sikh Guru.
Misal, A Sikh Sardar having troop.
Morcha, Agitation.
Nam, The divine name.
Nam-Semran, Repeating the divine Name of God.
Nihang, One who is free from anxiety and care.
Nirankar, Without form.
Pahul, The rite of Sikh Baptism.
Panj KAKKE, Five eternal symbols of the Khalsa or five K's (Kesh, Kachha, Kangha, Kirpan and Kara).
Panj Pyaras, The beloved five: the original Khalsa members.
Panth, A sect of religious beliefs and practices.
Patit, Lapsed Sikh.
Prasad, Gift received by devotee at Worship.
Sabad, Word from Sri Guru Granth Saheb.
Sangat, Religious congregation.
Sarbat Khalsa, The entire Khalsa Community.
Sevadar, A gurdwara attendant.
Singh, The title assumed by all male members of the Khalsa.
Takht, A seat of religio-spiritual authority.
Udasis, An order of ascetics; also a long tour.
Waheguru, Wonderful Lord.

1

Introductory

Of late traditional values are losing ground and secular values are taking hold of social life and social institutions buttressing factional and sectarian tendency. Hence it may directly or indirectly be the consequence of the modern scientific advancement that has begun to militate against the traditional character of our ethos. Though in a sense this phenomenon may be seen assuming large proportion in the case of Sikh shrines it appears to be in a low profile and is not easily observable. It raises a very pertinent question whether the Sikh shrines have landed in the process of institutionalisation, and are getting crystallised in their orientation and functioning under the influence of those who matter in managing the religious affairs. This vital question needs to be answered empirically in its entirety. The main objective of this attempt is to draw a comprehensive picture of the Sikh shrines (Gurdwaras) of Delhi with special reference to prominent Sikh shrines in the light of institutionalisation in the present situation.

We may look-upon 'The Process of Institutionalisation' as a crystallisation of different types of norms, organisation and framework, directing and controlling the processes of exchange of different commodities. It is truism that the process of institutionalisation is not random, fixed or unchanging. As a matter of course this process, by and large, takes off from several fixed starting points (which are given in the nature of the major institutional spheres and their structural core characteristics) and from the concrete organisational structure in the preceding situations implying thereby that they create the conditions for their own change.[1]

To elaborate, the institutionalisation of concrete form and pattern entails the development of new type of major institutional commodities and the crystallisation of varied norms and rate of exchange. As a natural corollary to it this process engenders organisational and behavioural patterns designed to cherishing and achieving certain goals and to regulate a flow of activities and resources.[2] However, it merits to be mentioned here that we hardly know any system wherein this process has equally influenced all the areas of social life and the groups involved in it.

The preceding paragraphs indicate that the institutionalisation of any social system (Whether social, economic religious, political, familial, cultural or stratification) means the setting up of certain values, sanctions and organisations that regulate access to different positions and establish certain norms of exchange.[3] According to H.M. Johnson, a social norm is said to be institutionalised in a particular social system when three conditions are met: first, a large number of the members of the social system accept the norm. Second, many of those who accept the norm take it seriously or they internalised it and last, the members of the system are expected to be guided by the sanctioned norm in appropriate circumstances.[4]

To elaborate the argument further the researcher may draw-upon the exposition and explanation of this concept as furnished by Parsons. The concept of institutionalisation is crucial to Parsons' conceptualisation of the system. Indeed, he regards institutionalisation as the fundamental integrative mechanism of social system. It is viewed both as a process and a structure. Institutionalisation builds up and maintains social structure. It also refers to stabilised patterns of interaction which are normatively regulated by the cultural system. It involves both structuralisation of value-orientations in the social system and the internalisation of value systems in the individual personality. The actor's internalisation of the cultural values and beliefs is the primary basis of institutionalisation.[5]

With no pretension of any scholarly attempt or in-depth analysis the researcher with the above theoretical formulations about the problem may now to come to the focus of the present study—The Process of Institutionalisation of Sikh Shrines. Here we are mainly concerned with the religious conservatism, doctrinnaire principles, dogmatic beliefs and the fundamental values for whose perpetuation, preservation and persistance the Sikh shrines are out to wage a grim and relentless fight. It may remind us of a long standing demand of the Sikhs to bind all the historic shrines in the country under one system of management to ensure uniformity of religious practices, goals and activities in all the religious places of the Sikhs. This process of institutionalisation is gradually and quietly creeping into the Sikh shrines who are using it as a mechanism and means for self-preservation, identity and separate entity. The ongoing institutionalisation of Sikh shrines is consciously and unconsciously creating a climate conducive to a collective mobilisation of the Sikhs and in-gathering of the faithful and in emerging as a force to reckon with in the present times. This process finds expression in their clamouring for a codification of personal law, adhering to their rites and ceremonies, rules of conducts, beliefs and practices and usages and procedures. It may add upto the Sikhs conservatism and fundamentalism. This process is reflecting among the Sikhs in their showing rigidity for a separate symbol, religion, separate pradhan (head of the state) and purity of faith threatening to culminate in demand for separate state. In this process of institutionalisation, the shrines are being used to revive the fundamental tenets, seminal beliefs, cultural practices hoping thereby that it will bring self-preservation and identity of the religion.

Added further institutionalisation may be taken as 'Standardisation of behaviour patterns and behavioural expectations in a collectivity.[6] It is in this parlance that there is growing evidence that the Sikh leaders and priests (both are the representative of the Sikh community), through their seats of power, are pulling their weight behind the uniformity of behaviour patterns, expectations and beliefs and practices. And probably it is this global urge which is becoming a rallying point among the Sikhs at home and abroad. Consequently now we find an upsurge brewing in their ranks for a distinct religio-cultural identity. It may be in the fitness of things to say that the present 'Dharamyudh' launched by the Sikh shrines is probably meant for crystallising and standardising their maintaining individuality of their religion. Efforts are a-foot for a uniform practicising of codes of conduct as enshrined in the 'Sri Guru Granth Saheb' (The Bible of the Sikhs) and the 'Khalsa' (initiated Sikh brotherhood).

Now to shift attention to the concept and institution Gurdwaras (Sikh Shrines) to the Sikhs, shrines have been more than mere places of worship. At different periods of Sikh history, the shrines have served a variety of functions. In the Sikh psyche, a shrine is associated with long history of bitter struggle and joyous victories of the Sikh against external and internal forces. The shrine or Gurdwara is also an inseparable part of the day to day social, charitable and religious life of the Sikhs both as individual and as a community. The Sikh community thinks of shrines as embodiments of goodness, morality, charity and collective identity.

The institution of Gurdwara has, at all stages, been central to the development of the Sikh's culture. These shrines or Gurdwaras are considered to be to Schools for the students, Centres of spiritual knowledge for the believers, Hospitals for the sick, Places of food for the hungry, Forts of security for the women folk and Inns for the travellers.[7] These shrines in their elementary form had begun to be set up during the life time of Guru Nanak (first Prophet and originator of the faith). Under exhortations of the Guru these places had emerged as a nuclei of social and religious life of the Sikhs.[8]

The institution of Gurdwara or Sikh Shrine is as old as Sikh faith.[9] It has been observed in the course of the study of the literature that the term 'Gurdwara' is now commonly used for a Sikh place of worship. As far as the Sikh texts are concerned 'the term Gurdwara' appears in the hymns even of the founder of the faith (Guru Nanak from 1469 to 1539 AD), as also in those of the third (Guru Ram Das) and the fifth Guru (Arjan Dev Ji), in the sense of 'Guru's Portal. [10] In early Sikhism the term Gurdwara was not in the sense in which it is used today. The Sikh literatures speak that a Sikh place of worship was called Dharamsal or Dharamsala.[11]

Basically the institution of Dharamsala was started by Guru Nanak with the aim of combating religio-cultural and ethnic diversities and disparities. This institution was the meeting place and later it was established by Guru Nanak in fifteenth century for preaching the basic tenets of his faith or meeting place for discussion of the faith.[12] Unlike the Hindu temple, it was not confined to the realm of religious worship and practices, it was and continues to be a socio-religious ensemble providing not only for religious and moral instructions but also food and shelter for needy.[13]

With the passage of time, these institutions of Dharamsalas began to be called Gurdwaras[14] and further developed into the centres of education, orphanages, and as resting places for travellers. It is in such Gurdwaras that religious congregations (Sangat) were socialised into the egalitarian tenets of Sikhism urging them to emancipate themselves from the clutches of caste prejudices and other social inequalities and from irrational beliefs and superstitions.[15] The essential feature of these shrines was the Guru-ka-Langar (free community kitchen). Free Prasad and meals were provided to the assembly (religious congregation) sitting in rows (Pangat) in defiance of the prevailing commensal taboos. Thus, Sikhism introduced a new social system within the larger society and offered an alternative to the existing stratification of caste and community.

The Sikh shrines had earned a recognition during the pontificate of the first four Gurus, particularly when these shrines began to be used as headquarters of the revenue divisions of the Panth. With the establishment of Harimandir (now known as Golden Temple), at Amritsar, particularly after the Sri Guru Granth Saheb was placed in it, the significance of these shrines increased enormously. Afterwards, these places began to be recognised by the Sikhs as a virtual abode of their Guru in the scriptural form.[16]

During Guru Gobind Singh's period (Tenth and Last Prophet of the Sikh Panth), 1666-1708 A.D., and until the execution of his stormy and dreaded petrel Banda Singh Bahadur (1716 A.D.), the management of the shrines was under the control of the initiated Sikhs. But following the period of persecution of Banda Singh Bahadur, the management of the shrines had passed into the hands of the Udasis, followers of a sect established by Baba Sri Chand, eldest son of Guru Nanak. They were preachers of Guru Nanak and the Gurus but dressed in a style distinctively different from the initiated Sikhs. These members of Udasi sect were highly respected by the Sikh masses for their saintly disposition.[17] They were allowed almost a free-hand in the management of the shrines under their control and the nomination of their successors. But in the course of time they began to be addressed as Mahants (head or manager of the sect or akhara).[18] The majority of the Sikhs opposed it because the Mahants of this sect refused to be called themselves as Sikhs. Instead they led a life of luxury and indulged in the misuse of the shrine's fund. This provoked the Akalis (immortals) to launch the Sikh agitation which received the blessings and support from Mahatma Gandhi and Jawahar Lal Nehru who were spearheading the freedom movement. As a result of this the British Government of Punjab had passed the Sikh Gurdwaras and Shrines Act on 8th July, 1925, handing over the control of 300 historic Sikh shrines in the Punjab to Shiromani Gurdwara Prabandhak Committee (S.G.P.C.) with then an income of over 20 lakhs of rupees a year. Since then the affairs of these shrines were being managed and guided by this committee.

As the provisions of the Sikh Gurdwaras and Shrines Act, 1925 was not applicable to the Sikh shrines outside the Punjab. The Historical Sikh Shrines in Delhi were also restored from the clutches of the Mahants by the movement of Singh Sabha and surrendered to the local committee, which was nominated by the local Sikh Sangats. This committee functioned for about a decade from 1925 till 1935, without any specified rules and regulations.[19] The rules and regulations for the management of the Historical Sikh Shrines of Delhi were framed in 1936 with the name Delhi Gurdwara Prabandhak Committee D.G.P.C. It became registered under the Societies Regulation Act No. XXI of 1850.[20] At present the name of this committee has been changed as Delhi Sikh Gurdwara Management Committee (D.S.G.M.C.).

At present there are 236 Sikh shrines are functioning in Delhi which 16 Sikh Shrines are managed by the Delhi Sikh Gurdwara Management Committee and remaining 220 Sikh shrines are managed by the Local and separate organisation of the Sri Guru Singh Sabha (SGSS).

Thus, it is not difficult to understand that the Sikh shrines provided a great inspiration and left deeper impact on the mind of Sikh Community as well as Indian mind. They formulated and perpetuated their own codes of conduct, beliefs and practices and usages and procedures called for its adherence strictly. These shrines also provided a vital contribution to the religio-cultural history of India. In the mind of the Sikhs, the question of purification and freedom of the shrines has always been associated with their national destiny and no sacrifice was considered too great to make for bringing them under the control of the Panth.

It has been keenly observed in the course of the present study that the Sikh shrines have in modern times taken up active social work in the field of education, health and welfare etc. These later developments have led them to have their own philosophy of living, rituals, ideals, institutions, initiation recruitment, authority, obedience, hierarchy of power and succession etc. This organisational form has given rise to a socio-economic base of these shrines for the propagation and promotion of their religion. Now, they have come to own vast resources and to be reckoned as a great force. And as such there was reason to understand their proper working and harnessing of resources was of far-reaching implications to our society as a whole. Their new role-orientations and new role-expectations and all what they entail in contemporary times constitute a mater of interest to a student of Sociology to make an objective and a scientific study of the process of Institutionalisation of Sikh Shrines in Delhi.

Now to deal with this specific nature of the study the investigator makes an apology that owing to the wide-range and most complex nature of the problem, the scope of the study has been restricted to the Delhi Sikh Shrines. Delhi has a long tradition of Sikh shrines with their historical moorings. To be specific, the study of Sikh shrines in the context of institutionalisation has mainly entered into the plan of the study.

A mention may be made here that in the empirical investigations the term 'Sikh Shrines' has embodied the historical Sikh shrines and the shrines of Sri Guru Singh Sabha as well. The historical Sikh shrines are directly associated with the life and martyrdom of Sikh Gurus and managed by the Delhi Sikh Gurdwara Management Committee, an organised and representative body of the Sikhs of Delhi. But the shrines of Sri Guru Singh Sabha were developed later to fulfil the religious, sectarian and congregational demand of the followers of the faith who were settled in far-flung areas of Delhi after the partition of the country. Now these shrines are managed separately by an independent body of Sri Guru Singh Sabha.

Relevance of the Study

Now to say a word about the relevance of the present study, it may be said that the institutionalisation of the Sikh shrines is little-studied from sociological point of view. Hence, this constitute almost an unexplored field which needs to be investigated to arrive at empirically established facts. This present spirit of scientific investigation combined with material civilisation of today demands a proper analysis and scientific assessment of these shrines. Hence, the investigator thought it appropriate to study the problem in detail from historical and empirical point of view. The historical perspective of the study contributed to the Sikh shrines as they were in the past and an empirical perspective of the study further contributed to explore the present existence with a varying degree of change in the structure of shrines from a scientific point of view. This provided a theoretical framework and logic for choosing the present problem for study for empirical validation of the above propositions and formulations.

Considering from the sociological stand point the present analysis aims to study the following aspects:

> First aspect deals with the structural-functional content of the Sikh shrines foiy is focussed at analysing the socio-economic bases of the Sikh shrines—the age, initiation, caste, education, term and role-expectations of the head priests and sources of income and items of expend'ture of the shrines.
>
> Thirdly, an attempt is made to know the mode of

management of the Sikh shrines and perceptions of the Head priests towards the members and organisations of the other sect in light of the socio-cultural matrics.

Fourthly, it endeavours to find out the process of crystallisation of norms and standardisation of behaviour patterns with reference to the Sikh shrines.

Fifthly, an effort has been made to analyse the pace of changes which are taking place into the shrines due to the orthogenetic and hetrogenetic factors.

Lastly, an analysis concentrates on knowing the dysfunctional trends which have crept in their administration.

It may also be in the fitness of things to add that owing to the descriptive and explorative nature of the study no well defined hypothesis has been formulated to test its validity. However, this study may provide useful material for further investigation and the formulation of more reasonable and more consistent hypotheses suited for empirical testing in undertaking later research in this vast field. However efforts have been made to establish relationship between historical and social factors giving rise to new and revealing development in their organisation and function.

Assumptions of the Study

First and one of the main assumption guiding and stimulating the present study was that the Sikh shrines—an integral part of the Sikhs as well as the Indian society—cannot remain neutral and indifferent to heterogeneous influences. They are capable of initiating and directing changes in their institutionalised patterns which have been stabilised into their structures.

In the context of second major assumption the researcher at the outset would like to point out that the sample of the study was to-layered. The collective data were analysed first in the category of historical prominent Sikh shrines and secondly in that of those shrines governed by the Delhi Sikh Gurdwara Management Committee (D.S.G.M.C.), a local affiliate to the Sri Guru Singh Sabha (S.G.S.S.). These categories were reported to have existent in other noted places of Sikh shrines. Therefore, our assumption has been that the major findings and conclusions of the present study will apply in a greater or lesser degree to the Sikh shrines existing in other places and thus falling outside the scope of our study.

To come to the third assumption it may be pointed out that the methodology and the mode of data collection and analysis as adopted in the present study will be more or less applicable to the study of the Sikh shrines at large and falling beyond the purview of the present enquiry.

Finally, it may be said that howsoever particularistic the present study may be, attention was focused on the on-going process of institutionalisation of the general Sikh shrines or in other words the structuralisation and crystallisation of value-patterns and norms and also their functional aspects of the shrines, the role they played for the community, the relationship they maintained with other institutions, groups and communities and to the socio-cultural milieu which exerted an influence over the centuries.

Plan of the Report

This work has been divided into nine Chapters for a systematic and scientific analysis of the problem.

The brief summary, relevance and assumptions of the study have been discussed in the first Chapter.

The second Chapter describes what tools and techniques for collection of data have been used.

An attempt is made to analyse how the Sikhism and the

Sikh shrines came into existence in the third Chapter.

The Chapter fourth illustrates the 'Social setting of the Study,' while the Chapter fifth describes the 'Socio-economic Structure of Sikh Shrines'.

The Chapter sixth evaluates the 'Mode of Management and Working of the Sikh Shrines.' The analysis of the 'Religio-cultural Beliefs and Practices' of Sikh Shrines is discussed in the Chapter seventh. Eighth Chapter is devoted to 'The Changing Patterns of Values of the Sikh Shrines.'

The findings and generalisations of the present investigation have been drawn up in the concluding ninth chapter.

REFERENCES

1. *International Encyclopedia of Social Sciences,* Macmillan Company, New York, Vol. 14, p. 414.
2. *Ibid,* p. 416.
3. *Op. cit.,* pp. 416-417.
4. Johnson H.M., *Sociology—A Systematic Introduction,* pp. 19-20.
5. (i) Abraham, M.F.: *Modern Sociological Theory,* p. 55; also,
   (ii) Parsons, T.: *The Social System,* p. 52; and also,
   (iii) Parsons, T. and Shils, Edward (eds.): *Towards General Theory of Action,* p. 150.
6. H.F. Reading, (ed.): *A Dictionary of Social Sciences,* First edition, *1977.*
7. Singh Kahan of Nabha: *Guru Shabd Ratnakar Mahankosh,* pp.16-17.
8. Dr. Singh Gobinder, *Religion and Politics in the Punjab,* p. 54.
9. Dr. Kaur Jitinder: *The Politics of the Sikhs,* National Book Organisation, New Delhi, 1986, p. 24.
10. Personal Information supplied by Prof. Harbans Singh, Editor in-chief Encyclopaedia of Sikhism, P.U., Patiala (Sept. 14, 1987)
11. (i) Dr. Singh Mohinder: *The Akali Movement,* pp. 1-2; and also
    (ii) Cole, W.O. and Sambhi, P.S.: *The Sikhs—Their Religious Beliefs and Practices,* p. 59; also
    (iii) Singh, Harbans, *The Heritage of the Sikhs,* p. 19; also

(iv) Mukherjee, P.N., *Punjab in Indian Politics—Issues and Trends*, p. 76; also

(v) Singh, Jagjit, *The Sikh Revolution*, pp. 108-109; and also

(vi) Singh, Khushwant: *The History of the Sikhs*, Vol. 2, pp. 193-194.

12. Singh, Mohinder, *op. cit.*, p. 23.
13. Mukherjee, P.N., *op. cit.*, p. 73.
14. In the time of sixth Guru, Hargobind Singh (1595-1694 A.D.) the Dharamsalas began to be called Gurdwaras. This information was supplied by Prof. Harbans Singh, renowned Sikh historian and the Editor-in-cheif, *Encyclopaedia of Sikhism*, Punjabi University, Patiala.
15. Mukherjee, P.N., *op. cit.*, p. 73.
16. Singh, Govinder, *op. cit.*, pp. 54-55.
17. Kapoor, Rajiv, A. *Sikh Separatism—The Politics of the Faith*, p. 43.
18. (i) Singh, Khushwant, *op. cit.*, p. 193; also

    (ii) Kapoor, Rajiv A., *op. cit.*, pp. 43-44; and also

    (iii) Singh, Teja, *The Gurdwara Reform Movement and the Sikh Awakening*, pp. 13-14.
19. Singh, Mohinder; *Guru Tegh Bahadur—Background and the Supreme Sacrifice*, Edited by Gurbachan Singh Talib, p. 70.
20. The Rules and Regulations of Delhi Gurdwara Prabandhak Committee, Delhi, 1936.

2

Research Design and Methodology

With the introduction of the problem, already discussed in Chapter first, now we may devote our attention to the research design and methodology.

A Sikh temple or shrine is popularly known as a Gurdwara, i.e. the 'house of God' or the 'house of Guru', where Guru dwells. Its most essential feature is the presence of the Guru. A Sikh Shrine or Gurdwara is built with the main concern for congregational worship. A group of devotees, small or large, living anywhere would generally have a shrine for them to participate collectively in religious or even social purposes. This is how these religious institutions continued to grow and thus a large number of beautiful and imposing shrines came into existence with a capacity of accommodating hundreds of devotees in the course of time.

It is learnt from an overview of the Sikh scriptures and other literature that a Sikh place of worship was called 'Dharamsal' and it was started by Guru Nanak in the fifteenth century. In fact, the Dharamsal was derived from Dharamsala in Sanskrit meaning a court of justice or tribunal. Basically, it was the meeting place where the followers of the particular faith could meet together and spread his message to others. With the passage of time, these Dharamsals developed into the centres of education and higher learning and shelters for the poors and needy. There was a huge contribution of such dharamsalas to remove the caste barriers and other social inequalities. It was made a strict rule in the Langar (the free community kitchen) of Guru Nanak, that all who came to take the food in the Langar, whether Hindu or Musalmaan, must sit in a line and eat together, the whole idea behind it was to narrow-down the sharp distinction and striking disparities among the followers of the faith.

It is patent fact of Sikh history that the Dharamsalas eventually became the gurdwaras, literally, the Guru's door or a house. The term Gurdwara came into general use after the Sikh Scripture, *Sri Guru Granth Saheb*, was proclaimed as Guru by the Tenth Master, Sri Guru Gobind Singh.

During the early eighteenth century and after the death of Guru Gobind Singh in 1708 A.D., the management of the Sikh shrines had passed into the hands of the Udasis. But in due course of time, these Udasis began to be addressed as Mahants. They became the owners of the Gurdwara assets and adopted an attitude of indifference towards the Sikh congregations. The demand for the restoration of their freedom of religious association and their right of control over the places of worship became the focal points for the Sikhs. A socio-religious awakening about the reformation of the shrines was brought out by the Singh Sabha Movement. The members of this Movement formed an Akali Party and militant actions were started by them. In a short span of five years (1920-25), the Akalis had succeeded to reform the religious places from the hands of Mahants. Thus, after these shrines were rested from the Mahants an attempt was made to formulate a progressive religious programme by the Sikhs.

Almost all the Historical Sikh Shrines in Punjab are managed by the S.G.P.C. and the shrines of remaining part of the country were being managed by the local management committees. The numerical base of the Sikh shrines expanded considerably with the assimilation of martial tradition in

Sikhism. The historical Sikh Shrines throughout the country and abroad were constructed at places visited by the Sikh Gurus, now these began to be erected in the memory of the Sikh Martyrs too.

With this background information the major focus of this study is on 'The Process of Institutionalisation of Sikh Shrines in Delhi'—with special reference to prominent Sikh Shrines. The present study is concerned with the religious fundamentalism, dogmatic beliefs and fundamental values for whose preservation and persistence the Sikh shrines are showing rigidity. Nowadays the Sikh shrines were being used as a mechanism and means for self-preservation and separate identity. It should be remembered here that there a long standing demand of the Sikhs was being emerged gradually to bind all the historic Sikh shrines in the country under one system of management so that uniform religious practices are followed in all the religious places of the Sikhs. And probably it is this global urge which has made a rallying point among the Sikhs in the country and abroad. It may be in the fitness of things to say that the present 'Dharamyudh' launched by the Sikh shrines is probably meant for cystallising and standardising their maintaining separate identity of the religious symbols.

From the very early times, the Sikh shrines played a vital role to remove the caste prejudices and other social inequalities and formed an egalitarian variety of norms and values. These later developments have led them to have their own vast resources for the propagation and promotion of the faith and now they came to be reckoned as a cementing force of the Sikh Society. And as such there was an essential need to understand their proper working and harnessing of resources in the orbit of the process of institutionalisation rocking these shrines.

The scientific investigation of the Sikh shrines began to be made only recently particularly after the Punjab problem was emerged. During this period and before a good deal of emphasis was laid on the study of Sikh shrines with a view to explore the dynamics of the Sikh society. Consequently a number of studies have appeared in this field over the past quarter of a century or so. Many Indian and western scholars had worded on the different aspects of the Sikh shrines. But the existing literature provide an only idea of historical perspective. No empirical attempt has been made so far to analyse the institutional aspect of the Sikh shrines. In an attempt to survey the literature in terms of orientation and approach to the problem we may classify it into the following works:

A pioneer attempt on the Sikh shrines was formulated by Prof. Teja Singh[1] in 1925. In this adventurous attempt, an early management of the Sikh shrines was discussed.

Another identical study has been made by Sri Sohan Singh Josh[2] in 1972 to project the political aspects of the shrine's movement alongwith its religious achievements. It was a successful attempt.

In India and abroad, studies of this kind have been made in the historical perspective particularly in the context of the national movement in this country. The similar study with slightly wider perspective and context is that of Prof. Ruchi Ram Sahani.[3] It provides a valuable insight into the notable role played by the Sikh shrines to organise the consciousness among the Sikhs.

Dr. Mohinder Singh's 'The Akali Movement'[4] is another scholarly inquiry which may be placed in this category. In fact it is an objective inquiry and milestone in the Sikh history. In this context, it surveys the importance of Akalis in reviving the Sikh church.

Due to the limitations of space a mere mention may be made of some other scholars and authors whose works have received greater attention in this area. They are: G.R. Sethi (1927)[5], Sangat Singh (1972)[6], J.B. Bali[7], Dr. Jitinder Kaur (1986)[8], and Dr. Gobinder Singh (1987)[9].

Our survey here shows that the institutionalisation of the Sikh shrines is a little studies field and, therefore, a need was felt to fill this gap by undertaking an appropriate micro-level study in the context of actual institutionalisation overtaking these shrines. There is a relatively a greater scope for such scientific probes into this rather potential but largely neglected area. More specifically, our study remains to the Delhi based Sikh shrines which have a long history and traditions creating curiosity for a study like the present one. This inquiry is largely descriptive-cum-exploratory. Considering the present portends and what is blowing in the wind as a straw it can very well be predicted that the present study will gain further relevance in the wake of the present crisis and conflict situations affecting these time honoured and hoary shrines and their institutional arrangements.

Objectives of the Study

In the light of the above discussion the study is focused at analysing the process of institutionalisation of the Sikh shrines. To be specific it undertakes to investigate and answer the following questions:

(i) To trace historically the growth of Sikhism and of Sikh shrines in India and its later developments.

(ii) To find out their religious system, affiliation, mode of maintenance, the religious hierarchy, mode of succession, action patterns and statuses and roles of the head priests.

(iii) It was also intended here to gather relevant details from the members of the management committee who were officially and directly involved in the working of these shrines.

(iv) To analyse the process of change in the elements of

traditions of the Sikh shrines.

(v) To examine the process of crystallisation of norms and organisation and of standardisation of behaviour patterns.

(vi) To know the processes, problems and prospects of variability of these shrines in the total ambit of their process of institutionalisation.

(vii) To explore the endogenous and exogenous factors for the emerging fundamentalism.

(viii) To explore the analyse the causes and consequences of the ongoing institutionalisation of the shrines from the community and national perspective.

(ix) To probe their changing patterns of values, goal-orientations and rab-expectations in changed situations.

(x) To know what disorganisational and dysfunctional trends have crept in their administration.

(xi) To evaluate their future and to suggest remedies to suggest remedies to restore the public confidence in and enthusiasm about them.

Hypotheses

At the outset it may be pointed out that the present study is, by and large, explorative and descriptive. Hence, no well defined or specific hypothesis has been formulated to test its validity or to support it to any rigorous cause-effect relationship. However, some specific hypotheses were formulated to establish the relationship between historical and social factors responsible for the unique developments in the shrines resulting from the process of institutionalisations.

To mention a few are:

(i) The Sikh shrines are striving for uniformity of religious beliefs and practices.

(ii) There is insistence on standardisation of behaviour

patterns and conformability to rigid rules of conduct.

(iii) These shrines are working for their cultural identity and separate entity with their going over-zealous ignoring sacrilege and desecration of their religious places.

(iv) The process of balkanisation, polarisation and crystallisation of forces marked by the regeneration and revival of the fundamental values is touching a new heigh.

(v) The role and functioning of these shrines is tradition-oriented making their credibility and respectability questionable in the modern context.

(vi) There is structural rigidity manifesting itself in the crystallisation of norms and standardisation of behaviour patterns.

(vii) These hoary shrines tend to become oblivious of their time-honoured roles and functions.

(viii) The priestly roles are also in drift.

(ix) Mutual discord and dissensions out-paced their commitment and loyalty towards the shrines.

(x) Controversy and criticism apart-these shrines still justify their existence and relevance.

Method

(i) Universe of the Study

Due to the wide-ranging and extensive nature of the problem the present study was restricted to Delhi Sikh shrines. And hence, the present study was conducted about the Sikh shrines located in proper Delhi.

After Punjab, the Delhi Territory has a long tradition of the shrines with historical moorings. From the very beginning, Delhi remained the powerful centre of cultural transmission. Consequently, almost all the Sikh prophets visited Delhi and passed their life to teach and preach their message to the suffering humanity and left strong impressions on Indian

Historical Sikh Shrines in Delhi

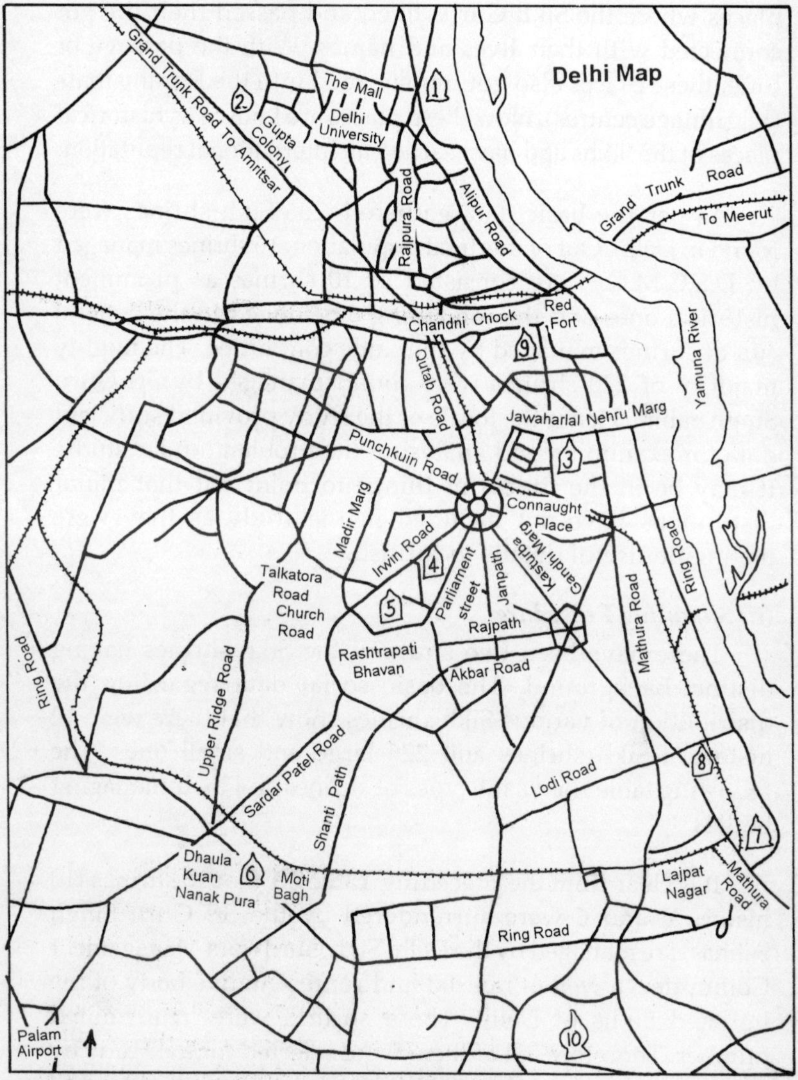

1. Gurdwara Majnu - Ka - Tila
2. Gurdwara Nanak Piao
3. Gurdwara Mata Sundri
4. Gurdwara Bangla Sahib
5. Gurdwara Rakab Ganj
6. Gurdwara Moti Bagh
7. Gurdwara Bala Sahib
8. Gurdwara Dam Dama Sahib
9. Gurdwara Sis Ganj
10. Gurdwara Banda Singh Bahadur

mind as well as the mind off the people of Delhi. Those very places where the Sikh Gurus lived and passed their life got connected with their lives and names. With the passage of time, these places also got transformed into the Karamsthals (Pilgrimage centres). Now these places are known as historical places of the Sikhs and have earned an international reputation.

As per the basic data gathered, 236 Sikh shrines were found in Delhi. Out of this total population, 16 shrines managed by D.S.G.M.C. were consisted of 10 shrines as prominent historical ones and the remaining 6 belonged to the general run of shrines managed by the same committee. The mighty majority of 220 shrines were found managed by Sri Guru Singh Sabha. Hence the locale of the study provided sufficient data for examining and analysing the problem under study. It may be in the fitness of things to point out that minor institutions have not included in the study as they were having no useful details to furnish.

(ii) Sampling Procedure

There have been two strata of the Sikh shrines having distinct background. The basic social data regarding the distribution of various Sikh shrines show that there were 10 historical Sikh shrines and 226 large and small ones. The following table shows the types of shrines and their managing bodies.

It is clear from the preceding Table 2.1 that 16 shrines (10 historical and 6 were surrendered by the Sri Guru Singh Sabhas) are managed by the Delhi Sikh Gurdwara Management Committee, a well organised and representative body of the initiated Sikhs of Delhi. These shrines were in a limited number. Therefore, all of them were selected for the study by census method. Further, 220 Sikh shrines large and small ones are managed by the separate and colonywise managing body of Sri Guru Singh Sabha. The sample selected for the study contained 50 Sikh shrines who may be representative of the whole universe. The break-up is as below:

TABLE 2.1

Types of Sikh Shrines in Delhi and Their Managing Bodies

The name of Managing Body of the Shrine	*Nature of the Shrines at all over Delhi*			
	Historical	*Surrendered by Sri Guru Singh Sabha*	*Colonywise independent Shrines*	*Total*
1. Delhi Sikh Gurdwara Management Committee	10	6	—	16
2. Sri Guru Singh Sabha	—	—	220	220
Total	10	6	220	236

TABLE 2.2

Sample Selected

Nature of the Shrines	*Their Managing bodies*	*Total No. of the shrines*	*Sample Selected*	*Percentage*
1. Historical Shrines	Delhi Sikh Gurdwara Management Committee	10	10	
2. The shrines which were surrendered by the Sri Guru Singh Sabha (who could not manage them)	-do-	6	6	6.8%
3. The shrines of Sri Guru Singh Sabha	Sri Guru Singh Sabha (Colony wise separately)	220	34	14.4%
Total		236	50	21.2%

It is evident from the Table 2.2 that the large supply of the shrines, 220 belonging to Sri Guru Singh Sabha when weighted against the available time and energy it was not found possible to include all the 220 shrines in the present study. Hence, 36 shrines were selected on the basis of stratified proportional random sample.

The actual units for investigation were selected at regular interval from a series of the shrines of Sri Guru Singh Sabha arranged in a systematic order. Thus from among 220 Sikh shrines every sixth item was selected. Thereby 34 shrines were picked out for the purpose of analysis and interpretation. Minor shrines ranging between 12 to 16 were leftout of account for their having no sufficient and worthwhile details to furnish. Hence the researcher excluded them from the sample without any detriment to the study. Thus, in total 50 cases were selected to draw relevant conclusions. This sample of 50 cases out of total supply of 236 shrines represented, approximately, 21 per cent sample which was considered adequate and properly represented to supply valid informations and to produce reliable results.

Explorations and observations were made to examine and analyse the process of institutionalisation by analysing and generalising the findings of these 50 shrines making the sample. In an attempt to make a probe into the process of institutionalisation the researcher interviewed and administered the schedule to 50 Head priests (one each from the shrines of the sample for discovering internal functioning of the shrine) and further 50 respondents were also administered the schedule who figured either as president and secretary on the managing body of each shrine (discovering external functioning). Thus the total number of subject stood at 100.

(iii) Tools and Techniques of Investigation

(A) Sources of Information

The data were gathered mainly by primary and secondary sources. Data from primary sources were collected by semi-participant observation, personal interviews, conference and meetings with professional persons having intimate knowledge and insight, correspondence from Sikh historians, interview schedule and other devices. The data from secondary sources were collected by library sources, archaeological sources, journals, official and unofficial statistics, newspaper accounts, magazines, census publications and reports etc. In this type both empirical and theoretical sources were used as a guide in the construction of tools, accumulation and analysis of pertinent data.

(B) Construction of Schedule

A structured interview-schedule was drawn up with pre-arranged and open-end questions giving choices to the respondents to show their first feeling reactions and also to show the internal consistency of the responses. At a few places the schedule contained close-end questions where the answers in yes or no served the purpose. The schedule was divided into the various areas of study ensuring the coverage of all aspects focused at under the study. Thus the sections into which the schedule was divided were mainly:

(I) Relational Informations
(II) Socio-economic Structure
(III) Mode of Management and Working
(IV) Religio-cultural Beliefs and Practices
(V) Changing Patterns of Values.

A pilot study covering five major or prominent shrines was also undertaken in order to pre-test the tool before applying it for the intensive study on a larger scale. As the pilot study progressed some new insights were gained and were made use of in re-framing and re-arranging questions in order to get the schedule more adaptable to the purpose of study. Later where it was found necessary editing was also done in order to make the tool more pointed, chiselled and responsive. Thus the idea behind pre-testing and editing was to make the tool more workable and useful and thus finally to avoid the low proportion of replies.

(C) Mode of Data Collection

Though the specific method of investigation used in the present study was the interview method. Generally speaking the present study was made mainly by using interview-schedule. However case-study was also adopted in the event of prominent or historical Sikh shrines in order to obtain in-depth and intimate details providing greater insight into these shrines.

The case-study approach was more similar to that of historico-cultural perspective than to a statistical one. To examine the institutionalised aspects and the general nature of the shrines at qualitative level, observational method was also used. For authentication of factual informations their economic structure was also studied supplementing the field data with checking out of the relevant official revenue records.

As warranted by the need and situation quasi-participant observation was also used in order to have a greater understanding of the socio-religious activities of the shrines.

As for the process of collecting data the researcher approached the Head priests of the shrines and the executive members of their managing bodies personally holding interviews with them. As a rule, the time and place was appointed with the subjects, whether head priests or the president and secretary, before approaching them for gathering the details. Mostly interviews were lasted about three hours each, and those respondents who could not give this much of time in a single sitting were also king enough to agree to give out the details in second sitting. Some depth interviews were performed six to eight hours and were spreadover two or three sittings.

The researcher during interviewing also tried to take care of the socio-cultural context and socio-temporal context pertaining to the study. The Sikh shrines had their own mode of life to which persons adhered or deviated from in some cases. In this context an understanding of behaviour-patterns both conforming and deviant and of the local norms was made. The researcher also tried to see the physical and the situational aspect of these shrines by making on-the-spot visits.

As for the socio-temporal context the study related to a definite period of time when the socio-political scene of the country since my field work was started from the month of January 86 to January 88) was some what disturbed. Some forces, external and internal, were in operation before and during the time of investigation requiring greater caution and care on the part of the investigator. And in this way an attempt was made to see the individual shrines in the specific setting of time and place.

(iv) Analysis and Presentation

The data in the present study were analysed analytically and statistically. The compilation of data was done on a number of sheets in a tabulated form by the investigator. But for construction of separate tables the data were marshalled variable-wise. Analytical tables were dealt with in various Chapters whereas the detailed and comprehensive tables were accommodated in appendices in the end of the book. In this study the scaling techniques—such as, Rating Scale and Thurstone Scale, were also used to measure the degree of internal-consistency, attitudes and reactions among the Head priests of the shrines and the officials of their managing bodies. The degree of social distance, between the Sikh priests and the people of other religion, was also measured by a Nine-point Scale of social distance constructed on the pattern of Bogardus' Social Distance Scale. Electronic calculator was also used for broad conclusions. All the quantitative data in the report were presented in a form of simple and multi-dimensional tables which were based on the reliable informations gathered through the interview-schedule. To enrich the data and give a objective flavour to the report, the observational and other data received through informal discussions were also reported accordingly.

(v) Difficulties and Limitations

It may not be out of place to mention here that the present study was a challenge for the investigator in the present circumstances and had been more complex after the Punjab problem was emerged. Hence, he encountered a great difficulty in collecting the relevant data from the different shrines which were established in far-flung areas in Delhi. However, with the help of a few educated and enlightened Sikh persons he could manage to get at the broad frame-work of the shrines and to develop a working relationship through their support. The investigator has also faced more difficulty to take the interview from the leaders of the managing bodies of the shrines, especially from the leaders of the D.S.G.M.C. Some respondents were very conscious of being important leaders (mainly—Jaswant Singh Kalka—Senior Vice-president of the D.S.G.M.C., Head Master Sucha Singh—General Secretary of D.S.G.M.C., Sardar Kulmohan Singh—Joint Secretary and Sardarni Nirlep Kaur, Executive Member of D.S.G.M.C.), they also discouraged the investigator by not keeping the appointment. Some of them gave as many as a dozen appointments but failed to keep even one. Ultimately, two respondents refused bluntly not to grant the interview.

All the same, the investigator has also posed a difficulty in gathering sufficient and valid informations from the historical prominent Sikh shrines (like as—Gurdwara Sis Ganj, Nanak-ka-Piyao, Majnu Tilla and Mata Sundari). This difficulty was all the more faced while holding interview with the Head Priests of historical shrines (except five Head priests of the historical shrines) who were unable to understand the language of Hindi and were also conservative and traditional in their approach to the problem.

Further, there was no proper record was found in the shrines of Sri Guru Singh Sabha whereas other large shrines of the same managing bodies were reluctant to give out required details. Hence, it was found possible to observe keenly their daily routine to draw the reliable conclusions about their income and expenditure.

Thus, some more intimate facts and classified, and insight informations were striven for but not much could be dug-out to most of the respondents going syncretic and resistant under such circumstance. The researcher had to rely on his own observations, impressions and practical experiences during the conduct of interviews. The same was supplemented with the relevant data obtained from scanning the published and non-published sources of data.

Despite all these difficulties and limitations the present study has been a fairly fruitful experience for the investigator. He has been able to collect the relevant fund of data and has done his best to present the same. By and large, the study ends on an more optimistic stand-point suggesting that the present study may provide a basis for deeper studies of the problem in future.

REFERENCES

1. Singh, Teja, *The Gurdwara Reform Movement and the Sikh Awakening.*
2. Josh, Sohan Singh, *Akali Morchon Ka Itihas.*
3. Sahni, Ruchi Ram, *Struggle for Reform in Sikh Shrines,* Edited by Dr. Ganda Singh.
4. Singh, Mohinder, *The Akali Movement.*
5. Sethi, G.R., *Sikh Struggle for Gurdwara Reform.*
6. Singh Sangat: *Freedom Movement in Delhi.*
7. Bali, J.B., *Sis Ganj—Story of the Historical Sikh Shrines of Delhi.*
8. Kaur, Jitinder, *The Politics of the Sikhs.*
9. Singh, Gobinder, *The Religion and Politics in Punjab.*

3

The Growth and Development of Sikhism and Gurdwaras

Similar to Europe and other parts of the world, India too reflected a dark and gloomy period in the fifteenth century and the early sixteenth century. The Indian society was tormented by fissiparous ten dencies of narrow feelings of caste, religion, language and region, and torn apart between two major sections of Hindu and Muslim. To worsen the situation there were inner dissensions among the Hindus and the Muslims with mutual jealousy and false sense of religious pride and thus they bogged down in empty rituals. These socio-political, economic and religious conditions paved the way for the revival of Bhakti Movement and ultimately for the rise of Sikh religion in India.

The natural consequence of it was that, in this background, the great seers spear-headed a powerful movement against all ills and evils then prevailing in the society and made it their mission to purify the hearts of the people. Sikhism, which emerged in the North-West of the country in the mid 15th century enriched the lives of millions.[1]

It vehemently opposed and rather uprooted the hardened traditional trends and rigidly fixed social alignments. More importantly, the Sikh faith set it face against the idolatry of Hinduism, the authority of Brahmins; and instead tried up the equality of all men ridiculing the cult of diverse gods and goddesses and thus preached monotheism, unity of God and equality of man before Him.

A long-left need of reversing the rigid and dogmatic trends and thwarting rigid and doctrinaire customs, stereotypes and such other fixed social alignments required a new and original ideology with a sense of purpose and direction marked by a committed organisation and determined leadership. This may briefly account for the rationale of the Sikh movement aimed at building up a society on egalitarian principles. It rejected caste distinctions and hierarchy, and came to be credited for its humanistic ends and objectives with an eye to the social involvement of the creed.

Sikhism: Origin

It may be commonly observed that all new religious movements have been produced and shaped by existing faiths and like offspring bore semblance of similarity to them.[2] Accordingly, Sikhism was born out of some sort of mutual relationship and of common ground between Hinduism and Islam after their having existed together for hundred of years.[3] At the same time, it deserve to be noted that after Sikhism was born, it, over the years developed its own personality and got crystallised into a distinct faith which barring slight semblance to both Hinduism and Islam came to have a substantive entity.

Now we have understand and take stock why and how Sikhism came into existence, what it is about, what it stands for, and what it has contributed to the religious thought of the mankind ? For it one needs and insight and a probe into the early history of Hinduism, its reactions to Muslim invasions and the stresses and strains it has undergone under the challenge of Islam. On the other hand, it also requires some knowledge how Islam traversed ground both rough and even and domesticated itself in India.

However, due to the limitations of space, the researcher,

in so far as the main focus of the study is concerned, would like to confine himself to discussing mainly the thesis, tenets and philosophy of Guru Nanak, the great founder and saviour of Sikhism, instead of walking into the welter of two rival faiths, Hinduism and Islam, how they clashed and how they compromised.

To come straight to the question, what were the conditions existed before the advent of Sikhism, we may here briefly give a passing reference to the Bhakti Movement and offspring of Hinduism's compromise with Islam and emergence of Sufi Mystics, Islam's compromise with Hinduism which made the climate conducive to the birth of Sikhism.

Dealing briefly with the Bhakti Movement this movement of renaissance and reformation started by Shankara (C.A.D. 800) exhorted return to the Vedas advocating monotheism and rejecting idol worship. It was Ramanuja (A.D. 1016-1137), who disagreeing with Shankara's purely logical approach advocated the path of Bhakti (devotion). Later, this creed was carried forward by Madhava, Vishnu Swami, Vallabha and above all Ramanuja. The influence of Bhakta order was far greater than that of orthodox Brahaminical Hinduism. And in actual practice it worked for a rapprochement with Islam, whose credit mainly goes to Kabir.[4]

However, for all the pronouncements and proclamations, Bhakti Movement could hardly build one comprehensible system putting precepts into practice.

Then come the Sufi Mystics who after learning about Christianity, Buddhism and Hinduism tested the religion of the prophet in the light of their own knowledge and experience. Contrary to Muslim conquerors who tried to convert non-believers and destroy their places of worship. The Sufis treated them as their brothers preaching the principles of the stirring together of hearts.

There were about a dozen orders of sufis in Northern-India till the beginning of 15 century with the Chisti, Qadiri, Suhrawardi, and presently—the Naqshbandi—as the most prominent.[5] However, in the 15th century the Punjab's religious and political climate was in total disarray and mess following Taimur's invasion in 1398 A.D. Consequently, the influence and the climate created by the Sufis preaching tolerance towards Hinduism and that of the Hindu Bhaktas advocating a sympathetic understanding of Islam was eroded and undermined. This political turmoil destroyed the social and religious fabric created by the combined efforts of the Bhaktas and the Sufis. And thus revived the fundamental values among Muslims and the dogmas and orthodoxy among the Hindus.[6]

Nanak added further, that the curse and bane of hate and falsehood so created, frustrated and supplanted the message of love of Sufis and the Bhaktas. Thus, needless to portrait that Guru Nanak (1469-1539 A.D.) initiated the separate faith by preaching a synthesis of Bhakti Hinduism and Islamic Sufism. Here, we find much similarity between the teachings of Guru Nanak and those of Bhakti Saints (Ramanand, Kabir, Vallabhacharaya and Chaitanaya etc.) and also between the Bhakti Saints and Sufi Saints (Baba Farid, Sheikh, Miyan Mir and Kabir etc).[7] Describing Guru Nanak as one of the most important reformer of his time, Prof. R.C. Majumdar says "He was a more courageous reformer and went further than Ramanand and Chaitanaya.[8] Ethne K. Marenco writes in his famous creation, "The culmination of the Sufi Movement of the Muslims and the Bhakti Movement of the Hindus was to be found in the doctrines of Guru Nanak."[9]

It can be inferred from the preceding analysis that it was the then socio-religious milieu which compelled Guru Nanak to organise the separate faith on separate ideological lines. Guru Nanak by correcting corrupt practices changed old beliefs into new one and projected his perennial wisdom into the stream of consciousness of their faith by telling the followers of other religions as to how they could become true Muslim and good Hindu? He called his faith or religion—Nirmal Panth (pure community), Sach ka Marg (path of truth) and Gurmat (Guru's wisdom).

Outstanding Features of the Faith of Guru Nanak

Guru Nanak, as a prophet and saviour, was a man whose life opened an era in the religio-cultural history of India and abroad. He left behind a unique tradition of holiness, humanity and tolerance. He not only initiated a new faith but also gave a new pattern of living and thinking. To understand the structural philosophy of the faith, the main features of Guru Nanak's teachings may be mentioned as below.

Conception of God

The teachings of Guru Nanak reflected that he was a strict monotheist. He taught his followers to submit completely before God's will because His appreciation and approval could be obtained only through complete self surrender. Nanak disapproved of the worship of idols and supported to Sat (truth and reality). Nanak's God was Nirankar. He used a variety of names for Him, as, Father (pita), Lover (pritam) and Giver (data). Nanak's God was neither Hindu nor Musalmaan but Ram, Rahim, Hari and Rub as well as True Creator (sat-kartar).

The Guru (The Perfect Prophet)

Nanak produced the institution of Guru (pivot of the religious system). Nanak believed that the personality of the Guru could pass into the disciple and prevent him from the narrow path of the religion. It is merely a Guru who removes the caste barriers and gives a status of equality. Guru Nanak emphasised that he was to be regarded as a guide not God or Prophet.

The Goal of Life

The religion of Guru Nanak was that of householder (grihastha), not monastic. His main goal of life was—raj main jog (to achieve enlightenment in the family life). He emphasised the Sadh Sangat (the company of holy men) and righteous conduct towards others.

The Name of God (Emphasis on Naam)

Contrary to the Tree Paths (marg) or salvation advocated in the Hindu religion: that of Karamamarg (action), Gyanamarg (knowledge) and Bhaktimarg (devotion), Guru Nanak emphasised only the path of Bhakti (bhaktimarg) and Name (namamarg). Nanak believed that the repetition of Name can remove the I-feeling (self or ego) what is the root of all evils. The True Name in the deep sense is not the word but an embodiment of power and wisdom. Guru Nanak gave new title to his God 'Wahguru.'*

Equality to All: (Association without Caste and Creed)

Guru Nanak revolted against the hierarchy or caste and the sectarian ceremonies among the people and took practical steps to demolish the vicious hold of caste by starting the Guru-ka-Langar (free community food) persuading his followers to eat together. The Guru-ka-Langar was not an assembly of sadhus and faqirs but the brotherhood consisted of people from every strata of society.

The foregoing lines may lead us to conclude that whatever the Bhaktas and Sufis stressed in their teachings, Guru Nanak accommodated all these into one system and took a clear organisational step in shaping a separate faith on distinct ideological lines. In his forty years' period as a Teacher and Prophet, Guru Nanak set up the centres in the form of

* The explanation of the term 'Wahguru' is that, Wah means—congratulation—and Guru means-great. Both words combined, therefore, means congratulation to the Great God.

Dharamsalas inside the country and abroad. These Dharamsalas (religious centres) were the centres where his followers met together and sang the hymns of Nanak in their mother-tongue, Punjabi. In his life time, Guru Nanak also introduced the institutions of Sangat (congregation of his followers with mutual equality and brotherhood), Langar (free community kitchen) and Manjis (seats of power). All these institutions helped inculcate equality, fraternity and brotherhood among his followers.

After having discussed the salient features of the faith and religion Guru Nanak propagated, now we have to understand briefly how the Sikh faith was developed later and institutionalised under the chain of his Nine Successors.

Growth and Development

After initiating and preaching the separate faith, Guru Nanak wanted his mission to serve posterity. Thus, he baptised and appointed Bhai Lehna, a devoted disciple, as Angad as his successor in preference to his sons (Sri Chand and Lakshmi Das) who after being deprived of Guruship founded his own creed as Udasi Sect. Guru Angad became the second Guru of the Sikhs in 1539 A.D. He carried forward the mission of his Master and emphasised among the followers of Nanak their own distinct identity, so that they might not relapse into Brahmanism. He strengthened the institution of Sangat and Langar and opened more centres for regular system of collecting offerings to meet the expenses. Guru Angad selected the appropriate 35 letters from the other scripts, popularised throughout Northern India as Lingua Franka[10] and called the new script 'Gurmukhi' (derived from the mouth of Guru). It was the revolutionary step and chief contribution of the Guru Angad; who gave the Sikhs a written language distinct from that of the Hindus and the Muslims. This proved an important land mark in the growth of this new creed.

Guru Angad, during his lifetime, nominated Amar Das,

a venerable old disciple, as his successor. He showed great devotion in forwarding the missionary work of Nanak and Angad. The institution of Sangat and Langar were further strengthened by him. Thus, the followers of the Guru not only grew in numbers, but also developed a sense of brotherhood among themselves. He also increased the numbers of Manjis (seats of preaching) whose main function was to preach the gospel of the faith and to collect the offerings.[11] In this way the Sikhs were given a well knit organisation.

In the time of Guru Amar Das the institution of Guruship had become hereditary. Guru's son-in-law, Bhai Jetha, a Khatri by caste, succeeded the Guru under the name of Ram Dass, Fourth Guru. He proved a true and devoted disciple and made a rapid progress in promoting the skin doctrines. Guru Ram Dass had created a town named 'Ram Dass Pura' which became famous as Amritsar (th Pool of Immortality).[12] It became later the religious capital of the Sikhs. Thus, under his leadership the Sikh faith drifted away from Brahmanism and developed its own rites and ceremonies and acquired a distinctive identity.

Guru Ram Dass had three sons but he shifted the Holy Ministry to his youngest son, Arjan Dev, Fifth Guru of the Panth, because he was practical philosopher and powerful organiser. During his Guruship he was determined to raise the Sikh faith from the status of sect to a fullfledged religion. For this purpose it was necessary that the Sikhs should have their own scripture like the Vedas, the Bible and the Quran.[13]

In this regard he collected the authentic hymns of the first Four Gurus (from Guru Nanak to Guru Ram Dass), Hindu Bhaktas and the Muslim Sufis. This remarkable task was completed in 1604 A.D. and the volume, known as Adi Granth, containing these hymns (now known as Sri Guru Granth Saheb), was installed in Harimandir (now known as Golden Temple). Another contribution of Guru Arjan Dev in the growth of the Panth was the reorganisation of the Mas and system (derived from the Persian Masnad, meaning couch, initiated in the form of Manjis by his predecessors) which was found useful in providing funds for making the growing requirements of big projects and Langar. Thus, Guru Arjan made the followers a totally distinct community in having their own scripture, pilgrimage centre and social customs. Now their dependence on Brahaminical texts ended.

After the martyrdom of Guru Arjan, the hereditary succession practice was transferred to Hargobind as Sixth Guru. In the new situation, created by his father's martyrdom, Guru Hargobind adopted a new way of conducting himself. At the time of ceremony of succession he wore to swords of Miri (temporal authority) and Piri (spiritual authority) and trained his disciples in military warfare.[14] During his Guruship the peaceful faith was converted into the militant faith. His specific and distinctive contribution to the evaluation of the faith was to synthesise the heroic and spiritual tradition. He trained nearly four thousand Sikh militants to face the intolerance and tyranny.

After the death of Sixth Guru, Hargobind, in 1644 A.D., his grandson, Hari Rai, succeeded him as Seventh Guru. He devoted most of his time in consolidating the faith among his followers. During his tenure of Guruship some notable princely families of Patiala, Nabha and Jind, embraced the tenets of Sikh faith and played a distinguished role in the building of Sikh power.

Guru Hari Rai was succeeded in 1661 A.D. by his younger son, Hari Kishan as Eighth Guru. He preserved only the Sikh culture as he inherited from his predecessors. The famous historical Sikh shrine of Delhi, Bangla Saheb, was established in his memory.

The Ninth Guru, Tegbahadur, was the youngest son of Guru Hargobind, Sixth Guru. He became Guru in 1644 A.D. and was a zealous preacher. To get freedom of worship, he incurred wrath of the Muslim Emperor, Aurangzeb, who asked the Guru either to accept Islam or face death. But the courageous Guru refused for which he was beheaded at Chandni Chowk in old Delhi in 1675 where the famous historical shrine Sis Ganj, stands. Guru Tegbahadur's martyrdom not only saved the Sikh church but also encouraged a spirit of fearlessness and sacrifice for the cause of Dharma and proved a baptism of fire among the followers of the faith.[15]

From the earlier discussions devoted to the Growth, Development and the institutionalisation of the Sikh faith, we may point out that all the nine earlier Gurus contributed a lot to the development of the Sikh community, yet Guru Gobind Singh's role in its socio-religious transformation was historically unique. In order to understand that how Guru Gobind Singh as compared to his predecessors succeeded in giving a new turn the Sikh psyche as well as Sikh practice, we must analyse and discuss the measures through which he brought a revolutionary change into the Sikh community as well as Sikhs as individual.

Transformation of the Faith

When Guru Gobind Singh, after martyrdom of his father, Guru Teg Bahadur, inherited the responsibility of guiding the Sikh faith in 1675 A.D. the Indian society was badly fragmented into a caste divisions, dominated by foreign rulers and exploited by high caste priests. Besides this, they had lost socio-cultural values. There was a complete degradation in social, economic, moral, intellectual and political field. They had lost even courage and ambitions for socio-political freedom.

Guru Gobind Singh's approach to the prevailing situation was multidimensional. In this respect Niharranjan's remark is apt, "Sikhism and Sikh society as they emerged from the transformation effected by Guru Gobind singh, may be interpreted as the most significant, direct and creative response to the challenge that medieval Islamic socio-religious creed and political authority offered to contemporary Indian Society."[16]

The Guru had to protect and reshaped the demoralised society. In this regard P.S. Gill remarks, "Guru Gobind Singh, as aiming at regenerating the decaying people, planned to lay the foundation of a new society based upon justice and freedom of conscience."[17] The basic motive of Guru Gobind Singh was to make the Hindus free from the clutches both of Muslim autocracy and Brahaminical hierarchical system of caste and to gather Channelised energy for political freedom.

In this direction Guru Gobind Singh reshaped the society by giving it new horizons. He had created a martial atmosphere and an expectancy of military action. He initiated the Khalsa Commonwealth in 1699 A.D. by assembling his followers at Anandpur Saheb and interestingly selected Five Beloved Ones known as Panch Piyarras. And they were declared the Khalsa meaning pure ones giving them new name with suffix male lion and female as Kaur or lioness. They were greeted with these words, "Wah Guru Ji Ka Khalsa—Wah Guru Ji Ki Fateh", meaning thereby the Khalsas are chosen people of God—victory be to God. Thus, the Khalsa brotherhood came into being and the final stage of militarisation was completed. This Khalsa Movement transformed the thinking of both man and society.[18]

Ideologically, the creation of Khalsa aimed at a combination of spiritual excellence and militant valour of the highest order. In the Sikh history, the creation of Khalsa Panth has become a most significant incident which stands for framming up a new society for which the outlines were first given by Guru Nanak. It should be remembered here that Guru Gobind Singh created a new brand of Sikhs, the 'Soldier Saints', who were to be guardians of the faith that had originated with Guru Nanak.[19] Guru Gobind Singh turned the saints into soldiers, i.e., strong in mind and body.

It may be inferred from the above discussion that Guru Gobind Singh was a great thinker, philosopher and practical organiser, who not only revolutionalised the Sikh's thinking but also inspired by showing a path how to live with dignity and how to die with honour. Thus, Guru Gobind Singh gave the institutionalised from to the Sikh faith. Before his death he also announced that he would have no human successor. Instead of that the Sri Guru Granth Saheb will be the only Guru of the Sikhs. In this way, the separate religious stream which had begun about two hundred years back was now completely institutionalised and the Sikh religion also became The religion of the Book.

Some modern writers and other scholars seem to undermined the importance Sikhism, having a separate entity, when they conclude that it is just and off-shoot of Hinduism. Dr. S. Radhakrishnan looked upon Jainism, Budhism and Sikhism as creation of the Indian mind representing reform movements meeting the special demand of various stages of the Hindu Faith. Going to its historicity, its distinctiveness stands quite clear in the first word of Guru Nanak as, "there is no Hindu and no Muslim meaning thereby that he pointed to a new path away from that of both Hindus and Muslims." Guru Gobind Singh opined, "the Sikh is to keep his observances distinct from those of other people of all the four Varnas." He should have dealing with everybody but his belief and style of life should be different all the same. Added further, Dorothy, Field rejecting it as an off-shoot affirms, "the pure teachings of Guru assumed a critical attitude to the three cardinal pillars of Hinduism—the priesthood, the caste system and the Vedas."[20]

We may infer from the above discussion that Sikhism may be passed for a universal religion emphasising the world -view of the fatherhood of God and brotherhood of man. Far from condemning other faiths it accepts the Hindu theory of

Karma, the Islamic principles of Raza and Christian tenets of Grace with some modifications and further accommodating some aspects of Budhism and Sufism over and above. Thus, it may go a sufficient way to explain a synthetic character of Sikhism showing its originality and Universality.

Sikh Shrines: Growth and Development

By way of General remarks we may point out that having analysed the growth and development of Sikhism, now we have to highlight the origin and development of Sikh shrines because the Sikh shrines are the most sacred places or worship where the Guru dwells himself. Now-a-days the Sikh shrines are the centres of religious, social and political life of the Panth. In the mind of the Sikhs, the question of the purification and freedom of the shrines has always been associated with their national destiny, and no sacrifice has been considered too great to make for bringing them under the control of the Panth. It is observed that the prominent or historical shrines (Gurdwaras) are either connected with one or another striking incident in the lives of the Gurus themselves, or they have been erected in the memory of the numerous martyrs who gave up their lives in defence of their faith. It is in this background, an attempt has been made to find out how these came into existence and developed later.

Early Beginnings

A survey of the Sikh literature followed by the investigator reveal that the Sikh shrine or the term 'Gurdwara', is now commonly used for Sikh place of worship. As far as the Sikh texts are concerned the term Gurdwara appears in the hymns even of the founder of the faith, Guru Nanak (1469-1539 A.D.), as also in those of the third Guru Amar Das (1479-1574 A.D.) and the fifth (Guru Arjan Dev, 1563-1606 A.D.), in the sense of Guru's portal. Among the early Sikhs, the term Gurdwara was not understood in the sense in which it is used today. Sikh literatures speak that a Sikh place of worship was called 'Dharamsaal'. It, orginally Dharamsala in Sanskrit meaning a Court of Justice, tribunal and charitable asylum, was the place where the followers gathered in the name of Akal (The Timeless Lord) for paying and singing the hymns of Guru Nanak.[21] This term began to be used metaphorically. In his book, 'Japu ji,[22] Guru Nanak described the earth as a Dharamsaal, i.e., the field for virtous action. Likewise, the human body was the Dharamsaal—an agent for good, pious deeds. As a place of worship, the first dharamsaal was established at Tulumba, now in Multan district of Pakistan. Dharamsaalas were also established in may distant places in the wake of Guru Nanak's extensives peregrinations. These dharamsaalas played an important role in the growth of the Sikh church. Dharamsalas eventually became the Gurdwaras, literally, the Guru's door or house.

Later Developments

Form the beginning of the Sikh faith in Mid fifteenth century, it began to be felt that Sikhs should have their own seat of religion and pilgrimage, so that it might not be necessary for them to go to the holy places (tiraths) of Hindus. Seeing the demand of separate church, dharamsalas were started by Guru Nanak. He left behind him a Sangat wherever he went with the injunction to built a dharamsal for the purpose of meeting in a common forum. The institution of dharamsal thus became Nanak's laboratory for both the demonstration and the practice of his teachings.[23] In this laboratory the devotees of Guru met daily in the morning and evening to hear and recite of the teachings of Guru and to sing his hymns.

These dharamsalas were the meeting places for the discussion of the faith where his followers could meet together and spread his message to others.[24] Gradually, they developed into the centres of education and higher learning, shelters for the poors and needy and the orphans and as resting places for travellers. There was an huge contribution of these dharamsalas to remove the barriers of caste and creed. It was made a rule in the Langar of Guru Nanak that all who came to take the food, whether Hindu or Musalmaan, must sit in a line and eat together.

All the disciples of the Guru were placed under the charge of a revered head or leader, appointed either by Guru Nanak himself or nominated by the Sangat or congregation. The succeeding Gurus farther consolidated and extanded these institutions of Dharamsaal, Sangat and Pangat (literally meaning one row or line).[25] Third Guru, Amar Das, systematised the work of propagation by setting up twenty-two Manjis (Centres for the propagation of th Sikh faith) in different areas. Persons of high religious calibre were appointed to these offices. They were incharge of the Guru's followers in an area and catered to their religious as well as secular needs. They were the links of the organisation and the two way channels of communication between the Guru and the Sangat. They collected the offerings and passed the same on the central treasury where these were used by the Guru for the purposes of the mission.

An increasing demand for money to carry out the missionary work and the development of the faith, the fourth Guru, Ramdas, established a new order of Sikh preachers called Masands (agents or deputy of the preaching authority). They were full time religious preacher. The masands were also required regularly to collect the donations from the followers in their respective areas. At the end of the year on the Baisakhi day, they visited Amritsar to render the offerings and to report on the progress of propagational work. The Fifth Guru, Arjan Devji, regularised this new order of Masands. He also fixed that every Sikh, in future, was to set a side Dasvandh (one-tenth) of his income for the Guru's fund and to remit it through an accredited Masand who, along with the Sangat of his area, was to visit and present the collection to the Guru in person on the Baisakhi Day.[26] These measures also resulted in the emergence of a larger number of new Sangats in the country.

In the early days of the Sikh tradition, these Dharamsalas did not look upon the offerings as their personal property. Instead, they utilised them for the purpose of running the Langars and other similar work for the welfare of the community. In the time of Sixth Guru-Hargobindji (1595-1694 A.D.), Dharamsalas began to be called Gurdwaras. This designation of Gurdwara became universal after the efforts made by Tenth Guru, Gobind Singh (1666-1708 A.D.), who installed the holy book, Sri Guru Granth Saheb, as Guru Eternal for the Sikhs.[27]

Management of the Sikh Shrines in the Past

In the days of Guru's the administration of these shrines was supervised by the Local Sangats or by the Masands. These Masands did not receive any monetary help unless they happened to be very poor or were found incapable of helping themselves. Thus, when the Tenth Guru, Gobind Singh, found that these Masands were misusing the offerings and had become forces of disruption in the Sikh community; he abolished the system of Masands.

During the early eighteenth century and particularly after the death of Guru Gobind Singh in 1708 A.D., the management of these shrines (Gurdwaras) passed into the hands of the members of the Udasi Sect (order of ascetics) or those who professed Sikhism but did not strictly conform to its outward symbols. The bitter persecution of the Sikh community (after the arrest and the subsequent execution of Banda Singh Bahadur in 1716 A.D.) by the Muslim Emperors of Delhi had forced large number of Keshdhari Sikhs (initiated Sikhs or who wore long or uncut hair) into exile and made the jobs of Granthi (scripture or granth reader) and Mahant of the shrines extremely hazardous. The Udasis, though professed Sikhism, escaped the tyranny and torture of the Muslim Emperors for their not strictly adopting the outward symbols of being the Sikhs. The Udasis rendered, at this time, an important service to the Sikh religion by keeping the shrines in good shape and good health. Mostly they were not attached into any particular shrine or wealth and property, but in some case they established institutions admitted Chelas and became heads of Deras, Akharas and Gurdwaras under the title as Mahants.[28] In earlier stage, these Mahants and their Chelas enjoyed the confidence and esteem of the Sangats of their areas for their maintaining good traditions of saintly character and standards of morality and uprightness. However, in the later period the tradition of purity and auteriety showed sings of deterioration following an increase in their income derived from the revenue free jagirs and other properties offered by Maharaja Ranjit Singh and other Sikh Misaldars.

With the advent of British Rule and followed by new settlements of records, Mahants were further advantaged in having the lands and properties of the shrines entered against their names. This naturally has left a distorting effect on their mode of life rendering them self-indulgent in worldly affairs. The natural consequence of it was that Sikhs at large got disoriented and suffered from a mass crisis of identity.

Socio-religious Awakening

After the annexation of the Punjab to the British Empire in 1849 A.D., most of shrines had passed into the control of the hereditary Mahants. And the government nominated managers and custodians and the religious leaders of the Sikh community had fallen prey to a number of social evils. It may be mentioned that no organised movement of reform could be launched against them for want of a general awakening among the Sikhs. Following the Akali struggle for reform the shrines in the early twentieth century arose from such purely provincial movements as the Nirankari, Namdhari and the Singh Sabha in conjunction with all India movements such as the Brahma Samaj, the Dev Samaj and the Arya Samaj. To add to it the socio-religious consciousness and response to nationalist upsurge also made a conducive climate. It was the culminative effect of these internal and external forces which provided inspiration and provocation among the Sikhs to reform their shrines.

Reformation

A socio-religious awakening brought about by the Singh Sabha Movement* made the Sikhs more conscious regarding their rights. The educated Sikh masses began to press gaining control of their shrines. There were no rules for the administration of the Sikh shrines. As prominent as their Sikh counter parts, Hindu Mahants in many of these shrines had asserted proprietary rights. For many years, Sikh associations carried on civil litigation against the Hindu Mahants. Then the impatience generated by the Ghadr and Nationalist Movement spurred the Sikh masses into jeltisoning methods of petition and redress form courts of the law. Following these developments the Sikh Sabhaties formed a new party of the Akalis (immortals) for offering non-co-operation and passive resistance. These Akalis, a militant order of ascetics, were nihang or reckless soldiers of the Akal, or Immortal, and played a significant role in the Sikh history. They ascribed their origin to the martial Guru, Gobind Singh, and served as self-appointed guardians of the faith. They adhered rigidly to Khalsa precepts and rejected Hindu rites.

The Sikhs realised well that any attempt at purification and improvement was not possible till the shrines were freed from the control of Mahants and British Government. Hence they in the early decades of 20th century got awakened to this situation and resented against the increasing influence and interference of the mahants and the Government agencies in administering the shrines. With the rise in the tempo of

---

* *Singh Sabha:* In 1873 A.D., prominent sardars, pujaris, mahants, gyanis, granthis, udasis and nirmalas and educated class of the sikhs in Punjab and the countryfounded an association called Singh Sabha. The mian aims and objectives of this Sabha were to reform the shrines, and to propagate and promote the principles of Sikhism.

the struggle, the Akalis got strongly organised to reform the important Sikh shrines even by force. The movement of Akalis gained impetus rapidly. The reformers did not have the patience to wait. They want to retrieve the important shrines immediately from the clutches of the Mahants. Militant actions were started by these Akalis to restore the prominent or historical shrines. With their militant efforts they occupied the important shrines one by one which were directly associated with the lives of the Gurus.

Due to these developments a need was being increasingly felt among the Akalis to form a central body for the purpose of reforming the shrines and coordinating their activities throughout the country. This brought the representative Shiromani Gurdwara Prabandhak Committee (S.G.P.C.) into existence.

The Establishment of Shiromani Gurdwara Prabandhak Committee

It was realised that in absence of any organised and careful line of action the reformers might be carried away by their zeal leading to irresponsibility, confusion and organisational anarchy. On November 15, 1920, a proclamation was made by the Akal Takht, Amritsar, to the effect that a committee of 175 members to be known as the Shiromani Gurdwara Prabandhak Committee (Central Gurdwara Management Committee—thereafter referred to by the initials—S.G.P.C.) was set up for the management of all the prominent shrines.[29]

The S.G.P.C. provided to the Akali Movement with a well-knit organisation. After the formation of S.G.P.C., it turned its attention to the establishment of a regular Akali organisation carrying on the work of reform in their respective areas. Consequently a central organisation was established on December 14, 1920 under the name of the 'Shiromani Akali Dal.'[30] Technically speaking the Shiromani Akali Dal and the bands of Akali volunteers under its control were supposed to work in the general frame work decided by the organisational wing, the S.G.P.C. Thus, the Shiromani Akali Dal, instead of being grouped in the category of subordinate organisations of S.G.P.C., developed a separate identity of its own working on more or less similar lines for the achievement of a common goal.

Thus in a short span of five years (1920-25), the Akalis succeeded in freeing their religious places from the clutches of the Mahants in 1925. In return for such mass sufferings and sacrifices the Akali Movement secured to Sikhs, the Sikh Gurdwara and Shrine Act. On 8 July 1925 the Sikh Gurdwaras and Shrines Bill of 1925 was passed by the Punjab Legislative Council.[31] The Sikh Gurdwaras Act 1925 provided an institutional structure for Sikh communal separatism in the new Shiromani Gurdwara Prabandhak Committee. Under this Act, the S.G.P.C. exercised jurisdiction over some 300 historic Sikh gurdwaras and shrines in the Punjab with an income of over 20 lacs of rupees a year in 1925. Later, however, a large number of Sikh gurdwaras and shrines were notified by the government as being connected with the Sikh history and traditions and brought under the authority of the S.G.P.C. Today there are several hundred such non-scheduled Sikh gurdwaras and shrines under the S.G.P.C.'s jurisdiction. They derived their income from religious property and estates associated with the shrines and the daily offerings of devotees. The annual budget of the S.G.P.C. from these sources was considerable and estimated to be more than Rs. 140 million (14 crore) in 1986.[32] Now this budget is reached approx 16 crore of rupees.

Restoration of Historical Sikh Shrines in Delhi

Now to shift to the Historical Shrines in Delhi, the central theme of our study, we may point out that after obtaining the control of all the shrines in Punjab, the S.G.P.C. approached the Mahants of the Gurdwaras of Delhi. These Mahants handed over easily the charge of the historical shrines to the S.G.P.C. In 1925 the Delhi Gurdwara Prabandhak Committee came into existence to manage them.[33] This committee functional for about a decade (1925-35) without any specified rules and regulations. These rules and regulations were framed in 1936 and the aims and objectives of the Delhi Gurdwara Prabandhak Committee were specified. In August 1938, the D.G.P.C. was registered under the Societies Regulation Act No. XXI of 1850. At present the name of this committee has been changed as Delhi Sikh Gurdwara Management Committee (D.S.G.M.C.).

Development of Sikh Shrines in Delhi

It was collected from the Sikh literature and Archaeological reports that the Sikh Shrines of Delhi were established in the form of Dharamsaal and came into existence as Historical Gurdwaras or Shrines after the death of Sri Guru Gobind Singh in 1708 A.D. when Baghel Singh (a true devotee of Sri Guru Gobind Singh) captured Delhi in 1790 A.D. and secured the promise from Shah Alam II to restore all the historio-prominent places connected with the lives of Sikh Gurus. Accordingly he succeeded to locate the existing historico-sacred places of the Sikhs in the late eighteenth century. Further, it was also find out that these historical and sacred places were demolished many times and mosques were established by Mughal Emperors. Ultimately the fascinating symbolic buildings of historical Sikh shrines in Delhi—such as Gurdwara Sis Ganj, Bangla Saheb, Rakab Ganj, Nanak Piyao, Majnu Tilla, Bala Saheb, Damdama Saheb, Mata Sundari, Moti Bagh and Gurdwara Banda Singh Bahadur—were designed and constructed in 1925 and later.

It was also gathered that there were 10 historical Sikh shrines in Delhi and each of which were found connected with the lives of Sikh prophets. Nowadays 16 shrines were managed by the Delhi Sikh Gurdwara Management Committee in which 6 shrines were surrendered by the local disputed Sri Guru Singh Sabhas.

Along side the foregoing discussions of the historical shrines in Delhi, it may be only relevant here to touch-upon briefly the other category of Sikh shrines turned as 'Local Shrines' (the shrines of Sri Guru Singh Sabha) included in our sample of the study.

It was observed that the shrines which are managed by the separate body of Sri Guru Singh Sabha called Local Shrines.' These shrines came into existence when the large number of Sikh victims came from western Punjab and became settle in the different areas of Delhi particularly, after the partition of the country in 1947. It was also discovered that prior to the partition of the country, there was no existence of these shrines and as such those followers of the faith used to be accommodated by the historical Sikh shrines in their religio-sectarian congregations and other ritualistic observances. After sometimes, these followers of the faith felt increasingly inconvenienced in attending the congregational worship in the historical shrines. Hence a great need was felt among the followers of the faith for having their separate institutions of worship. The stimulus for it was provided by those who wanted to establish their religio-social identity among the Sikhs of Delhi. Consequently, the Amritdhari Sikhs (who were initiated) formed an independent body of Sri Guru Singh Sabha and the management of these shrines was handed over to this elected and representative body. It will not be out of place to mention here that these shrines have no historical existence but, at present, they have developed their own well defined ideals, tenets and institutionalised religio-cultural functioning similar to historical shrines. Now they have their own system of management functioning, with the principle of universal equality and brotherhood.

REFERENCES

1. *Sikhs in the Mainstream of National Life*, published by (DAVP, Ministry of I&B, Govt. of India). New Delhi, p. 1.

2. Desai, A.R., *Social Background of Indian Nationalism*, pp. 240-241.
3. Singh, Yogendra, *Modernisation of India Tradition*, p. 45.
4. (i) Singh, Khushwant, *A History of the Sikhs*, Vol. I, pp. 22-23; also
   (ii) Desai, A.R., *op. cit.*, p. 21.
5. Singh, Khushwant: *op. cit.*, p. 28.
6. *Ibid.*, pp. 28-29.
7. Mukherjee, D.P., *Modern Indian Culture*, p. 28.
8. Prof. Majumdar. R.C., *The Cultural Heritage of India (ed.)*, Vol. IV (Religions), p. 60.
9. Marenco, K. Ethene, *The Transformation of Sikh Society*, p. 24.
10. Mcleod, W.H., Quoted in *Encyclopaedia of World Religions*.
11. Singh, Harbans,: *The Heritage of the Sikhs*, p. 36.
12. *'Imperial Gazetteer of India'*, Provincial series (Punjab), Vol. I. (Superintendent of Govt. Printing Press, Calcutta, 1908), p. 28.
13. Banerjee, Indu Bhushan, *Evolution of the Khalsa*, Vol. I. p. 193.
14. Kapur, Rajiv Alochan, *Sikh Separatism—The Politics of Faith*. p. 3.
15. Singh, Gurcharan, *Guru Tegh Bahadur—Background and the Supreme Sacrifice* (edtd.), p. 25.
16. Roy, Niharranjan, *The Sikh Guru and the Sikh Society*, p. 148.
17. Gill, P.S., *History of Sikh Nation*, p. 207.
18. Massey, James, in *Studies in Sikhism and Comparative Religion*, Vol. VI, p. 77.
19. Kaur, Ravinder, Quoted in *Contribution to Indian Sociology*, Vol. 20, p. 226.
20. Singh, Harbans and Lal Mani Joshi, Quoted in: *Studies in Sikhism and Comparative Religion*, Vol. VI. (April 1987), pp. 46-47.
21. Prof. Singh, Harbans, Quoted in: *Studies in Sikhism and Comparative Religion*, Vol. I, p. 10.
22. It is most revered book in Sikh religion and recite daily in the morning prayer.
23. Singh, Mohinder: *The Akali Movement*, p. 2.
24. Information supplied, through personal letter, by Prof. Harbans Singh, Editor-in-Chief, Encyclopaedia of Sikhism, (Punjabi University, Patiala, on September 4, 1987).
25. Singh, Fauja, *Development of Sikhism under the Gurus in Sikhism*. pp. 5-6.
26. Singh, Teja and Ganda Singh, *Short History of the Sikhs*, p. 27.

27. Information given by the Prof. Harbans Singh, Sikh historian and Editor-in-Chief, *Encyclopaedia of Sikhism*, (Punjabi University, Patiala).
28. Singh, Mohinder, *op. cit.*, p. 4.
29. Singh, Khushwant, *op. cit.*, Vol. II, p. 198.
30. Shiromani Akali Dal was a political body. The main function of it was to train the Akali Volunteers for wresting the prominent historical shrines from the clutches of the Mahants.
31. Dr. Kappor, R.A., *op. cit.*, p. 190.
32. Article, 'Shiromani Gurdwara Prabandhak Committee Ke Chunav', in *Saptahik Hindustan* (weekly), Hindi, Nov. 23-29, 1986.
33. Kaur, Dr. Jitinder, *The Politics of the Sikhs*, p. 26.

4

Social Setting of the Study

Having discussed the growth and development of Sikhism and Sikh shrines in the Chapter III, it was considered appropriate to devote attention to describing the social surroundings and the direction of flow of social life in the city of Delhi, the area of our study. Hence in popular terminology this chapter is devoted to the social setting of the study. Here our main interest was to deal with the etymological, historical, demographic and economic aspects of the area of study. Demographic aspect lays stress on the migration of population particularly the immigration of persons in Delhi from Punjab following the partition of the country and the consequent impact on the socio-cultural ethos of the Delhi population. Similarly the economic aspect includes, in the main, the economic life and organisation of the Sikh community at large.

Besides the discussions of the above aspects, the researcher also thought it fit to deal with some case studies of historical prominent Sikh shrines in this chapter. Hence it is attempted here to deal with these facets in a consistent manner point-wise.

Delhi, the capital of Indian Union and the third largest city of India, is situated in North-central India (within the Union Territory of Delhi covering an area of 1483 sq. kilometers) standing on the west (right) bank of Yamuna River, a tributary of the Ganga.[1] The Union Territory is bounded on the East by the State of Uttar Pradesh and on the North, West and South by Haryana. Taking all the locations into consideration the triangular area of about 112 kilometers is called the Delhi triangle with its two sides bounded by the Aravalli range in the West and South and the third by the river Yamuna. The Union Territory of Delhi consisting of Old Delhi (occupying 14.8 square kilometers), Delhi Cantonment (27.2 square kilometers) and New Delhi (25.6 square kilometers) lies at an attitude between 700 and 1000 feet above sea level.[2] It constitutes a focal point in India's transportation network lying about 160 kilometers to the South of the Himalayas.

Etymological Aspect

In etymological parlance, it is popularly held that the city was named after Raja Dhilu, a King of a the Mauryan Dynasty, reigning in the first century B.C. The various names, Delhi, Dilli and Dhilli, may be looked upon as the corruptions of this name.[3]

It has been the capital city of a succession of mighty empires with ruins marking both ancient and medieval sites. It is popularly entertained that the city has changed its locality seven times with still others claiming it fifteen times.

The famous epic *Mahabharata* carries a reference to a settlement at Delhi calling it as Indraprashta built about 1400 B.C. between the historic Purana kila and the Humayun's Tomb. As mentioned earlier Raja Dhilu built this city near the Qutub Minar site and named it for himself.[4] Later Delhi faced many ups and downs and remained in low profile until twelfth century A.D.

Historical Aspect

Delhi did not came into prominence until the Chauhana ruler, Prithviraja, made it his capital in 12th century. After the defeat of Prithviraja Delhi passed into the possession of Muslim Rulers.[5] The Muslim Emperor, Qutub-ud-Din Aybak, founder of Muizza (slave) dynasty and builder of Qutub Minar, also chose the city of Delhi as his capital. Ala-ud-Din-Khalji (1296-1316) built the second city of Delhi at Siri, three miles North-East of the present Delhi. Delhi was habituated third time by Ghiyas-Ud-Din Tughluq (1320-25) at Tughlakabad. The fourth city of Delhi was expanded the fortified by Muhammed Ibin Tughluq (1325-51) under the name of Jahanpanah. These new settlements were located between the old city near the Qutub Minar and Siri Fort. Firuz Shah Tughluq (1351-88), the successor of Mohammed Ibin Tughluq, however, abandoned this site altogether and in 1534 moved his capital farther North near the ancient site of Indraprastha and founded the fifth city of Delhi, Firuzabad.[6] It is known now the Kotla Firuz Shah area.

When Timur invaded Delhi in the later half of the 14th century, the last of the Sultan Kings moved the capital to Agra. And Babur, first Moughal ruler, re-established Delhi as the seat of his Empire in 1526.[7] Again Humayun, the son of Babur, Built a new city, Din Panah, on the site between Kotla Firuz Shah and the Purana Qila. Sher Shah razed Din Panah to the ground and built his new capital, the Sher Shahi (Purana Qila), as the sixth city of Delhi.

The city suffered a setback in the late 16th and early 17th centuries when the Moughal Emperors Akbar (1556-1605) and Jahangir (1605-27) moved their headquarters to Fatehpur Sikri and Agra respectively. Again seventh city of Delhi was built by Shah Jahan, Akbar's grandson, as Shahjahanabad.[8] It is presently known as Old Delhi. Thus, the city of Delhi was restored to its former glory and prestige in 1638. The greater part of this city is still confined within the space of Shah Jahan's walls, and several gates built by him, as Kashmiri Gate, the Delhi Gate, the Turkman Gate, and the Ajmeri Gate still exist and are the mute reminders of their hoary and historic past.

With the fall of Moughal Empire during the mid-18th

century, Delhi again faced many ups and downs until the arrival of Britishers in 1803. Under British rule of the city of Delhi flourished by leaps and bound and Mughal rule ended with the last Mughal Emperor, Bahadur Shah Zafar. In 1912 the Britishers moved the capital of British India Calcutta to the new city of New Delhi.[9] Delhi was a Chief Commissioner's province until 1947. It became a centrally administered state in 1952 and finally it has become a Union Territory in 1956.

Demographic Aspect

It is needless to say that the demographic details and materials constitute basic social data which is vital for making the study worthwhile and coherent. To add further the study of demographic characteristics is useful not only from the point of view of population composition but also from the stand point of the relation of demographic characteristics to the life organisation of the individuals and to their struggle for living. Naturally enough the population composition of a place exercises a great influence over the social life of the area. Hence without elaborating the point further we may appropriately give the analysis of the following Table 4.1 showing the growth of the population of Delhi and the corresponding increase in Sikh population of the city counting it from the year 1901 to date.

The Table 4.1 clearly reflects a demographic trend that the population of Delhi in 1901 had increased nearly ten fold by 1971. Further it is also clear that between 1901 and 1941 the growth of population was comparatively slow, but between 1941 and 1951 the population was a little less than doubled. The specific reason of this increase in population was the immigration of a large number of refugees into the city at the time of Independence. The demographic trend further shows the fastest growth rate in population after 1971. To shift to the population growth among the Sikhs, the table suggests that there is a continued rise in their numbers and especially their population exhibits a phenomenal rise after their massive immigration here following the partition of the country. And this may be attributed to a spurt in their socio-religious activities. The following table throws an ample light on this aspect:

TABLE 4.1

Growth of the Population of Delhi and Corresponding Increase in Sikh Population*

Year	*Total Population of Delhi*	*Total Population of the Sikhs in Delhi*
1901	4,05,819	294
1911	4,13,851	2,985
1921	4,88,452	4,335
1931	6,36,246	6,437
1941	9,17,939	—
1951	14,,44,072	1,37,086
1961	26,58,612	2,03,916
1971	40,65,698	2,91,123
1988	82,00,000 (Approx.)	8,20,000 (Approx.)

*Source: (i) *Delhi District Handbook*, 1961, p. 15, and Census 1971, *Delhi District Census Handbook*, Series-27.

(ii) *Gazetteer of India* (Delhi), April, 1976, Delhi Administration.

It may merit special mention here that the immigration of a large number of refugees into Delhi has materially affected the population size and composition with 56 per cent of the its inhabitants in 1961 coming from outside the Territory. The religious composition of the population also showed variation and the Sikhs emerged as the second largest community (about 10 per cent) after the Hindus (about 85 per cent).

It may lead us to opine that though Punjab is their religious and emotional home but Delhi also is no less dear to them because after the partition of the country this is the only home most of them have known. This crucial position of the Delhi Sikhs makes them vulnerable to the developments in Punjab. Their political situations and the consequent perceptions are largely influenced by the happenings and currents going on in Punjab. The Punjab Sikhs being in a majority may afford strong political ambitions in the governance of the state. On the other hand, the Delhi Sikhs too may be seen reflecting growing political awareness and confidence. They may be seen alternating between cooperation with the Central Government and alienation from it depending on the course of events.

It may also be in the fitness of things to add that as the Delhi Sikhs form a part of the Punjab Sikhs they may individually and collectively be observed taking interest in the Sikh politics in Punjab, and on the other hand it may also find expression in their showing anti-government sentiments and propensities in Delhi. Such tendencies of collaboration and dissidence have resulted in strains within the Sikh community in Delhi and outside. They were seen clamouring for codification of personal law, a distinct religious identity, ego-centrism, ethnic and racial entity and a growing tendency to link religion with politics. For attaining these strong propensities and ambitions they are pulling their weight behind crystallising and internalising their religious norms aiming towards institutionalisation of their shrines. Hence the above discussions show that the demographic factors have their own share to contribute to forming a socio-political climate and ethos of a locality.

Along side the foregoing discussions of the historico-demographic aspects of the study, now we may touch upon briefly a few incidents relating to Sikh shrines which may explain the demographic as well as the historical importance of Delhi from the Sikh point of view.

It was gathered from the Archaeological reports and Sikh literature that 236 Sikh shrines were working in Delhi.

Among those, 16 shrines were managed by the Delhi Sikh Gurdwara Management Committee (D.S.G.M.C.), a religious and representative body of the Sikhs of Delhi, in which 10 shrines were historical prominent in nature plus 6 shrines were surrendered by the local disputed managing body of Sri Guru Singh Sabha. It was also explored that the historical prominent shrines in Delhi were established in the form of Dharamsaal by the Sikh Gurus and came into existence as prominent historical shrines after the death of Sri Guru Gobind Singh in 1708 A.D.. But these shrines faced many ups and downs during the rule of Mughal Rulers. The existing places of these shrines were demolished many times and mosques were established by Mughal Rulers. The reminders of the historical prominent places of the Sikhs in Delhi were located by Sardar Baghel Singh. Ultimately, the fascinating buildings of these prominent places were designed and constructed in 1925 and later. On the other hand, the Local Shrines of Sri Guru Singh Sabha came into existence when the large number of Sikh refugees came into Delhi particularly, at the time of Independence.

Hence in a nutshell, it may be said that the Delhi Territory has a fine array of Sikh shrines and is fairly represented by many organisational and structural bodies. In view of a large following and wide recognition of these shrines Delhi stands out in prominence considering the size and magnitude of the Sikh shrines.

Economic Aspect

A sizable ratio of Delhi's working population is engaged in various services including public administration, the professions, the liberal arts, various miscellaneous personal, domestic and unskilled labour services. The city has, over the centuries, been a dominant trading and commercial centre. Today it has also acquired the status of a manufacturing centre having small- and medium-scale industries. As the national capital it has shot into prominence as a banking, wholesale-trade and distributive centre.

It may be relevant to our purpose here to briefly discuss the financial position of the Sikhs and their economic life and organisation and then to examine and analyse how it is responsible for their socio-political collective consciousness, mobilisation and strength.

Though no empirically verifiable and confirmatory data were forthcoming during the period this study was undertaken, our observation was that the per capita income of Sikhs stood higher in comparison to that of other members of the communities in Delhi. They were found almost monopolising many trades like transport, spare-parts, machinery, contractorship, type trade and so on with their domination in many markets. They have a significant share in the army personnel with a good number of them holding many key positions in civil administration also. By design and orientation they are distinguished by a natural aptitude of practical trade and crafts having a good number of engineers, craftmen and architects among them. Those belonging to non peasant class who were observed showing an easy adaptability to business, trade and commerce. Consequently there were some very prosperous traders and contractors. Their relative prosperity combined with their collective consciousness and occupational mobility has enabled them to get their position entrenched and to weild many positions of power and pelt in the socio-political structure of the city. This is also amply reflected in their making handsome donations, endowments, charitable offerings and so on in the name of their shrines which a mass vast properties and immense wealth. Hence we can very well infer that their sound financial position and their occupying key positions in different walks of life provide a spurt to their religio-political activities in the civic affairs of Delhi and outside and as such they have come as a force to reckon with.

As mentioned earlier in the chapter, now we would like to shift our attention to deal with case-studies of some historical prominent Sikh shrines. For it the researcher has taken in-depth and focused personal interviews, consulted relevant documents, ledgers and has taken the help of semi-participant observation. The Tool used for collecting the data was unstructured, uncontrolled and non-directed interview guide containing loose headings and broad points relating to the general and common features of the shrines.

Among others these case-studies mainly pertain to: Gurdwara Sis Ganj, Gurdwara Rakab Ganj, Gurdwara Bangla Saheb and Gurdwara Punjabi Bagh, Delhi.

CASE NO. 1

This is about Gurdwara Sis Ganj situated at Chandni Chowk in old Delhi. The head priest of this shrines was Bhai Gurbachan Singh Chhadah when the study was conducted. It is built at the hollowed spot where Ninth Guru, Tegbahadur, was beheaded on the 11th of November, 1675, under orders of the contemporary Moughal Emperor, Aurangzeb. It is most revered and sacred pilgrimage centre for the Sikhs of India and abroad.

The sacred place of Ninth Guru's martyrdom where the Gurdwara Sis Ganj exists passed into oblivion till 1790 when one of the Sikh Misaldar, Baghel Singh, captured Delhi and secured promise from Shah Alam II to restore all the places where the Sikh Gurus lived and sacrificed of the community. Accordingly, he made out to locate the existing place where Guru Teghbahadur was beheaded. Ultimately, he looked through the existing place with the kind help of the wife of Bhisti (waterman) who had sprinkled water on the particular spot where the execution of the Guru had taken place. But under the British rule, the reminders of the execution place were demolished by the Muslims and mosque was built there. Sardar Baghel Singh sent the information to the king to demolish the mosque and its replacement by a gurdwara. Later, the Muslims obtained a decree from the High Court of Calcutta and the gurdwara was again replaced by a mosque. The Sikhs appealed to the Privy Council against the judgement of High Court, and Raja Ranbir Singh of Jind won the case in the Privy Council and built a gurdwara in 1861 with a jagir of Rs. 4000 granted by the king from a village named Pipli.

The existing fascinating building of the Gurdwara Sis Ganj was constructed in 1930 as a result of the efforts of Gurdwara Prabandhak Committee, Delhi, headed by Sardar Bahadur Narayan Singh. Remaining disputed part of the Kotwali just adjoining the gurdwara, where Ninth Guru, Tegbahadur and some of his disciples were imprisoned by the Aurangzeb, was also handed over to Delhi Sikh Gurdwara Management Committee by the Central Government on 14th June, 1983.

The trunk of the tree under which the Guru was martyred has been preserved in the Gurdwara. The well where the Guru had taken his bath before his martyrdom exists still.

The Gurdwara Sis Ganj is highly honoured by the Sikh Community due to its being the martyrdom place of the Guru Tegbahadur. Consequently, more than fifteen thousands devotees from India and abroad including foreigners visit daily and bow with great reverence to the shrine and offer lacs of rupees by way of donations. Mostly Sikh followers coming from different parts of the country join the service to the humanity into the shrine and the Langar. It, in comparison to other historical prominent shrines, is run by the largest staff including 2 Head priests, 5 Priests, 1 Kirtan jatha with 8 Musicians, 5 Panch Pyarays, 6 Storekeepers, 8 Clerks, 4 Jathedars, 83 Sewadaars, 7 Sweepers and 4 Lady sweepers. The Head priest of this shrines called Class-I officer and has the highest status with more privileges and amenities. The monthly income of this shrine was estimated at Rs. 10 lacs when the study was undertaken. On the occasion of

Gurupurbs, big congregations are held here and the incidents from the lives and sacrifices of the Gurus are narrated.

A Higher Secondary School for girls, a rich library for readers and an information office, where the informations are given about the shrine and its History, headed by Sardar Indra Pal Singh, were functioning on the first floor and the ground floor respectively. It also houses the offices of the Delhi Sikh Gurdwara Management Committee, a religious and representative body of the Sikhs of Delhi, which manages the historical shrines and the other religious, educational and charitable institutions in Delhi.

CASE NO. 2

This is related to the 'Gurdwara Rakab Ganj'. This beautiful building of white marble existing opposite Parliament House on one side and North Block of the Central Secretariat on the other. Gurdwara Rakab Ganj marks the place where the beheaded body of the Ninth Guru, Tegbahadur, was cremated. In Moughal Period, the existing place of Rakab Ganj was a village inhabited by Banjaras (the carriers of grain by their horses in Moughal's Emperor's Rule). They were always in the rikab or company of the king's camp to supply the rations. Hence the village came to be known as Rikab Ganj. To add to it we may refer to the Archaeological Reports suggesting that where the Gurdwara Rakab Ganj exists used to be the residence of the king's bodyguards during the Moughal period. At this place there was a store house for Rakabs or stirrups from which the Gurdwara derives its name, Rakab Ganj.

Like the martyrdom place of Guru Tegbahadur, Gurdwara Sis Ganj, this sacred place of the cremation of the Guru's body also fell into oblivion. The present site of this shrine was also located by Sardar Baghel Singh with the help of Begum Samru—who called Baghel Singh her brother—and of the wife of the water sprinkler.

In 1857, at the time of Mutiny, the Muslims once again demolished the Gurdwara and replaced it by a mosque. The matter was taken by the Sikhs to the High Court and later to the Privy Council. The case was decided in their favour and a gurdwara building was constructed at the site.

In March 1914, a dispute arose between the British Government and the Sikhs with regard to the boundary wall of the Gurdwara. The British Government demolished the boundary wall of the Rakab Ganj to provide a straight road to viceregal lodge. The great resistance was offered by the Sikhs and a Morcha was launched under the leadership of Harchand Singh and S.S. Caveeshar. Ultimately, the government had to yield to the popular will and the demolished portion of the wall was rebuilt by the Sikhs.

A new fascinating building of this Gurdwara has recently been constructed. The frontage on all the four sides is the same with several steps leading to the hall where congregations are held. Several domes, some big, some small, adorn the two-storeyed structure.

A unique, big and marbelled Diwan Hall is also constructed inside the Gurdwara premises. All the congregations on Gurupurbs and Martyrdom days collect here and proceed from the Diwan Hall of Rakab Ganj. A few weapons are also kept here of Guru Gobind Singh like two Swords, one of them two edged Khanda, a Daggar, and two Katars.

An outstanding feature of this shrine is the school of religion. Only are the initiated children of the Sikhs admitted here and the knowledge related to religion and the religious books is given to them. After completing this religious education the degree of 'Gyani Course' is granted to the scholars. It is an essential qualification to them who wanted to serve in the shrine as priest.

Gurdwara Rakab Ganj is run with adequate staff of 1 Head priest, 3 Priests, 2 Jathedars, 23 Sewadaars and 1 Sweeper. The Head priest of this shrine, Gyani Balkar Singh, was found highly educated with the degree of B.Sc. (Ag.) and M.A. in Guru Granth Saheb studies from the Guru Nanak Dev University, Amritsar. This shrine has also earned an international reputation due to its being the cremation place of the Ninth Guru. It is visited by thousands of devotees every day. An individual income of this was estimated approx. 2.5 lacs per month. The daily Langar is also run inside the gurdwara premises and thousands of devotees and needy eat in the Langar without any caste and creed.

CASE NO. 3

The study of this case is concerned with the 'Gurdwara Bangla Saheb.' It is situated on half kilometer from Cannaught Place and close to the Gole Post Office, New Delhi. On this site once stood a place of Maharaja of Jaipur. It is one of the important prominent historical shrine and dedicated to the Guru Hari Kishan, 8th Prophet of the Sikh Religion. It was headed by Gyani Hem Singh when the data were collected. Originally, he was a Hindu Jat but due to the familial circumstances he embraced Sikhism. Now he has established his own identity and international fame for presenting best analysis of the hymns from the Sri Guru Granth Saheb as well as performing the melodious kirtan.

It was gathered that when Guru Hari Kishan visited Delhi, he was entertained as a royal guest by Mirza Raja Jai Singh of Ambhar in his Haveli (residence), the existing site of Gurdwara Bangla Saheb. The Guru had come to meet the Moughal Emperor, Aurangzeb. While the Guru was staying at the Raja's Bunglow the Small Pox and Cholera broke out in Delhi. A large number of people suffering from the disease came to the Guru for his blessings. They were given water from the well in the house. This place is now called 'Chobacha Saheb'. The water is still regarded by the faithful as a cure for all the diseases. Many seriously ill persons are reported to have been healed. Raja Jai Singh dedicated his Bungalow to his sacred memory and since his death it has been the place of worship of the Sikhs and is known in the name of Bangla Saheb.

One Museum and an Art Gallery is also housed inside the Gurdwara premises dedicated to Sardar Baghel Singh. On display are 45 large paintings by leading Sikh Artists which depict historical events connected with the Ten Gurus and Sikhism in general. One distinguished feature of this shrine is the Guru Hari Kishan hospital where the patients are touched by the kindness and gentleness of the medical staff and are treated with a faith in the healing power of the Guru's name.

The golden dome of this shrine is also visible from a distance of kilometers and covered with Gold in kilograms. The functioning of this shrine involves a hoard of employees such as—1 Head priest, 5 Priests or Granthis, 3 Storekeepers, 7 Clerks, 3 Jathedars, 54 Sewadaars, 5 Sweepers and 8 Lady sweepers. The monthly income of it was estimated approximately 13 lacs. This income was found highest of all others. The Head priest of this shrine told without any hesitation that the income of this shrine was increased more than double after the Hindu-Sikh riots in November 1984, in Delhi.

Some outstanding features of this shrine are the silent as well as huge donations in cash and kind even gold and diamond, where more than 30,000 devotees visiting daily and performing Langar with consumption of 100 bags of flour per day.

Along side the case-studies of above three prominent historical shrines, it will be relevant here to study of one shrine of Sri Guru Singh Sabha another managing body, to make the study broad-based and objective.

CASE NO. 4

This is related to 'Gurudwara Punjabi Bagh' situated in the West Colony of Punjabi Bagh, Road No. 5. There was no historical background of this shrine. The name of this shrine or gurdwara was put on the name of colony and is also run by the separate body of Sri Guru Singh Sabha. This Sabha is elected by the members of the colony. The structure and constitution of the Sri Guru Singh Sabha was formed as per provisions of the Societies Registration Act.

The standing of this shrine is not more than 45 year old. It was established when the refugees came from Punjab particularly after the Independence. But now it has developed its own vast resources for its day to day running and religious functioning.

Shrine was headed by Sardar Amrik Singh and managed by Sardar Santokh Singh when the study was conducted. The source of income of this shrine was 'Golak' and public donations by demand. The monthly income of it was calculated Rs. 6000 plus Rs. 3000 from performing Katha and Kirtan. The same religio-cultural activities, functioning and philosophy is adopted by this shrine as is in the case of the prominent historical shrines. The Langar was not found as a regular feature of this shrine.

The prominent feature of the managing body of Punjab. Bagh's Sri Guru Singh Sabha was the Guru Nanak Public School run by it from L.K.G. to Higher Secondary. In this school 2300 students were found registered in the session of 1987-88 and their result was found 100%. It was also observed that the Hindu Children were registered in greater number than the Sikhs.

It is a well-established and organised shrine and found having a link with the prominent historical shrines. It joins prominent historical shrines when the birth anniversaries

(Gurupurbs) and the Martyrdom days of the Sikh Gurus are celebrated collectively. Hence while maintaining a separate entity the shrine moves into collectivity and commensality on the common festive occasions.

It may be worthy of note here that through these case-studies the researcher got new insights and thus was able to make some specific hypothetical formulations which guided the course of enquiry and in the final analysis some of these hypotheses were tested through the analysis and interpretations of field data.

REFERENCES

1. *The New Encyclopaedia Britannica,* Vol. 5th, ed. 15th, p. 570.
2. *Ibid.,* p. 571.
3. (i) *Ibid.,* p. 570, also;
   (ii) *Imperial Gazetteer of India,* Provincial Series, Vol. I, p. 280.
4. *New Encyclopaedia Britannica,* p. 570.
5. *Report on the Administration of Delhi Province for the year of* 1913-14.
6. *Op. cit.,* p. 571.
7. *Gaztteer of the Delhi District,* 1883-84.
8. *The New Encyclopaedia Britannica,* p. 571.
9. (i) Garr, Stephen in *Asiatic Society's* Journal Supplementary Number of Vol. XXXIII.
   (ii) *General Cunningham's Archaeological Reports,* specially I, pp. 132 to 231, and IV—I to XVI.

5

Socio-Economic Structure of Gurdwaras

A. SOCIAL STRUCTURE

Having studied the social setting of the sikh shrines we may now devote this chapter to the socio-economic structure of the sikh shrines. The social structure of any institution plays a decisive role in determining the actual behaviour patterns, network of relationships, goal setting and opportunities of their achievement and moulding one's attitude with value-orientations. This chapter, therefor, signifies the socio-economic background of sikh shrines.

It was observed that the internal functioning of the shrines is governed by the Head priests. These priests are directly associated with the entire functioning of the shrines and influence the socio-cultural matrics. Consequently, our purpose here is to highlight the social aspects of life and philosophy of the head priests. In social aspects we have taken into consideration as Present Age, Caste Distribution, General and Religious Education, Occupational Group, Nature of Local Dilect, Marital Status and Nature of Habitation etc. These general characteristics of the Head priests reflect and serve as an introduction to the subsequent data and solid base for making differential analysis of their life-style, Succession practice, Orienting factors, Role-expectations and Attitudes of the Head priests. Relevant discussions here may contain as:

(i) Basic Social Data

Age Distribution

Among the various bases for the ascription of status, age holds an important place. It is most important biological need for social fabrics. It determines one's physical and psychical maturity. It defines the cluster of rights, duties, obligations and privileges. Therefore, the data regarding the age distribution of the respondents were tabulated and analysed as under.

TABLE 5.1

Age Distribution

Age Groups in years	*Respondents*	
	No.	*Per cent*
20-29	6	12
30-39	20	40
40-49	12	24
50-59	7	14
60 and above	5	10
Total	50	100

TABLE 5.2

Calculations of Mean or Average Age

Age Groups		*Respondents*		
	(m)	*(f)*	*(mxf)*	*Per cent*
20-29	24.5	6	147.0	12
30-39	34.5	20	690.0	40
40-49	44.5	12	534.0	24
50-59	54.5	7	381.5	14
60-69	64.5	5	322.5	10
Total		N=50	2075.0	100

$$m^* = \frac{mf}{f}$$

$$= \frac{2075.0}{50}$$

$$= 41.50 \text{ years}$$

*m indicates Mean or Average Age.

The Table 5.1 shows that the age of the Head priests ranges between 20 to 60 years. However, the majority of them falls within the age group 30 to 49 (64 per cent) and slightly less than one fourth strength of the Head priests falls within the age group of 50 to 60 and above (24 per cent) and insignificant (12 per cent) of Head priests for a minority of them.

The statistical calculation reveals that the mean age of the respondents was 41.5 years (Table 5.2). From the data it can be concluded that an overwhelming majority of the Head priests belong to the young age. It may also be pointed out from the data here that the sikh tenets require the Head priests to attain the age of maturity and wisdom before aspiring for the office of the head priests. This may also has been considered fit in view of the onerous duties of the Head priests requiring physical fitness, alertness and alacrity.

Caste Distribution

Caste in India has always played a dominant role. The impact of caste on Indian social system can be clearly seen by looking into the political, cultural, economic, occupational and other social aspects of Indian society. From the point of view of the individual member of a caste, the system provides him from birth with a fixed social milieu from which neither wealth nor property, success or disaster can remove him, unless of course he so violate the standards of behaviour laid down by his caste. He is provided in this way with a permanent body of association which controls almost all his behaviour and contacts. The practice of caste dictates to each member customs to be observed in the matter, diet and the observance of ceremonial uncleanliness. It prescribes to some extent rituals to be observed at birth, initiation, marriage and death.

The caste system enables the caste to act corporately and to control the behaviour of its component members. But by organisation and propaganda a caste can change, as it exists today, its name and in the course of time get a new one accepted, and by altering its canons of behaviour in the matter of diet and can increase the estimation in which it is held.[1] In this connection we observed that the same process was adopted by the different caste living in Punjab in the fifteenth century. Thus, these castes have succeeded in getting themselves generally known by 'The Sikh' or Shishyas who were formerally less known to the rituals, myths and other rudimentary properties of the caste.

However, occupation of an individual caste in modern India is not restricted to either caste hierarchy or sub-caste occupational status. Therefore, we have classified the macro-structure of caste into the five social aggregates as Brahmins, Kshatriya, Vaishya, Jats and Harijan. Sikh religion embraced a large proportion of the Jats and Shudras, though the former have not prominently fallen discretly into the major caste divisions. The word 'Shudra' representing untouchable caste and scheduled caste has been replaced now the term by 'Harijan' (the people of God).

In the above context, it was found worthwhile to study the caste-structure of the respondents before initiation. The data collected in this regard are shown in the Table 5.3.

The analysis here indicates that our of 50 Head priests, 20 respondents or Head priests (40 per cent) were Jats before initiation. The respondents belonging to Harijan (16 per cent) were the second highest number in descending order. Further the respondents belonging to Brahmins and Kshatriyas were only 8 and 6 per cent respectively. To the contrary, 30 per cent gave no reply and liked to be treated as sikhs only.

TABLE 5.3

Caste Distribution of the Head Priests Before Initiation

Caste Categories	*Respondents*	
	No.	*Per cent*
Brahmins	4	8
Kshatriya	3	6
Vaishya	—	—
Jats	20	40
Sikhs	15	30
Harijans	8	16
Total	50	100

From the data, it can be concluded that the majority of the Head priests belonged to the Jats and Harijan caste before initiation. Also the evidences of various observers of the sikh history suggest that the Jats and Harijan continued to join the Khalsa in large numbers following the death of the Tenth and last Guru, Gobind Singh in 1708 A.D.

Extent of General Education

Education in a broad sense is a vital mean of social control, and its significance has been greatly enhanced in the last two decades by the rapid expansion of education at all levels in the developing countries, and by the equally rapid growth of secondary and higher education in the industrial countries. Through education new generation learns the social norms and the penalties for infringing them.

For want of good level of education one can not understand the basic principles, values and rituals of the particular religious group or community. A disciple having good educational standard may become an effective agent for the growth and development of the religious aggregate or community. It is in this wider perspective an attempt has been made here to find out the general educational standard of the Head priests.

It is evident from the Table 5.4 that the education of the Head priests was not very high. Only were 6 per cent respondents found possessing graduate and post-graduate level of education. It was also clear from the table that majority of the respondents (60 per cent) obtained education upto below matric, matric and intermediate standard. And remaining 28 per cent respondents were literate and 6 per cent illiterate. The data are mentioned in the Table 5.4.

TABLE 5.4

Level of General Education

Educational Standard	*Respondents*	
	No.	*Per cent*
Illiterate	3	6
Literate	14	28
Below Matric	16	24
Matric or equivalent	16	32
Intermediate or equivalent	2	4
Graduate	2	4
Post-graduate	1	2
Total	50	100

It may be summed up from the above table that the general education of the head priests was not very high. Mostly head priests of the shrines obtained the education upto high school standard.

Extent of Religious Education

As the study pertains to inquiry about sikh shrines through religious heads, our interest here was also to find out the level of their religious education equipping them with necessary knowledge and orientation for managing the shrines.

Religious education helps to integrate not only the society but also the human behaviour. The human behaviour is in large part of social product. This education also gives the individual a sense of social identity with the distant past and limitless future. It expands ago by making his spirit significant for the universe. It establishes moral and social attitudes which helps people to develop integrity. It originates also an inter-communal understanding or emotional integration. Therefore, attention was focused here on the religious education of the Head priests.

TABLE 5.5

Level of Religious Education

Religious Educational Standard	*Respondents*	
	No.	*Per cent*
Attending the Daire	3	6
Training in Damdami Taksaal	3	6
The Gyani Course	8	16
Only reading the Sikh scriptures and performing the Katha and Kirtan	36	72
Total	50	100

It is evident from the Table 5.5 that the majority of the respondents (72 per cent) obtained only essential religious education. In other words we can say that out of 50 respondents, 36 respondents were known only reading the Sri Guru Granth Saheb and other scriptures and performing the Katha and Kirtan. 16 per cent respondents was completed Gyani course. And only were 6 per cent respondents took the diploma from Daire. The remaining 6 per cent of them also took the religious training from Taksaal.

It may be concluded from the Table 5.5 that the majority

of the Head priests (72 per cent) acquired only the minimum level of religious education like—reading the Sri Guru Granth Saheb and performing the Katha and Kirtan. Hence, it may broadly be inferred that the level of both general and religious education among the religious heads did not receive that importance and thrust.

At the time of interview from the religious heads, the researcher observed that the necessity and importance of education particularly the religious education has recently dawned upon the community leaders of the sikhs and they were found keen on starting some better schools and academies catering to the need of good education.

Occupational Background of the Head Priests

An occupational group of the individual plays an important role in determining his aspirations, motivations, social values as well as a socio-economic status. An occupation is also a supplement of his cultural environment. Therefore, an occupational background of the respondents is discussed here.

It is evident from the Table 5.6 that the majority of the respondents (70 per cent) came from the farming occupation, 14 per cent came from teaching occupation, 10 per cent respondents were found having background of service, and only 6 per cent respondents' family were engaged in business occupation before becoming head priests. The data are mentioned in the Table 5.6.

It amply demonstrates that the farming occupation was predominant as overwhelmingly the Head priests belonged to the farmers families. This may also suggest of their having largely a rural background with fewer opportunities of their exposure to modern education, urban influences and soon. This also got reflected in their orientation towards managing the affairs of the respective shrines.

TABLE 5.6

Occupational Background of the Head Priests

Occupational Background	*Respondents*	
	No.	*Per cent*
Teaching	7	14
Service (Govt., Semi govt. and private too)	5	10
Farming	35	70
Business	3	6
Industry	—	—
Any other	—	—
Total	50	100

Local Dialect

Dialect is a powerful media of communication. Without it we can not transfer of culture. It represents the experiences, ideas and feeling to which meanings become attached. It is also the most vital symbolic tool used by man. Because of dialects, interacting persons can organise past, present, and even future experience to bear on a present situation in which it is necessary to assign meanings in social interaction. Therefore, it was found necessary to focus attention on this aspect of respondents. The data were collected and analysed on the basis of dialect combinations formulated according to field observations. These were represented in the following table.

Table 5.7 suggests that 60 per cent respondnts use the combination of Gurmukhi and Hindi dialect, 32 per cent use the combination of Gurmukhi, Hindi and Urdu dialect and only 8 per cent respondents use the combination of Gurmukhi, Urdu and English dialect.

It may be summed up from the above table that the majority of the Head priests use the combination of Gurmukhi and Hindi dialect. It was supported further by the fact that their Sikh Gurus also adopted and patronised the Gurmukhi and Hindi combination. It was observed that Gurmukhi of the language of sikh scriptures had its roots in Hindi and Sanskrit. And therefore, this Hindi and Gurmukhi combination of dialects still commands its preponderance over other dialects.

TABLE 5.7

Local Dialects Used by the Head Priests

Name and Combination of Particular Dialects	*Respondents*	
	No.	*Per cent*
Gurmukhi-Hindi	30	60
Gurmukhi-Hindi/Urdu	16	32
Gurmukhi-Hindi/Urdu/English	4	8
Total	50	100

Marital Status

Marriage is not only a socially sanctioned sex relationship but also a status giving device in the society. Indeed marriage is one of the principal indicator that one has moved into a new status of adulthood. Marriage gives higher status to the family, occupation and the community. It supports also one's responsibility, new values and role—expectations. In this regard an attempt was made to find out required details regarding this aspect.

Table 5.8 indicates that the overwhelming majority of the respondents (80 per cent) were found married and only 12 per cent single or un-married. An remaining 8 per cent was that of widower.

It is clear from the preceding table that the percentage of married respondents was highest. An interesting fact was that the practice of desertion and judicial separation or divorce was almost a non-issue. It shows that the family bonds among the Head priests came to be well established.

TABLE 5.8

Marital Status of the Head Priests

Marital Status	*Respondents*	
	No.	*Per cent*
Single	6	12
Married	40	80
Re-married	—	—
Separated	—	—
Divorced	—	—
Widower	4	8
Total	50	100

Nature of Habitation

Nature of habitation is played an important role in the individual's life and culture. Habitation is a process in which people unconsciously adapt their way of thought to the social conditions under which they live. In this way, habitation comes to the aid of indoctrination. Through indoctrination and habitation men achieve a sense of solidarity and a feeling of attachment to a particular social order and the codes that regulate it.[2] Therefore, it was attempted to findout the nature of habitation of the respondents.

The data indicated that the majority of the respondents (84 per cent) were found migrant. Whereas the natives were 16 per cent only. As for migrants they mostly migrated from Pakistan, Rajasthan and Kashmir. The fact that they have already spent a number of years in their status and role as that of the Head priests. They were no longer found having any visible traits, properties and characteristics of their native states. The data in this regard are presented in the Table 5.9.

TABLE 5.9

Nature of Habitation of the Head Priests

Type of Habitation	*Respondents*	
	No.	*Per cent*
Native	8	16
Migrant	42	84
Total	50	100

(ii) Life-Style and Succession Practice of the Head Priest

Life-style is a design for living or a mode of life or a blue print for behaviour gives us an idea towards an understanding. It is the entire complex of ideas and social objects that the people of a society use to carryout their collective life. The life-style is also the outer and inner environment of social man. The outer culture or environment includes his material culture in the form of comforts and conveniences. The inner culture or environment embodies traditions, institutions, life-orientation, nature of attachment, role-expectations and attitudes. The total life-style is closely associated with different social positions and statuses. Any individual can be ranked on various criteria such as, power, age, income, prestige, style and so on, and all these ranking are uniformly recognised in the society.[3] It is in this wider perspective, an attempt was made here to findout the life-style and succession practice of the head priests. The relevant data were given in the following dimensions and tables.

Age of Being Initiate

Baptismal Initiation (Amrit Chakhna) in the sikh religion is of a nature of a sacrament whereby the recipient of Amrit undergoes an inner change in holy communion with the divine. It was a new revolutionary approach that provided social equality moral sanctity, political legitimacy and vertical mobility for the lower castes and sections of the society in their own right, and with their own self-identity. This practice was started and supported by Guru Gobind Singh through the baptismal ceremony of Amrit. This process of initiation symbolises the new value-system institutionalised by the Tenth Prophet, Guru Gobind Singh through the sacrament of Amrit.[4] This practice originated from the Hindu Sanskar of Upnayana (second birth).

In the present investigation an attempt was made to know the actual initiation age of the Head priests. According to the codes of conduct in the sikh religion a person should be initiated over fourteen years of age but there was an ample evidence of young children being initiated in the Punjab. It was also observed in the course of investigation that this practice held its own even now.

Table 5.10 indicates that the overwhelming majority of the Head priests (62 per cent) were initiated in the age group of 10-19, 20 per cent were initiated in the age group of 20-29, 10 per cent were initiated in the age group of 0-9 and only 8 per cent were initiated in the age group of 30-39. None of the respondent was initiated in the age 40 to 59.

TABLE 5.10

Age of Being Initiate

Age Group	*Respondents*	
	No.	*Per cent*
0-9	5	10
10-19	31	62
20-29	10	20
30-39	4	8
40-49	—	—
50-59	—	—
Total	50	100

Average or Mean Age of Being Initiate

TABLE 5.11

Mean Age of Being Initiate

Age Group	Respondents			
	(m)	*(f)*	*(mxf)*	*Per cent*
0-9	4.5	5	22.5	10
10-19	14.5	31	449.5	62
20-29	24.5	10	245.0	20
30-39	34.5	4	138.0	8
40-49	44.5	—	44.5	—
50-59	54.5	—	54.5	—
Total		50	954.0	100

$$m^* = \frac{mf}{f} = \frac{954.0}{50} = 19.8 \text{ years}$$

*m indicates Mean or Average Age.

TABLE 5.12

Age of Being Head Priests

Age Group	Respondents	
	No.	*Per cent*
0-9	—	—
10-19	—	—
20-29	4	8
30-39	10	20
40-49	20	40
50-59	9	18
60-69	7	14
Total	50	100

It may be summed up from the Table 5.10 that the majority of the respondents took their initiation at the age of 10 to 19. It has also been attested from the Table 5.11 that the average initiation of the head priests was calculated 19.8 years.

Age of Being Head Priests

In this enquiry an attempt was made to draw the real age of being head priests. According to the rule of D.S.G.M.C. it is only after the age of 35 years one can shouldered the responsibility of the Head priest.

It is clear from the Table 5.12 that the majority of the respondents (40 per cent) became head priests at the age of 40 to 49 years, 20 per cent respondents became Head priest at the age of 30 to 39 years, 18 per cent at the age of 50 to 59 years and only 14 per cent respondents shouldered the responsibility of the Head priest at the age of above 60 years. Those who became the head priests at the age of 20 to 29 years (only 8 per cent), they were found in the shrines of Sri Guru Singh Sabha because no age restrictions were followed strictly in the working of Sri Guru Singh Sabha. It was also discovered that, in some cases, the initiates with age ranging from 10 to 19 became straight way the Head-priests whereas in some cases they became head priests after crossing the age of 30 years and above and they under went initiation again.

Mean or Average Age of Being Head Priests

TABLE 5.13

Mean Age of Being Head Priests

Age Group	Respondents			
	(m)	*(f)*	*(mxf)*	*Per cent*
0-9	4.5	—	4.5	—
10-19	14.5	—	14.5	—
20-29	24.5	4	98.0	8
30-39	34.5	10	345.0	20

40-49	44.5	20	890.0	40
50-59	54.5	9	490.5	18
60-69	64.5	7	451.5	14
Total		50	2294.0	100

$$m = \frac{mf}{f} = \frac{2294.0}{50}$$

$$= 45.9 \text{ years}$$

It may be concluded from the Table 5.12 that the majority of the respondents took over as head priests at the age of 40 to 49 years. It is also evident from the Table 5.13 that the mean age of being head priest was estimated at 45.9 years.

Psyche and Orientation

Dealing with this aspect the researcher was mainly concerned with those psychological and cultural factors that resulted in their being Head priests. Orientation is a directional or motivational process. It was found necessary to know the directional and motivational factors responsible for their becoming Head priests. In this regard our observation is that there were some religio-spiritual motivating factors that persuaded respondents to embrace the basic tenets and doctrines of the sikh religion. The relevant data of these orienting factors were presented in the following.

The data in Table 5.14 suggested that maximum number of the respondents (36 per cent) identified themselves with this profession drawing aspirations and encouragement from their forefathers engaged in the service of these shrines. 28 per cent respondents were found taking interest in the upkeep and development of the shrines from the very childhood. In the third category came those respondents (20%) who were seen distinguished by inherent desire and will to join the sikh fold and to offer their services for the cause of sikh shrines. The teachings of the Ten Gurus were dialectical and Logico-meaningful which attracted the mind of the respondents. Consequently 16 per cent respondents joined this fold with 8 per cent to serve the Panth, 4 per cent to better next life and 4 per cent with collectivity orientation. These details are given in the following table.

TABLE 5.14

Orienting Factors for Head Priests

Factors	*Respondents*	
	No.	*Per cent*
Self Orientation	10	20
Family background	18	36
Influence of philosophy of Ten Gurus	14	28
Service of the Panth	4	8
Betterment of next life	2	4
Collectivity Orientation	2	4
Total	50	100

Nature of Attachment

Having analysed the orienting factors, now attention is focused on the nature of attachment of the head priests. The nature of attachment is the state of being attached or close adherence or the liking which binds one person to another. Therefore, an attention was drawn on this aspect.

The figures in the Table 5.15 show that the largest majority of the respondents (40%) joined this profession with a goal to propagate the ideals set by the Ten Gurus. 32% respondents admitted, without any hesitation, that they devoted themselve to propagate the divine knowledge enshrined in the Sri Guru Granth Saheb. Further, 12 per cent respondnts admitted that they joined for attaining peace. 10 per cent advocated that they joined for leading an ascetic life. Remaining respondents (6%) frankly acknowledged that they joined this profession to follow the way of Truth.

TABLE 5.15

Nature of Attachment of the Head Priests

Main Objectives	*Respondents*	
	No.	*Per cent*
Devoting yourself for the propagation of the divine knowledge enshrined in the Sri Guru Granth Saheb	16	32
Propagating the ideals of Ten Gurus	20	40
Attaining peace	6	12
Passing ascetic life	5	10
Following the way of truth	3	6
Total	50	100

It may be concluded from the table that the majority of the Head priests got themselves attached to this profession for propagation of the ideals set by the Ten Gurus.

Tenure of Office

Tenure is manner or right of holding property. It is also a status granted to one after serving a certain period of time in a particular position which assures of his permanency in that position. Therefore an attention was focused on this dimension.

Table 5.16 exhibits that the majority of the respondents (66%) were found attending their office temporarily and remaining respondents (34%) were permanent in nature. Those who were holding office temporarily they were the employee of the body of Sri Guru Singh Sabha. These respondents frankly accepted that there was no protection of their job in this body. Further, it was clear from the said table that 34 per cent head priests were holding their permanent status because they were the employee of Delhi Sikh Gurdwara Management Committee. This majority of the Head priests reacted that there job was on a permanent basis having the facilities of residence, medical and the like. These respondents also told that their job was under full protection of Delhi Sikh Gurdwara Management Committee.

TABLE 5.16

Tenure of Office of the Head Priests

Nature of Tenure	*Respondents*	
	No.	*Per cent*
Temporary	33	66
Permanent	17	34
Total	50	100

The conclusion drawn from the Table 5.16 is that the majority of the head priests (66%) were holding a temporary office and only approximately one-third strength of them, particularly belonging to Delhi Sikh Gurdwara Management Committee, Conveyed a sense of protection of their job.

Age of Retirement

A certain age is fixed for retirement in every walk of life. Therefore, an attempt has also been made here to findout the exact position of the age of retirement of the head priests. The relevant data may classify the position in the following table.

TABLE 5.17

Age of Retirement of the Head Priests

Age (in years)	*Respondnts*	
	No.	*Per cent*
Fixed (60 years)	17	34
Not fixed (as long as they want)	33	66
Total	50	100

We find from the above data that the age of the majority of the respondents (66%) was not fixed. These respondents can hold their office as long as they wish to continue. It deserve to be mentioned that this category of Head priests (66%) were associated with the Sri Guru Singh Sabha's shrines where the formation of rules and regulations about protection of job was not in vogue. Remaining respondents (34%) belonging to Delhi Sikh Gurdwara Management Committee were bound by the restrictions of minimum age for eligibility to become Head priests and whereas the retirement age was fixed at sixty years. It was also observed that in case of satisfactory performance of the Head priests there was a possibility of his being given extension in period of service.

Hence, an obvious inference derived from it is that there is a protection of service of those Head priests who were under the umbrella of Delhi Sikh Gurdwara Management Committee and contrarily the Head priests of the shrines falling in the management of Sri Guru Singh Sabha did not enjoy any such protection.

Term and Nature of Job

In the present investigation an attention was also devoted to knowing the term and nature of job of the Head priests. The data are presented in the following table.

TABLE 5.18

Term and Nature of Job of the Head Priests

Nature of Term	*Nature of Job*							
	Paid		*Honorary*		*Voluntary*		*Missionary*	
	No.	*P.C.*	*No.*	*P.C.*	*No.*	*P.C.*	*No.*	*P.C.*
Transferable	17	34	—	—	—	—	—	—
Non-transferable	33	66	—	—	—	—	—	—
Total	50	100	—	—	—	—	—	—

It is clear from the Table 5.18 that 34 per cent respondents were found holding a transferable job from one shrine to another and rest of the respondents (66%) were holding a non-transferable job. To add to it, it may be said that those respondents whose job was transferable they were attached with the prominent or historical shrines, and whose job was non-transferable were associated with the shrines of Sri Guru Singh Sabha.

Further, it is also evident from the data that the Head priests were found paid in their job and as such they were not found performing their duties with honorary, voluntary and missionary in nature.

Our finding here regarding the paid or honorary job of the Head priests is both intriguing and instructive and is in contrast with the Mahants, Mahamandleshwaras and other their religious counterparts attached with the Hindu *Maths* and Ashrams.

Grade Structure

Attention was also devoted to knowing the grade structure among the respondnts indicating their class ranking. This class ranking categories into class I, class II and class III, was termed and accepted by the governing bodies of the sikh shrines in the popular sense of the term in the domain of sikh shrines. Hence, the researcher has used these classes as such confining them to the present analysis. The Table 5.19 may clarify the position.

The different classes and ranks based on the pay scales, as showing in table, cover the Head priests and other officials of both the prominent historical shrines and those managed by the Sri Guru Singh Sabha. However, in the case of minor and so well-off shrines, particularly belonging to the Sri Guru Singh Sabha, it was observed that their economic conditions did not allow to follow this popular practice. And instead only one or two officials were found serving there and the title of the Head priest carrying class-I position was mere titular.

TABLE 5.19

Table Showing Grade-Structure* Among the Head Priests and Other Officials

Hierarchy among the officials into the shrine	*Rank of service*	*Grade and increment (in Rupees)*
Head Priest	Class-I	480-20-580-25-705-30-825
Priest (Senior)	Class-I!	350-15-425-20-525-25-625
Priest (Junior)	Class-II	250-10-300-15-375-40-475
Sewadaar	Class-III	150-5-190-8-254

Eligibility Criteria for Appointment

An eligibility criteria is a recognisation of talent and power of an organisation that determine the direction of the activities of the members. In this context an analysis was made to know the specific eligibility criteria for appointment of the successor of the head priest. The following table gives necessary details about it:

TABLE 5.20

Main Eligibility Criteria for Appointment of the Successor

Eligibility Criteria	*Respondents*	
	No.	*Per cent*
Spiritual knowledge and experience	22	44
Excellent record of service	12	24
Undoubted integrity	9	18
Competence for running the shrine	7	14
Total	50	100

* Source: *Accounts Department of Delhi Sikh Gurdwara Management Committee,* Sri Guru Tegbahadur Niwas, Chandni Chowk, Delhi.

It may be seen from the above Table 5.20 that a majority of the respondents (44%) identified the spiritual knowledge and experience as the most important consideration for the appointment of the successor. The second largest number of them (24%) laid emphasis on the excellent record of service; and 18 per cent respondents stressed undoubted integrity as the main basis of appointment. And remaining 14 per cent went in for competence for running the shrine as an out weighing consideration for it.

Our inference here is that the possession of spiritual knowledge and experience figures up prominently as compare to other bases.

Attainment of Status

While discussing the eligibility criteria one may legitimately ask about the question of status of a Head priest. The status of the head priest is highly esteemed in the Sikh Society. In this context it may be relevant to find out how does a Head priest attain his status and moves upward in the building of his career. The relevant data have been analysed in the following table:

TABLE 5.21

Attainment of Status of the Head Priest

Bases	*Respondents*	
	No.	*Per cent*
Merit	8	16
Promotion	39	78
Direct appointment	3	6
As per convention	—	—
Education	—	—
Total	50	100

Our data suggest that a largest majority of the Head

priests (78%) attained the status by promotion, 16 per cent respondents were appointed as head priest on the basis of merit, and a meagre (6%) were selected through direct appointment.

It may be summed up from the table that a largest majority of the Head priest were promoted from the lower status of Sewadaar and priest which reflects a trend of their going traditional instead of being open in an assigning status to a Head priest.

(iii) Attitudes and Reactions

Discussions under this head shall evidently be related to the attitudes and reactions of the head priests to the socio-political and institutional aspects of the organisation and structure of the shrines. Closely related to this aspect is the concept and meaning of role-expectation. Hence, a word about the same will only be relevant here.

Role expectation is the part of culture as well as pattern of real behaviour. It is also a pattern of several norms which is closely related to values. It may be understood in relation to others behaviour. Expectations of any role are definitions of how its incumbent should act towards others.[5]

Now shifting to the meaning and concept of attitude, we may say that an attitude is an enduring system that includes a cognitive component, a feeling component and an action tendency.[6] The majority of attitudes held by a person are acquired from the members of the family and from the peer-group in early childhood and later. Thus, other people are generally the sources for the formation of attitudes. Most of our attitudes develop within the group to which we belong. The behavioural component of attitudes is greatly influenced by social norms which are ideas held by a group regarding what is correct behaviour and what is not.

In this perspective an attempt has been made to know

the attitudes of the Head priests towards the following aspects. The data are presented as below.

Attitude Towards Kinship Relations in the Staffing

Kinship in social relationship based on real, *putative* or *factative consanguinity*; or on the model of *consanguine* relations.[7] The relevant data are mentioned in the following table:

TABLE 5.22

Attitudes of the Head Priests Towards Kinship Relations

Degree of Attitudes	*Respondents*	
	Responses	*Per cent*
Strongly Reject	4	8
Reject	5	10
Indifference	7	14
Support	16	32
Strongly Support	18	36
Total	50	100

It is evident from the Table 5.22 that an overwhelming majority of the respondents (68%) supported the kinship relations in the staffing of the shrines ranging from moderate support to strong support. Those who rejected strongly or mildly were 18 per cent. And remaining 14 per cent were found indifferent.

It may be inferred from the data that the majority of the Head priests supported the kinship relationship in the staffing of the shrines. It may also be noted here that the majority of the respondents, who supported, have claimed their strong voice in the managing body and were found powerful to gain favours from the managing body. On the contrary, those who were against this practice were not found able to secure any favour from the members of the managing body because this attitude adopted by the Head priests did not serve the interests of the managing body in maintaining hold and authority over the affairs of the shrines.

Further, the study reveals that the members of the managing body were guided by this consideration that a close rapport and working relationships, between them and the head priests, was necessary for their holding the position of power and authority who were administering the affairs of the shrines. Therefore, they did not mind the Head priests having their way in selecting the successor of their choice. This practice of appointing the kin in the staffing of shrines was found limited to the prominent shrines while a far greater number of them (specially run by Sri Guru Singh Sabha) did not favour this practice.

Attitude Towards the Principles of Governing

Here an attention was also devoted to knowing what was the mode of administering the affairs of the shrines. To put it in other words, what the guiding principles of head priests were observed by the Head priests in their dealings with the Sangat (congregations) and the lay public. The relevant data given in Table 5.23 indicate that 58 per cent majority of the respondents advocated the principles of Sarve Dharam Sambhave or universal equality. Those who favoured democratic principles were 30 per cent.

The logical inference emerged from it is that overwhelming majority (88%-58% for universal equality and 30 per cent for democratic principles) of the Head priests were found humanist and democrate in their dealing towards the Sangat and the lay public.

However, a notable observation here is, though the data supplied by the respondents make it clear, that they are great protagonist of the universal and democratic values, in actual practice it was found that in the present state of affairs in the country their rituals, observances and other religious ceremonies largely attracted and rather allowed the members of their own faith to join and take part in the deliverations and serious discussions. It may go to show that some sort of rigidness and chilliness has entered into their working.

TABLE 5.23

The Head Priests and Their Attitude Towards the Principles of Governing

Principles of Governing	*Respondents*	
	Responses	*Per cent*
Universal Equality	29	58
Democratic Principles	15	30
Subjective	—	—
Dictatorial	—	—
No reply	6	12
Total	50	100

Attitude Towards Their Position of Power and Authority

When the question was asked how did they feel about their present office and station, majority of them reacted showing a sense of religious pride and privilege in adorning such an important seat. They were found enthusiastic about and alive the position of trust and responsibility given to them. However, somewhat opposite picture emerged from the details gathered about those Head priests, though less in number, who were somewhat uncomfortable and afraid about the very survival of the concerned shrines for having no dependable and tangible economic support and other patronage. Table 5.24 may clarify the exact position about the attitude of the Head priests towards their liking and disliking of the office.

Attitude Towards Organisational Activities

It is attempted here to discover the attitude of the Head priests towards the management mechanism and the power-

TABLE 5.24

Head Priests and Their Position of Power and Authority

Degree of Attitude	*Respondents*	
	Responses	*Per cent*
Strongly like	20	40
Like	10	20
Indifferent	5	10
Dislike	8	16
Strongly dislike	7	14
Total	50	100

structure in administering the affairs of the shrines. The data collected about it are given in the following table:

TABLE 5.25

Head Priests and their Attitude Towards Organisational Activities

Attitude	*Respondents*	
	Responses	*Per cent*
Organisational rally	—	—
Demonstrations	5	10
Agitations	3	6
Election conversing	7	14
Election	—	—
Never took part	35	70
Total	50	100

Our data suggested that an overwhelming 70 per cent of them were found not enthusiastic about the management and power-apparatus in the shrines. Only were a meagre of 30 per cent of them found involved in capturing and maintaining power and hold-in running the shrines. To serve these ends they were seen in truck with the members of the managing body and thus both develop a convenient understanding and relationship between them. Their main interest lay-in dividing and contriving measures to maintain their swipe over the shrines.

Uniform Civil Code

The data regarding the Uniform Civil Code for the community exhibit that an overwhelming 90 per cent of them reacted favourably towards an uniform civil code made by the sikh community. They considered it to be most essential for the welfare of the community. And remaining 10 per cent were found indifferent.

An inference may be drawn from the data mentioned in the Table 5.26 that almost all the Head priests supported the Uniform Civil Code with one voice at home and abroad. The study further reveals that the head priests of all the shrines were found much conscious about the uniformity in behaviour-patterns, religious beliefs, values and goals and activities.

TABLE 5.26

Head Priests and Their Feelings Towards Uniform Civil Code

Attitude	*Respondents*	
	Responses	*Per cent*
Strong Support	28	56
Mild support	17	34
Indifferent	5	10
Mild Oppose	—	—
Strong Oppose	—	—
Total	50	100

Sikh Separateness

We identify the sikhs today as a distinct and separate people. The majority of the common men as well as the sikhs themselves have also sanctioned the proper place to the sikhs as separate people and community. In this respect, an attempt has been made to explore the right meaning of sikh separateness. The responses are dealt with in the following table:

TABLE 5.27

The Head Priests and Their Opinion Towards, Sikh Separateness

Weightage of opinion	*Respondents*	
	Responses	*Per cent*
Quom	32	64
Race	—	—
Class	10	20
State	—	—
Nation	—	—
No reply	8	16
Total	50	100

Our data indicate that 64 per cent majority of Head priests identified the sikhs as a separate *quom*, 20 per cent admitted as a class and remaining 16 per cent were found unable to opine.

The inference emerged from the data is that, excepting a slender minority of them, a large number of them have enclaimed, without any fear and hesitation, the sikhs, belonging to separate people, having a separate identity in their behaviour and symbols.

Khalsa Raj*

An outstanding feature may be noted here that on the conclusion of each prayer in the sikh shrines, Ardas (supplication) is repeated and recited daily with its following tail:

*Khalsa Raj: The rule of initiated one's.

Raj Karega Khalsa, Aqi Rahe Na Koe

(The Khalsa shall rule no repel shall exist)

The data gathered about this aspect are given in the following table:

TABLE 5.28

Estimation of the Head Priests Towards 'Khalsa Raj'

Estimation	*Respondents*	
	Responses	*per cent*
Azad hasti	15	30
Khalsa Victory	5	10
Keeping alive their independent Traditions	20	40
No reply	10	20
Total	50	100

It is clear from Table 5.28 that 70 per cent majority of the head priests (40% of keeping alive traditions plus 30% for Azad hasti) were vocal and emphatic that the meaning of Khalsa Raj was to keep alive their separate and independent identity, and a meagre 10 per cent admitted it as Khalsa victory. And remaining 20 per cent were found indifferent.

It may be summed up from the data that the majority of the respondents wished that the Khalsa, founded by Sri Guru Gobind Singh, who shared a set of separate symbols, rituals and practices, might not be relapsed into any community all over the world. It may also be noted that majority of the Head priests asserted that the 'Khalsa Raj' was a spirit of internal solidarity and consciousness among the sikhs.

B. ECONOMIC STRUCTURE OF THE SHRINES

Having analysed the social structure of the shrines

(preceding part of the chapter), now attention is devoted on the Economic Structure.

Economic activities, like all other kinds of social action, make different markedly from one structure to another. Economic structure like all other structures does handle the function of production, distribution and consumption. Now-a-days every type of social action in a group which is oriented to economic considerations and every associative relationships of economic significance involves to some degree a particular mode of division and organisation of human services in the interest of production. A mere glance at the facts of economic action reveals that different persons perform different type of work and these are combined in the service of common ends in the most varied ways.[8]

In the light of the above, it may be said that the sound economic base is essential for the smooth and constructive working of an organisation. Hence, speaking from economic point of view, the sikh shrines not only fulfil the religio-sectarian demand of the followers of the faith but economic too. It was observed that the economic structure of shrines is based on the religious offerings and open endowments. Consequently the Dharamsaals of yester years have been shaped as a 'Gurdwara system' strengthening and crystallising with the institutions of 'Karha Prasad' and the 'Langar.' It will not be out of place to mention here that the network of shrines spread throughout the country particularly after the partition of the country expanding with 12,000 sikh shrines and 100 crore of rupees. Now the network of shrines has been developed as an estate within the state serving the purpose of an armour and shield for them.

In view of the importance of the Economic Structure, we endeavoured here to findout the sources and amount of income and expenditure. First it is attempted to discuss income and later, the expenditure is dealt with. Besides this, it is also attempted to assess the present financial status of the sikh shrines of Delhi.

An examining and analysing the above aspect now an attention is devoted to the following sub-areas.

Let us now examine the various sources of income of the sikh shrines (prominent historical and the shrines of Sri Guru Singh Sabha).

I. Sources and Amount of Income of the Shrines

(a) Prominent Historical Shrines

It was observed that there 16 prominent historical sikh shrines (10 purely historical plus 6 surrendered by local disputed Singh Sabhas) were managed by Delhi Sikh Gurdwara Management Committee. It was also gathered that these historical shrines were main sources of income and employ different methods for it. Thus, on the basis of sources of income of the prominent historical shrines, the various sources of income may conveniently be classified as under: (i) Ritualistic offerings like as—Charat, Prasad, Langar and Paths. (ii) Rent and Property. (iii) Charitable and Miscellaneous donations.

The investigator has also collected the Annual Budget for last 30 years from the official sources of accounts from the Delhi Sikh Gurdwara Management Committee, Delhi. It was collected to observe the contribution of the shrines to the religion as well as national production. It may further be explained with the help of the separate added tables.

It is clear from the Table 5.29 that the main sources of income of D.S.G.M.C. were the various Charats, Karha Prasad, Langar, Paths, Rent from property and other miscellaneous religious donations such as donation for Dharam Prachar (propagation for the religion), Guru Purabs (Guru's Anniversary) celebrations, cultural centres and charitable institutions.

The investigator has collected this Budget passing through

various problematic circumstances. It was collected since the statements were available from the period 1956-57 to 1986-87. The main goal of the investigator was to find out whether there had been an increase in the income of historical shrines; if so, to what extent it had increased and what were the factors which contributed towards this increase in the income. For the purpose of clarity and to show a trend over a period of time, every fifth year's budgetary figures have been taken into account.

It was also gathered that the historical prominent shrines receive an enormous amount of money from the popular base in the form of offerings. These shrines enjoy a massive economic support from the sikh community. It is also evident from the Table 5.29 and graphical Figure 5.1, that between 1956-57 and 1986-87 the income of the sikh shrines in Delhi increased from rupees 8.49 lacs to about rupees 3.79 crores. This increase in income was due to the liberal donations by the sikhs, increase into the sikh population of Delhi mainly due to the disturbances in the Punjab, and increase in the number of sikh institutions, inside the gurdwara premises, which were a source of economic help to the organisation. The donations for Langar and Paths are given only by the rich sikhs. Further, it is also evident from the table that the popular sentiments for langar, it is considered very sacred into the sikh community, do not show any appreciable rise.

This fact was also brought to light during interviews from the respondents that the income of the shrines of Delhi increased suddenly after November 1984's communal riots in Delhi. The reason for it may be a sudden wave of enthusiasm and a spurt in religious sentiments and activities provoking the sikhs at large to make a strong economic base to face any future hazard or danger to them.

Further individual actual annual income with monthly too is also calculated which is shown in Table 5.30. It is clear from the table that the Bangla Saheb (one of the major historical

TABLE 5.29

Sources and Amount of Income (in Rupees) of Prominent Historical Sikh Shrines

Income During Last 30 Years from 1956-57 to 1986-87*

Year	*Charats and Shabad Offerings*	*Prasad*	*Langar*	*Paths*	*Rent and Property*	*Grants Fees and Relief Fund*	*Miscella-aneous*	*Total*
	Amount	Amount	Amount	Amount	Amount	Amount	Amount	Amount
1956-57	323922	341900	21152	32093	72027	33308	24494	848896
1961-62	524552	616598	31829	100453	35534	—	34257	1343223
1966-67	1228319	1448285	83558	242585	69047	—	182062	3253856
1971-72	2191249	2794187	150819	508540	119297	—	141873	5906066
1976-77	4334518	5327917	327591	898603	837987	—	144612	11470228
1981-82	9927989	11042438	1044503	2170059	451766	—	180630	24817365
1986-87	16904164	13723445	1334620	1859211	119582	3702809	228745	37872576

* Source: Department of Accounts, Delhi Sikh Gurdwara Management Committee, Chandni Chowk, Delhi, 1987.

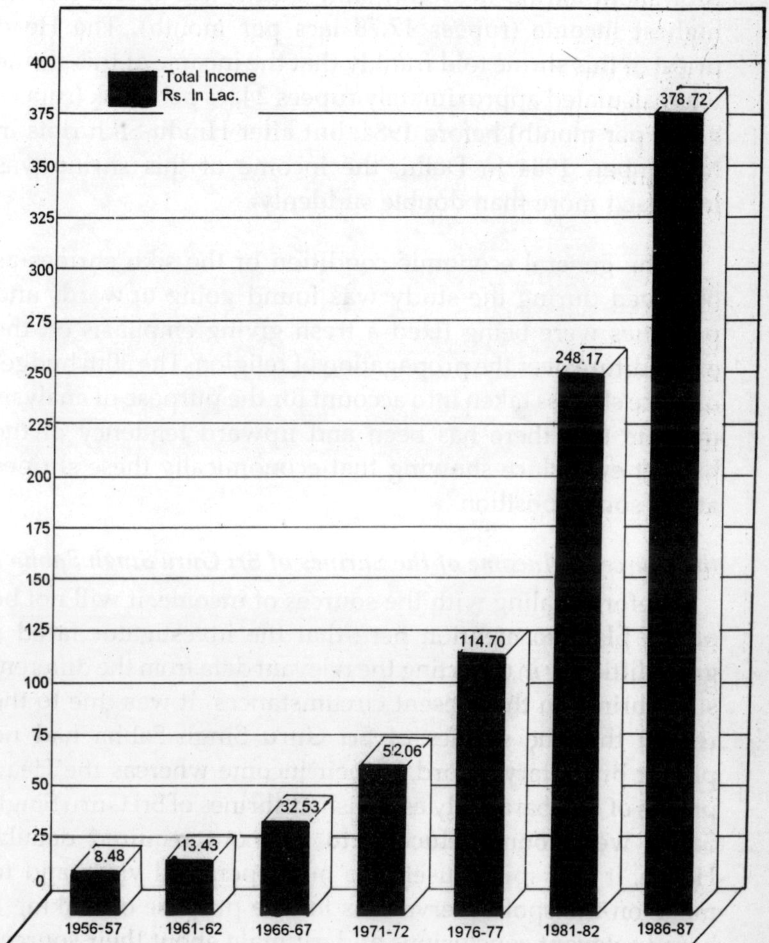

Graph 5.1 Income of Prominent Hisorical Soilj Shring during Last 30 Years Grahh 5.1 (Ref. Table 5.29)

prominent shrine in Delhi) sikh shrine was found having highest income (rupees 17.78 lacs per month). The Head priest of this shrine told frankly that the income of this shrine was calculated approximately rupees 2 lacs per week (rupees 8 lacs per month) before 1984, but after Hindu-Sikh riots in November, 1984 in Delhi, the income of this shrine was increased more than double suddenly.

The general economic condition of the sikh shrines as observed during the study was found going upwards and priorities were being fixed a fresh giving emphasis on the expenditure over the propagation of religion. The 30th budget of these shrines taken into account for the purpose of analysis indicate that there has been and upward tendency of the budget ever since showing that economically these shrines are in sound position.

(b) Sources of Income of the Shrines of Sri Guru Singh Sabha

Before dealing with the sources of income, it will not be out of place to mention here that the investigator faced a great difficulty in collecting the relevant data from the different sikh shrines in the present circumstances. It was due to the reason that the shrines of Sri Guru Singh Sabha had no proper budgetary record of their income whereas the Head priests of comparatively established shrines of Sri Guru Singh Sabha were found reluctant to give out required details. Hence, it was found useful to make personal visits and to make on-the-spot observations for the purpose of making a broad relevant conclusions and estimate about their sources of income.

It was observed in their case that the Charats were the significant part of their income. Daily visitors, followers and regional devotees were found offering charities and donations. The researcher also observed that the large shrines of Sri Guru Singh Sabha such as—Punjab Bagh Singh Sabha's shrine, Tilak Nagar's, Lajpat Nagar's and Greater Kailash's shrine of Sri Guru Singh Sabha, raised their income through offerings

TABLE 5.30

Prominent Historical Sikh Shrines and Their Individual Actual Annual Income (Income Calculated on the Financial Year from April 1986 to March 1987) Sources of Income (in Rupees) on March, 1987*

Name of the Shrines and other Institutions	*Charat*	*Prasad*	*Langar*	*Paths*	*Shabad Kirtan offerings*	*Buildings*	*Miscella-neous*	*Total*
Historical Prominent Shrines	*Amount*	*Amount*	*Amount*	*Amount*	*Amount*	*Amount*	*Amount*	*Amount*
1. Gurdwara: Sri Sis Ganj Saheb	472942	383132	41176	47708	48489	510	2495	996452
2. Gurdwara: Sri Bangla Saheb	661784	925733	65415	72790	42935	2000	7784	1778441
3. Gurdwara: Sri Rakab Ganj	121764	84116	7398	19264	—	575	1870	234987
4. Gurdwara: Sri Nanak Piyao	66528	71092	6650	16563	9578	—	3133	173544
5. Gurdwara: Karolbagh	21017	1781	—	1505	—	—	—	24303
6. Gurdwara: Sri Bala Saheb	34323	8632	1830	11739	—	—	339	56863
7. Gurdwara: Sri Damdama Saheb	9383	2085	1680	9632	6298	—	—	29078
8. Gurdwara: Moti Bagh	21741	6864	2677	12341	—	—	200	43823
9. Gurdwara: Majnu Tilla	5241	3038	309	1505	3574	128	500	14295
10. Gurdwara: Mata Sundari Ji	9340	241	—	8127	8526	—	—	26234
Shrines Surrendered by the Sri Guru Singh Sabha								
11. Gurdwara: Darya Ganj	4548	625	—	3010	9787	—	—	17970
12. Gurdwara: Dhaka Dhirpur	3324	—	—	—	4979	—	—	8303
13. Gurdwara: Pahari Dheeraj	—	—	—	—	—	—		

14. Gurdwara: Banda Singh Bahadur	—	—	—	—	—	—		
15. Gurdwara: Pipal Mahadev	—	—	—	—	—	—	3709	3709
16. Gurdwara: Badarpur	—	—	—	—	—	—		
Other Institutions								
Guru Purabs	—	—	—	—	—	—	11238	11238
Guru Har Kishan Hospital (Inside G. Bangla Saheb)	—	—	—	—	—	—	2936	2936
Electronic Institute (Inside G. Nanak Piyao)	—	—	—	—	—	—	12788	12788
Property	—	—	—	—	—	—	511	511
Religious Propaganda	—	—	—	—	—	—	100245	100245
Relief Fund	—	—	—	—	—	—	183495	183495
Chanani	—	—	—	—	—	—	8511	8511
Total Income on the Month of March 1987	1431935	1487339	127135	204184	134166	3213	339754	3727726
Income from April 1986 to Feb. 1987	14100718	12236106	1207485	1655027	1237345	116369	3591800	34144850
Total Income of D.S.G.M.C.** on the financial year 1986-87	15532653	13723445	1334620	1859211	1371511	119582	3931554	37873576

* Source: Department of Accounts, Delhi Sikh Gurdwara Management Committee, Chandni Chowk, Delhi.

** D.S.G.M.C.: Delhi Sikh Gurdwara Management Committee which manages 16 sikh shrines in Delhi.

(two type of offerings—one common offering plus other Shabad-Kirtan offering) and charities. But on the other side, those shrines of Singh Sabha which were small in structure, followers and devotees, they were fighting still for their economic existence. The income of these small shrines was very low so the authority of these shrines did not pay much attention towards the daily routine of these shrines. The Head priests of these shrines distressingly tried to raise their income through Katha and Kirtan visiting the residences of the devotees.

The researcher found several Singh Sabhas which had no proper record of their income. This was the reason that the researcher faced a great difficulty in collecting the data regarding the offerings, and thus no statistical analysis of the income could be possible here.

From the above discussions of the sources of income of both the categories of the shrines (historical prominent and the shrines of Sri Guru Singh Sabha) this significant conclusion can be drawn that more than 50 per cent sikh shrines of Delhi enjoy sound financial position and remaining were fighting for their financial existence. The prominent historical shrines mainly raise their income from various type of offerings, rent and property, charity and miscellaneous donations. But the large shrines of Sri Guru Sigh Sabha drive their income only through offerings and religious endowments and small shrines raise their income through public collection.

II. Sikh Shrines and Their Items of Expenditure

After discussing the sources of income of the shrines it is deemed necessary to know their items of expenditure.

The investigator has already mentioned that 16 sikh shrines in Delhi are managed by the Delhi Sikh Gurdwara Management Committee. The present annual budget (1986-87) of D.S.G.M.C. was estimated at rupees 3.79 crores in which approximate 90 per cent income (approx. 3.4 crores) was derived from prominent historical shrines only.

The expenditure made by the Delhi Sikh Gurdwara Management Committee can broadly be categorised into two parts—(i) Customary expenditure (ii) Present day existing requirements.

The study reveals a variety of items of expenditure, however, seven items have taken into account in the present study as under:

(i) Dharam Prachar (it entails like—Prasad, Langar, Paths and Guru Purabs celebrations).
(ii) Salaries of Gurdwara employees.
(ii) Construction and Maintenance of Gurdwara Property.
(iv) Education.
(v) Welfare.
(vi) Administration and Management.
(vii) Miscellaneous expenditure.

It is clear from the Table 5.31 and Table 5.32 that since 1956-57 'Dharam Prachar' was the main item of expenditure. The Dharam Prachar entails expenditure on items like—Prasad Langar, Paths and Guru Purabs celebrations etc. From the point of view of making expenditure on different items, the first important item of expenditure was Dharam Prachar. It is further clear from the Table 5.31 that between 1956 and 1986, the expenditure on this item increased from rupees 24.69 lacs to approx. rupees 1.19 crores. The second place of expenditure was occupied by three items as salaries of employees, construction and maintenance of gurdwara property and education. It is also evident form the said table that the salary of the employees increased suddenly in 1966-67 from rupees 82.8 thousand to rupees 3.29 lacs. It was due to the expansion of the sikh institutions. On the other hand, the D.S.G.M.C. increased its expenditure on the construction of buildings for shrines and educational institutions. After

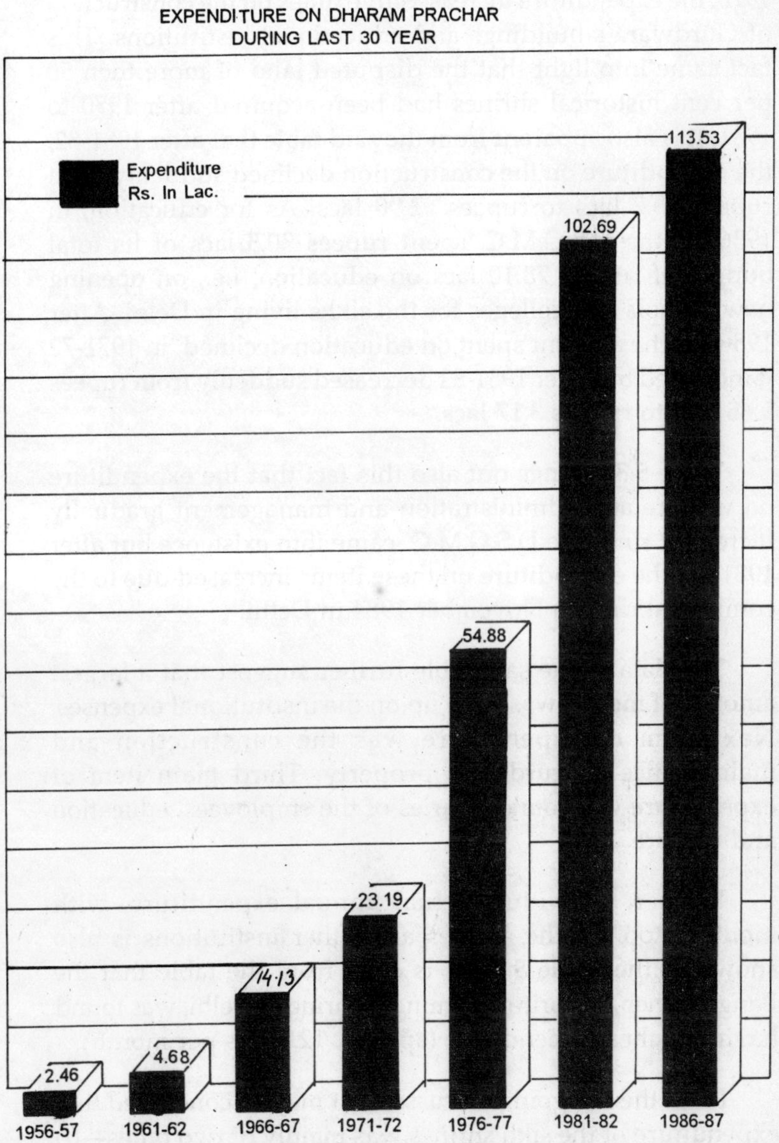

Graph 5.2. (Ref. Table 5.31).

1970, the expenditure increased five times on the construction of Gurdwara's buildings and educational institutions. This fact came into light that the disputed land of more then 50 per cent historical shrines had been acquired after 1970 to 1981. It is also apparent from the said table that after 1981-82, the expenditure on the construction declined suddenly from rupees 78.7 lacs to rupees 52.90 lacs. As for education, in 1956-57, the D.S.G.M.C. spent rupees 30.5 lacs of its total budget of rupees 78.10 lacs on education, i.e., on opening new schools and colleges for the sikhs living in Delhi. After 1956-57, the amount spent on education declined, in 1971-72 it increased but after 1981-82 decreased suddenly from rupees 9.65 lacs to rupees 3.17 lacs.

Table 5.31 brings out also this fact that the expenditure on welfare and administration and management gradually increased since the D.S.G.M.C. came into existence but after 1981-82, the expenditure on these items increased due to the communal riots in November 1984 in Delhi.

The data in the said table further suggest that a largest amount of money was used up on the institutional expenses. Next item of expenditure was the construction and maintenance of gurdwara property. Third main item of expenditure was found salaries of the employees, education and welfare.

Further, individual actual annual expenditure, with monthly too, on the shrines and other institutions is also shown in the Table 5.32. It is clear from the table that the Bangla Saheb, historical prominent shrine in Delhi, was found having highest expenditure (approx. 12.5 lacs per month).

From the foregoing discussions it may be concluded that expenditure of the sikh shrines was mainly of two types—(i) Customary expenditure, (ii) Present day or existing expenditure. The customary expenditure was mainly on Karha Prasad, Langar, Paths and Shabad-Kirtan and present day or

TABLE 5.31

Degree of Involvement of Prominent Sikh Shrines on Different Items of Expenditure (in Rupees) 30 Years' Expenditure Shown from 1956-57 to 1986-87*

Year	*Dharam Prachar (Prasad, Langar Path and Shabad offerings)*	*Salaries of the employees*	*Construction and Maintenance of Gurdwara Property*	*Education*	*Welfare*	*Administration/ Management*	*Miscellaneous*	*Total*
	Amount	*Amount*	*Amount*	*Amount*	*Amount*	*Amount*	*Amount*	*Amount*
1956-57	246857	82805	77956	304368	7370	27293	42528	789177
1961-62	468664	156620	248041	213260	23853	43935	85330	1239703
1966-67	1413282	329148	348839	213516	261425	89161	144838	2799809
1971-72	2319564	615489	1732288	374892	329015	209331	201605	5782184
1976-77	5488601	1134770	3244607	481154	667132	307550	319076	11642890
1981-82	10269020	3139150	7868476	965184	1183666	461669	1755173	25642338
1986-87	11352996	5303243	5290068	316582	516931	478905	8956917	32215642

* Source: Department of Accounts, Delhi Sikh Gurdwara Management Committee, Guru Teg Bahadur Niwas, Chandni Chowk, Delhi, 1987.

existing expenditure was mainly on construction of buildings, education and welfare.

It may be summed up from the items of analysis of expenditure that maximum amount of expenditure is being spent on Dharam Prachar on institutional items.

III. Shrine's Funds, Accounts and Audit

It was gathered that the funds and all receipts were found credited. The donations are received against proper receipts which are counted for through respective registers, cash-books and ledgers. The amounts received by the cashier from all sources are deposited with the banks approved by the Executive Board. The cash required for meeting out the routine expenses is, however, retained by the cashier of the managing body of the shrine who maintain a cash-book showing the day-to-day receipts and expenditure. All entries in the cash-book are carried to respective ledgers under proper heads. Receipt books are also maintained by the Head priests of all the shrines to issue receipt for the accounts they receive for Paths and Karha Prasad and by way the other, donations. These Head priests or priests record the amounts in the receipt registers and finally deposit the same with the cashier of their managing bodies against the proper receipt. The Golak (treasury), in which the money offered by the people is kept, of all the shrines is opened periodically in the presence of members of the Golak Committee, and amount received is recorded in the Golak-Register. There are four of five clerks who issue receipts for Karha Prasad and deposit the money in the central pool (this process was observed only in the historical prominent shrines); and income from the Paths is deposited with the cashier by the respective priest. Miscellaneous donations for buildings and community's development and welfare are also received by the priest and deposited with the cashier of their management committee.

It has also been observed during the collection of financial

TABLE 5.32

Prominent Historical Sikh Shrines and Their Individual Actual Annual Expenditure*
(Expenditure Calculated on the Financial Year from April 1986 to March 1987)
Items of Expenditure (in Rupees) on March, 1987

	Name of the Shrines and other Institutions	*Prasad*	*Langar*	*Paths*	*Shabad*	*Mainte- Kirtan buildings*	*Salaries nance of Gurdwara Employees and others*	*Electri- of the water charges*	*Misce- city and Accounts of Expen-diture*	*Total llaneous*
	Historical Prominent Shrines	*Amount*	*Amount*	*Amount*	*Amount*	*Amount*	*Amount*	*Amount*	*Amount*	*Amount*
1.	Gurdwara: Sri Sis Ganj Saheb	162953	66718	30000	21922	55712	141883	42376	55015	576579
2.	Gurdwara: Sri Bangla Saheb	553114	69602	50099	23954	36669	101855	16798	400960	1253051
3.	Gurdwara: Sri Rakab Ganj	2953	60032	11040	—	54032	29063	1691	19743	178554
4.	Gurdwara: Sri Nanak Piyao	34911	29142	13920	2302	82888	29667	—	5336	198166
5.	Gurdwara: Karolbagh	5849	—	3655	—	60913	6711	3381	560	81069
6.	Gurdwara: Sri Bala Saheb	9972	17384	9970	—	14198	12544	—	3816	67884
7.	Gurdwara: Sri Damdama Saheb	1651	1906	3380	3149	—	7756	1615	533	20090
8.	Gurdwara: Moti Bagh	—	4037	9000	—	9050	6826	—	3963	32876
9.	Gurdwara: Majnu Tilla	3103	3114	750	1787	11518	6841	—	1634	28747
10.	Gurdwara: Mata Sundari Ji	3435	—	4250	4263	3621	8220	2488	606·	26883

Shrines Surrendered by the Sri Guru Singh Sabha									
11. Gurdwara: Darya Ganj	3	—	490	4894	—	6291	—	96	11774
12. Gurdwara: Dhaka Dhirpur	964	—	—	2490	—	5120	9683	137	18394
13. Gurdwara: Pahari Dheeraj	—	—	—	—	—		—		
14. Gurdwara: Banda Singh Bahadur	—	—	—	—	—		—		
15. Gurdwara: Pipal Mahadev	—	—	—	—	—	4920	—	1062	5982
16. Gurdwara: Badarpur	—	—	—	—	—		—		
Other Institutions									
Guru Purabs	—	—	—	—	—	—	—	392069	392069
Vehicles	—	—	—	—	—	—	—	12660	12660
Daily Expenditure	—	—	—	—	—	—	—	250	250
Cases	—	—	—	—	—	—	—	328	328
Hospitals	—	—	—	—	—	10527	—	11338	21865
Electronics Institute	—	—	—	—	—	10527	—	12786	23313
Interest	—	—	—	—	—	—	—	11243	11243
Gratuity	—	—	—	—	—	—	—	14940	14940
Property	—	—	—	—	—	—	—	2613	2613
Propogational Work	—	—	—	—	—	—	—	100557	100557
Office	—	—	—	—	—	—	—	21863	21863

Relief Fund	—	—	—	—	—	—	—	368435	368435
Help to Victims of Riots	—	—	—	—	—	—	—	148496	148496
School/College	—	—	—	—	577625	—	—	306055	883680
Total Expenditure on the Month of March 1987	778908	251935	136554	64761	906226	388751	78032	1897194	3502361
Expenditure from April 1986 to Feb. 1987	6184848	2226932	1100965	608093	4383842	4914492	373280	8920829	28713281
Total Expenditure of D.S.G.M.C. on the financial year 1986-87	6963756	2478867	1237519	672854	5290068	5303243	451312	10818023	32215642

* Source: Department of Accounts, Delhi Sikh Gurdwara Management Committee, Chandni Chowk, Delhi.

statement from the office of the Delhi Sikh Gurdwara Management Committee that he budget is estimated in every financial year and placed before the committee and duly passed. In this regard some members of the Delhi Sikh Gurdwara Management Committee were found dissatisfied regarding the funds were utilised.

REFERENCES

1. Hutton H.J., *Caste in India,* p. 112.
2. Maciver, R.M., and Page, C.H.: *Society,* pp. 145-146.
3. Bates, A.P., and Julian, J.: *Sociology—Understanding and Behaviour,* p. 155.
4. Ahluwalia, Jasvir Singh: Baptismal Amrit—a Sociological Significance, *(Studies in Sikhism and Comparative Religion),* pp. 82-83.
5. Parson, Talcott: *The Social System,* p. 40.
6. Kuppuswamy, B.: *Elements of Social Psychology,* p. 95.
7. *Dictionary of Sociology,* edited by G.D. Mitchell, p. 104.
8. Weber, Max: *The Theory of Social and Economic Organisation,* edited by T. Parsons, pp. 218-19.

6

Mode of Management and Working of the Sikh Shrines

After discussing the socio-economic structure of the Sikh shrines in Chapter 5th, now an attempt has been made to discover and examine mode of management and working of the Sikh shrine. Speaking in general terms there have been various modes of management in the society to run the organisation, such as, autocratic management, bureaucratic management, defensive management, systematic management and so on. But the main philosophy behind these managements is to draw best output from their employees. It may lead us to say that the strength of any organisation depends largely on its management. If the organisation is to remain strong, it must be given to the development of human assets. It may be in the fitness of things to add that the development of any individual in the organisation depends, to a large extent, upon the attitudes of his superiors. It needs to be emphasised that the superiors can not develop subordiantes; they must develop themselves. Nevertheless, the superiors can provide the atmosphere in which subordinates can experiment and grow. Hence we may deductively say that the entire organisational survival depends upon its mode of management and working.

Now shifting our attention to the main theme it may be pointed out that both the processes of management and working of the Sikh shrines must be taken into account, if the process of institutionalisation is to be understood in its correct light. Therefore, one of the focal point of the present investigation was to study the mode of management and working of the Sikh shrines in the surveyed area. It is in this context an attention here has been shifted mainly to discuss the aspects as: Internal Management, Daily routine of the shrines, External Management, Size and Composition of the Managing Body, Qualification of the members, Election procedure, Working of the Committee, Power-structure and Decision Making and Activities of the Management Committee of the shrines. Now these aspects may be discussed in essence in this chapter.

I. INTERNAL MANAGEMENT OF THE SHRINES

As the investigator said earlier that the institutionalisation of any institution or organisation is both process and result and may be scientifically tested after the management and working of the organisation is observed. In this respect the investigator has studied the internal and external management and working of the shrines. The internal management is structured with adequate staff of Head priest (Head granthi), priest (granthi), Pathi (reader of Sri Guru Granth Saheb), Kirtan Jatha (the band of musicians), Jathedar (supervisor of the Sewadaar) and Sewadaar (maker of different services in the shrines). On the contrary, the external management is joint effort of executives, representatives and their officials. Now to take the internal management in the first instance and external in the second. In this connection we have interviewed Head priests of the shrines and the executives of their managing bodies. And thereby the inferences were drawn through analysis and interpretations.

In an attempt to make an explanation and clarification of the term 'Head priest' in our frame of reference, we had two categories of interviews. In the first category were included those who were actually designated as Head priests (as in the case of 12 historical and prominent shrines (24%) drawing salary and other perquisites going with this office. In the second category included those who were having a mere semblance and a title of Head priest but virtually they were not getting salary and privileges accordingly. The reason for it was found that in all these cases (applying to an overwhelming number of Sikh shrines approximately 76%) there was one priest assisted by a small number of juniors. And thus we have treated them as Head priests and included them as such in our sample for the sake of convenience.

Now to analyse what are the rights and power-structure of the Head priests. The relevant data may be manipulated logically in the following pages.

Rights Vested in Office of the Head Priests

Here an attention was focused on finding out what are the various rights and their structures which the Head priests were armed with. The researcher would like to categories as administrative rights, supervisory rights, obligatory rights, corporate and collective rights. In the administrative rights we have included those who were related the matter of general administration, keeping or removal of petty staff, maintaining general discipline and order and the like. Our study reveals that these rights were in evidence only in the case of the Head priests belonging to 10 historical and prominent Sikh shrines. Among the rest these rights paled into insignificance. To came to the supervisory rights covering the daily working of the shrines, taking an order with the daily services and monitoring other routine matters, it was observed that they were quite improminence. To shift to the obligatory rights going with the laying down and prescription of rules and norms of the office held by them they did not have wide incidence. However the corporate or collective rights had somewhat greater incidence among them. The following table may throw some light on the extent and magnitude of these rights vested in the Head priests:

TABLE 6.1

Rights Vested in the Office of the Head Priests

Nature of Rights	*Respondents*	
	No.	*Per cent*
Administrative	10	20
Supervisory	25	50
Obligatory	5	10
Corporate/Collective	10	20
Total	50	100

Main Functions of the Head Priests

For the purpose of our study here we have mainly aimed a collecting the data on some of the important functions being performed by the Head priests. The typology, functions and their corresponding data we dealt with in the following table:

TABLE 6.2

Main Functions of the Head Priests

Types of Functions	*Respondents*	
	No.	*Per cent*
Alloting Duties	10	20
Monitoring and Supervision	15	30
Dealing with the problem of devotees	5	10
To strengthen and keeping working system healthy	20	40
Total	50	100

Table 6.2 illustrates that the main function of the majority of the respondents (40%) was to strengthen and keeping working system healthy of the shrines. The 20 per cent of

them had the main function alloting the duties to their inmates. The rest 40 per cent of the respondents were seen performing mainly the function of monitoring and supervising the various activities and programmes of the shrines.

Viewing these various functions, it can easily be inferred that in majority of cases of Head priests were concerned with the function of keeping the organisation healthy and strong. And for it they frequently devised new ways and mechanism Considered expedient to the demand of the situation and requirement of the time. It may reflects that their mode of functioning tends to get oriented to the process of institutionalisation.

Mode of and Right to Punishment

It was attempted to find out what were the various mode of awarding punishment and the right thereto among the Head priest. Though, not much data were collected in this regard, however, it may be pointed out that a sizable majority (80%) the Head priest reacted confining themselves only to giving warning to the erring persons. On the other hand only a slender number 20 per cent of them reacted to the choice of terminating the erring persons. The following table may clarify the position:

TABLE 6.3

The Head Priests and their Rights to Punishment

The Mode of Punishment	*Respondents*	
	No.	*Per cent*
Giving	40	80
Giving order for menial services	—	—
Termination	10	20
Total	50	100

TABLE 6.4

Daily Routine of the Sikh Shrines

Timings	*Ritualistic Activities*	*Conceptual Clarification of the Term*	*Special Services and Routine Activities*
(I) Morning Routine			
2.30 a.m.	Timings of the opening of the Kiwars	Opening of the enterance doors	1. *Akhand Path:* Non-stop reading of the holy book
2.45 a.m.	Prakash	To burn the pure ghee-fed lamp just near the Sri Guru Granth Saheb	2. *Karha Prasad:* The gift of God to his devotees
3.00 a.m.	Vak or Hukam Arambh	To draw the holy ward from the holy Sri Guru Granth Saheb	3. *Langar:* Free community kitchen to all
3.15 a.m.	Starting of the Path of the Sukhmani Saheb		4. *Piyao:* To distribute the water without any caste and creed
6.00 a.m.	Completion of the Path of the Sukhmani Saheb		5. *Dispensing:* To distribute the medicines to the needy, helpless and the poors.
4.30 a.m.	Time of starting of the Asa-waari (after two hour of the opening of the Kiwars)	Procession of the holy book of the Sri Guru Granth Saheb from the resting place of the holy book (Ground of first floor)	
6.00 a.m. to 8.00 a.m.	Asa Di War	Morning Prayer in the Sikh religion	

8.00 a.m. to 9. 00 am	Katha	To analyse the hymns of the holy book
9.00 a.m. to 10.00 a.m.	Kirtan	Praise of the God presented by best Raagi Jatha (Musicians)
10.00 a.m.	Aardas	Sikh prayer performed at the conclusion
10.30 a.m.	Samapti	Completion of the morning routine
(II) Evening Routine (By Sunset)		
600 p.m. to 9.00 p.m.	Path of Rah Ras Saheb	Evening prayer in the Sikh religion
9.00 p.m. to 10.00 p.m.	Kirtan Sohilla	Late evening prayer
10.30 p.m.	Ardas and Samapti	Prayer and completion of the Evening Routine
10.45 p.m.	Time of the return of Asawari Saheb	To keep out of the holy book, Sri Guru Granth Saheb at his resting place with religious practices
11.00 p.m.	Closing of the Kiwars	Closing of the enterance doors

II. DAILY ROUTINE OF THE SHRINES

Having analysed the rights and their structures among the Head priests it was found of interest to examine the Daily Routine of the Shrines. Our main interest here was to investigate and discover their emphasis on the religio-cultural patterns and activities being directed to attaining universal equality and other matters of catholicity. In order to gather the relevant data we have divided the daily routine of these shrines into two categories—Morning Routine — starting from 2.30 A.M. to 10.30 A.M. or from the openings of the Kiwars till Samapti— and Evening Routine beginning from 6 P.M. to 11 P.M. or from evening prayer till closing of the Kiwars.

It needs to be emphasised here that, while dealing with the daily routine, various such terms have been used which have a special meaning for the Sikhs and or popular with them in their religious parlence. Hence, they need to be explained and clarify to make them understandable to the lay public. The relevant Table 6.4 carries the necessary explanation of these vernacular and local terms concerning their routine.

Morning Routine of the Shrines

It was gathered that there was a fixed daily routine in the historical prominent shrines but no fixed daily routine was observed in the shrines of Sri Guru Singh Sabha. The Sikh shrines, mainly historical prominent, remain open throughout the day except for a short interval of approx. four hours (11 P.M. to 2.30 A.M.). This time of routine may be fluctuate during the changed seasons. Daily routine includes chiefly ritualistic and institutional activities, reading and analysing of the Holy Book, Sri Guru Granth Saheb and teaching and preaching for the benefit for the congregration.

In the above context, it may be noted here that the morning routine of the shrines was bound with some subinstitutions, such as — Vak, Kirtan, Ardas, Karha Prasad, Akhand Path and Langar etc., as an essential features of the faith. The relevant analysis based on keen observations is given on the following:

(i) Kiwars and Vak

It is clear form the Table 6.4 that the preliminaries of the shrines ranging from the opening of the Kiwars to Vak or Shabad (Hukum Arambh) were seen taking place between 2.30 A.M. to 3.00 A.M. The Vak (word or shabad) carries some sanctity and significance in the routine of the shrines. It is believe that the Vak is derived from the mouth of the Guru. To elaborate it may be added that the Vak constitute the basis of innerlife with inner treasure of wisdom and knowledge. It was observed that those attending the congregation go first to show respect and salute the Vak—the religious and pious citation displayed on the outer wall of the shrines connecting to enterence of the shrine. And this goes on among the devotees as and when they enter the shrine for congregational purpose. And thus the Vak has assumed the character of a near — institution.

(ii) Kirtan

Another important activity observed was the practice of Kirtan. The kirtan starts and goes continually till the gates are closed for the night and the Guru Granth Saheb is taken back to its place of rest (Sukhasan). The regularity of this practice was more visible in the case of prominent historical shrines and was not so among the shrines belonging to Sri Guru Singh Sabha. The kirtan observed as an essential part of the religious service in the shrines. The efforts are made to secure the services of the best Ragi Jathas (the band of musicians) for the purpose. At present there were found many trained Ragi Jathas in the Gurdwara Sis Ganj Saheb (most revered shrine where the Ninth Guru Sri Tegbahadur was beheaded) who perform the melodious Kirtan into the different prominent historical shrines and also the shrines of Sri Guru Singh Sabha. It was observed that the only Shabads from the Sri Guru Granth Saheb were permitted to be sung in the shrines. In the morning session the kirtan is followed by recitation of Asa Di War (morning prayer of the Sikh religion) which goes on till the sun rises. After the morning prayer was over the Head priests perform the Katha (analysis of the Holy Book) with musical instrument before the congregation.

(iii) The Ardas

Proceeding further with the daily routine of the shrines, we may now discuss the usage and procedure of the service of the Ardas (prayer). The Ardas — the prayer invoking Almighty's benedictions — is observed as an most essential feature of the every shrines. It is offered by three times a day. The first Ardas goes up immediately after the formalities in connection with the arrival of the Holy Book, from the resting place to the main plateform. Second Ardas goes up on the completion of the recitation of the *Asa Di War* and third Ardas goes up at *Samapti* (completion of the morning routine), when *Ragis* (reciters) finish the recitation of Anand Saheb (the final prayer at the time of Ardas).

(iv) The Karha Prasad

In the daily routine of the Sikh shrines the practice of Karha Prasad also occupies an important place. The Karha Prasad is made form plain floor with desi ghee and sugar. The hymns of sacred scriptures are sung during its preparation. It is distributed among the Sangat without any discrimination. It was observed, particularly in the case of historical prominent Sikh shrines, that the Karha Prasad on sell at the counter near the shrine. The devotees generally purchase this Karha Prasad and get it offered before the Holy Scripture, Sri Guru Granth Saheb, through the priest who later gives back some of it to the devotees. It was further observed that the Karha Prasad thus collected by way of its being offered to the Holy Book is taken outside for its being distributed among the devotees while leaving the shrine.

(v) The Akhand Path

Our observation in this regard is that the arrangements for performing the Akhand Path from the Holy Book were made at the request and bid of the devotees meeting the expenses incurred on it. It was also observed that the Akhand Paths were permitted on the happy occasions not on the occasion of grief, e.g. death etc. These Akhand Paths were commemorated only in the historical prominent shrines, e.g., Gurdwara Sis Ganj, Bangla Saheb and Rakab Ganj etc. The regular practice of these Akhand Paths may be seen twenty-four hours on the ground floor or first floor of these shrines. This practice was not observed as a regular feature in the small shrines both belonging to the category of prominent historical shrines and those of Sri Guru Singh Sabha. A person desirous of availing himself of this privilege and gratifying experience must deposit a fix amount with the office of the local committee after which his name will be registered and the Akhand Path will be performed when his turn comes.

(vi) The Langar

Lastly in the daily routine, we may discuss the institution of Langar. The study revealed that the Langar was as old as Sikh faith. It is born-out by the Sikh scriptures that the Guru-ka-Langar played a vital role in removing the caste barriers and social inequalities in the society at large. It was observed that still it is valued greatly by and is rated high among the followers of the Sikh faith and thus the shrines whether large or small were seen giving due importance to it. The organising and funding part of the Langar is entrusted to the local managing committee of the shrines. The study revealed that the Langar was performed daily by prominent historical shrines but on the contrary this practice was not observed as an regular feature in the small shrines. To sight a most prominent example we may here quote the Head priest of the Bangla Saheb Shrine, most sacred and prominent shrines of the Sikhs in Delhi situated at Cannaught Place, saying that 90 bags of wheat floor were consumed daily in the Langar entertaining thousands of devotees and lay persons to it with no discrimination of caste and creed.

Evening Routine of the Shrines

It was observed that after the morning routine was over, in the case of prominent historical shrines, a regular Kirtan goes on continually till the gates are closed for the night and the Sri Guru Granth Saheb is taken back to its place of rest. But this regular and continuous practice of kirtan was observed only in the large Sikh shrines. In small shrines an evening routine starts after the sunset with the Path of Rahras Saheb (evening prayer) through Kirtan. After this prayer was over, the kirtan is resumed again and goes on till (as also clear from the Table 6.4). This makes the last Kirtan of the day and daily routine ends with it. After this routine, the Holy Book is taken back at his resting place with religious practices and Kiwars are closed.

Some inferences may be drawn from the 'Daily Routine' of the Sikh shrines:

First, it was observed that there was strict enforcement of the codes of conduct for the daily life in the prominent historical shrines in Delhi.

Secondly, it was found that the Daily Routine of the shrines, from morning to evening was institutionalised with the sub-institutions such as — Vak, Kirtan, Ardas, Karha Prasad, Akhand Path and Langar etc. taking place widely and almost uniformly.

Thirdly, it was gathered that the Sangat were found completely surrendered to their shrines. Everybody who joins the shrine, morning or evening, wants to share every type of service. The priority was given to Sewa (service towards the humanity) in the shrines which also assumed the character of being internalised and standardised.

Lastly, it may be inferred that the Daily Routine of all the shrines is getting restricted day by day to the community and the concept of universal equity and brotherhood in the Sikh panth is declining gradually.

III. EXTERNAL MANAGEMENT OF THE SHRINES

Here an attempt was made to examine the External Working or Management of the Shrines in the surveyed area. In this context the investigator has covered 50 members of the executive body of the shrines who figured as President or Secretary (some were members of the various committees) of the managing bodies.

Out of 46 Elected Members in the Delhi Sikh Gurdwara Management Committee (D.S.G.M.C.), 16 members (32%) were interviewed and 34 (68%) — taking one each colonywise belonging to Sri Guru Singh Sabha — members were interviewed from Sri Guru Singh Sabhas. The relevant data are given in the following paragraphs.

Aims and Objectives of the Managing Body

The main aim and objective of an organisation is to give the direction and determine the activities of its members and the pattern of their interaction. Keeping in view the significance of these aims and objectives for an organisation, the members D.S.G.M.C. and Shri Guru Singh Sabha Delhi were asked to identity the main aims and objectives of their organisation which they liked most. The following table may clarify it.

It is evident form the Table 6.5 that a majority of respondents (66%) of both the managing bodies identified the propagation of the Sikh religion as most important objective. Some members have gone so far as to say that now we have to live and die only for the propagation and welfare of the community. The second largest number of the members (20%) stressed the safe custody of the funds of the shrines. As a meagre 10 per cent were found disposed towards educational institutional and charitable facilities.

TABLE 6.5

Aims and Objectives of the Managing Bodies

(As Identified by the Members)

Aims and Objectives	*Respondents*					
	Members of the D.S.G.M.C.		*Members of the Shri Guru Singh Sabha*		*Total*	
	No.	P.C.	No.	P.C.	No.	P.C.
Propagation of the Sikh religion	8	16	25	50	33	66
Ensuring safe custody of funds of the shrine	4	8	6	12	10	20
Providing educational, institutional and charitable facilities	2	4	3	6	5	10
Establishing welfare programme	2	4	—	—	2	4
Total	16	32	34	68	50	100

On the basis of data the inference may be drawn that two objectives which had greater attention form the members of the Delhi Sikh Gurdwara Management Committee and the Sri Guru Singh Sabha were the propagation of the Sikh religion and the ensuring of safe custody of funds and property of the shrines.

A. Composition and Size of the Managing Bodies

(i) Delhi Sikh Gurdwara Management Committee

The formation of Delhi Sikh Gurdwara Management Committee is base don the Delhi Sikh Gurdwaras Act, 1971, approved by the Govt. of India, Ministry of Law and Justice.[1] According to the Act, the D.S.G.M.C. consists of fifty five members, out of which 46 members are elected from the various wards into which Delhi is divided and 9 members are co-opted by the elected members, the Co-opted members include two representatives of the registered Singh Sabhas[2] of Delhi who are chosen by draw of lots from among the Presidents of the Sabhas. The Head priests of the Four Takhts[3] are also co-opted as members. The remaining three members include one nominee of the Shromani Gurdwara Prabandhak Committee, Amritsar, and two representatives of the Sikh community of Delhi. The term of office of a member of the Committee is four years from the date on which the first meeting was held.

(ii) Shri Guru Singh Sabha

The formation of Sri Guru Singh Sabha is based on the Societies Registration Act XXI of 1860 (Punjab Amendment Act, 1957). According to this Act every Sri Guru Singh Sabha consists of 21 members. These all members of the Sabha are elected by the Sangat of the particular colony. Each colony has its own Sri Guru Singh Sabha on the name of his colony. After every two years, the followers of the faith and those who are members of Rs. 6 collect in the shrine and elect the members of the sabha. If the working performance of the Sabha is good the time may be extended by the same Sangat.

(iii) Composition and Size of the Executive Board

Both of the managing bodies have maintained a hierarchy of power and same pattern is followed to form the Executive Board. The Executive Board is the highest organ and takes all the decisions. The Board of both the managing bodies consists of five office bearers — President, Senior Vice-President, Junior Vice-President, General Secretary and Joint Secretary and ten members. All these fifteen members of the Board are elected by the elected members of both the managing bodies.

(iv) Qualifications of the Members

According to the Delhi Sikh Gurdwara Management Act, 1971, a person to be member of the Committee should attain the age of twenty-five years; should be a citizen of India; should be an Amritdhari Sikh (initiated); should not trim his beard or shave his Keshas (hairs); should not take alcoholic drinks; should not smoke; should not be of sound mind; and should be able to read and write Gurmukhi language.

It was observed that the same critaria of qualifications were followed by the managing body of Sri Guru Singh Sabha.

It may be concluded that the condition for membership of both the managing bodies affirms its concern for a high level of personal morality and a distinct Sikh identity. It was also found that a sound ethical code and physical appearance is a must to fight the election of the managing body.

Political Mobilisation and Voting Behaviour

The study revealed that the managing bodies of Delhi Sikh Shrines took interest of Sikh politics and participate in their action programme. The top leaders of these managing bodies have always been taking keen interest in active politics.

It is clear from the above account that these managing bodies of the Sikh shrines of Delhi are not only purely a socio-religious bodies but also quasi-political ones. Therefore an attempt has bene made to find out the political mobilisation and voting behaviour of the members of these bodies. To explore their interest in casting their vote for their candidates they were asked, "what does influence you while casting your vote"? The Table 6.6 indicates that 80 per cent of the respondents cast their vote in favour of candidate of their religion. They advocated strongly that only initiated Sikh (who adopted Khalsa) could fight the electin of the body. They also admitted that the candidature of the candidate is already defined by the Delhi Sikh Gurdwara Act, 1971. Against it, 8 per cent were in favour of personal popularity and remaining 12 per cent showed their interest in personal competence.

TABLE 6.6

The Political Mobilisation and Voting Behaviour of the Members

Deliberations of the members	*Respondents*	
	No.	*Per cent*
Belonging to your religion only	40	80
Regional loyalty	—	—
Party support	—	—
Personal popularity	4	8
Perosnal competence	6	12
Total	50	100

It may be inferred from the Table 6.6 that an overwhelming majority (80%) have given the top priority of their religion and religious person while casting their vote in the election of the managing bodies.

An Eligibility Critaria for a Candidate Seeking the Highest Status

In order to further explore the main eligibility critaria of the candidate seeking the highest status an attempt has been made to discover the qualifications and conditions laid down for it.

It is interesting to note that 76 per cent majority of the members have given the first priority to religious affiliation. They acknowledged that without the religious affiliation the members of the committee could not aspire for higher status. Against it only 6 per cent of them have admitted the critarion of party support, 8 per cent about personal competence and remaining 10 per cent about economic prosperity.

A significant finding here is that the party support and money power both played an important role in the election and also in seeking the highest status in the managing bodies.

TABLE 6.7

Eligibility Critaria for Seeking the Highest Status in the Bodies

Eligibility Based	*Respondents*	
	No.	*Per cent*
Religious Affiliation	38	76
Party Support	3	6
Personal Competence	4	8
Economic Prosperity	5	10
Total	50	100

Though our data may not sufficiently bare out it, but the researcher, on the basis of his own experiences during the study and his insight knowledge, may conclude that the party support and money power also these days appeared and gathering ground in influencing the election politics.

IV. WORKING OF THE MANAGING BODY

There are various modes of working to run the organisation such as traditional, modern, democratic, dictatorial and so on. The working of the organisation plays an important role to establish an identity in the society. After watching the working or functioning of an organisation we could recognise easily either the organisation is traditional or modern. The working of an organisation must be understood if the institutionalisation of an organisation is to be understood. Therefore an attempt was made here to examine the working of the Sikh shrines in Delhi.

It was gathered that the working of the D.S.G.M.C. and Sri Guru Singh Sabha is carried out through various Committees constituted by the Executive Board. The Executive Board can constitute as many sub-committees from amongst its members as it thinks fit and for such purposes as it may decide. Generally, sub-committees of D.S.G.M.C. consists of ten or fifteen members. Against this, the sub-committee of

Sri Guru Singh Sabha comprise of 2 or 3 members depending upon the purpose for which it is constituted. The office of both the managing bodies is managed by the Manager according to rules and byelaws of the body and instructions issued by it form time to time through its secretary.

The Pattern of Leadership

It is clearly evident form the Table 6.8 that 52 per cent majority of the respondents reacted that the pattern of leadership, in both the managing bodies, was democratic. They advocated that the decision are taken through process and by majority of opinions. Against this 34 per cent of the respondents reacted that the present leadership was power and money oriented. One respondent frankly said, "our present leadership is greedy and main goal of it is to spend money levishly." And remaining 14 per cent told that the present pattern of leadership was self-oriented and also significantly spoken that the present pattern of leadership was selfish and should be changed. There was no response to the idea of the dictatorial and collectivity oriented leadership.

TABLE 6.8

The Pattern of Leadership of the Managing Committee (as Identified by the Members)

Nature of Leadership	*Respondents*	
	No.	*Per cent*
Democratic	26	52
Dictatorial	—	—
Power and money oriented	17	34
Self oriented	7	14
Çollectivity oriented	—	—
Total	50	100

It may be summed form the data slightly more than fifty per cent (52%) of the respondents favoured the democratic pattern of leadership.

The Pattern of Management

In order to further explore the working of the Committee an attempt has been made to know the pattern of management. It is evident from the Table 6.9 that the majority of the respondents (76%) preferred the religious minded management. Against it 20 per cent favoured highly educated and experienced and remaining 4 per cent preferred honest and morally bound management.

TABLE 6.9

The Pattern of Management for the Welfare of the Sikh Devotees

Pattern of Management	*Respondents*	
	No.	*Per cent*
Religious Minded	38	76
Highly educated and experienced	10	20
Honest and Morally bound	2	4
Total	50	100

To sum up, it may be inferred that the management carried on by religious minded people drew the greatest notice.

Reactions of the Members about the Present Set-up of the Managing Body

Responses to the question, "Do you think that the present set-up of the Committee and Sabha is not giving right path to the shrines?" Were presented in the following Table 6.10 suggest that 20 per cent of the respondents were strongly satisfied with the existing set up of the D.S.G.M.C. and Sri Guru Singh Sabha; whereas 14 per cent were partly satisfied. The number of those who felt dissatisfied with the present set-up was as high as 30 per cent and 20 per cent members were strongly dissatisfied. Remaining 16 per cent of the members gave not reply.

TABLE 6.10

Reactions of the Members Towards Present Set-up of the Managing Bodies

Reaction	*Respondents*	
	Responses	*Per cent*
Strongly satisfied	10	20
Partly satisfied	7	14
Undecided	8	16
Dissatisfied	15	30
Strongly dissatisfied	10	20
Total	50	100

In conclusion, we may say that the majority of members of the managing bodies were not satisfied with the existing set-up of the bodies.

Factors of Organisational Weakness

To the question, "Do you feel any organisational weakness?" Table 6.11 shows that 50 per cent respondents admitted that the organisational weakness was in evidence due to the greedy leadership; whereas 20 per cent attributed lack of unity to it creating vested interests vitiating the vary atmosphere in the organisation. In descending order 18 per cent of them were dissatisfied with power performance of the members and remaining 12 per cent acknowledged about the groupism as the reason for it.

In summing up, it can be said that the largest majority of the respondents reacted that the dysfunctional trends in the managing bodies threaten to find their way into the working and management of these shrines.

TABLE 6.11

Identified Factors for Organisational Weakness

Factors	*Respondents*	
	Responses	*Per cent*
Lack of Unity	10	20
Greedy leaderships	25	50
Dissatisfaction with the power performance	9	18
Groupism	6	12
No reply	—	—
Total	50	100

Changes Suggested by the Members

To the question, "what kind of change would you like to make the working more effective?" The Table 6.12 exhibits that 40 per cent respondents suggested that the total managing body should be changed to make the working more effective. A negligible number, 10 per cent, suggested regarding the executive board. These respondents also advocated that more powers should not be deligated to the members of the executive board; it should have only advisory powers and the approval to its proposals should be given by the General House. 20 per cent of the respondents suggested that the old rules of the managing bodies should be changed. They stated that the old rules are not fit into the existing structure of the managing bodies. Remaining of the respondents pointed out that the mode and body of financial management should be changed. These respondents suggested that the persons in dealing with the financial matters should be transferred; so that they may not come to occupy a monopolistic position in this regard. The relevant data are given in the Table 6.12.

It is clear from the table that the affairs of the Delhi Sikh Gurdwara Management Committee were not in sound health and this needed proper handling. Contrarily, the shrines belonging to the Sri Guru Singh Sabha give somewhat a better picture.

TABLE 6.12.

The Changes Suggested by the Office-bearers of the Managing Bodies

Changes suggested	*Respondents*	
	No.	*Per cent*
An overhaul of the Management Committee	20	40
An Executive Board	5	10
The Rules	10	20
The Financial Management	15	30
Total	50	100

Emergence of Groupism and Factionalism

Mostly, in all the socio-religious organisations different type of sub-groups emerge and stabilise. The sub-groups influence the leadership and the style of working of the organisation as a whole. In respect of the managing bodies of both the categories of the shrines, it is attempted here to examine and discuss the trends of groupism and factionalism creeping into these shrines. Our observation here is that the Sikh shrines affiliated to Sri Guru Singh Sabha were not affected much by groupism and factionalism. Hence no investigations were made about these shrines on the aspect of groupism. Our findings hence mostly related to the shrines run by the Delhi Sikh Gurdwara Management Committee. The analysis of data are given in the following lines.

It is clear from the Table 6.13 that 32 per cent of the respondents the existence of two or three rival groups which were suggested at cross purposes. Mainly, one such group was led by late Jathedar Santokh Singh (assassinated former President of D.S.G.M.C.) and the other by the Shromani Akali

Dal. Some members frankly told that all the groups existed on the basis of personal loyality to the leaders and similarity of the economic interests.

Rest 68 per cent majority of the respondents significantly conceded that mostly the Singh Sabhas were free from the groupism. The main reason of it was in sufficiency of the income from the shrines.

TABLE 6.13

The Emergence of Groupism in the Bodies

No. of Groups	*Respondents*	
	No.	*Per cent*
0 - 1	—	—
1 - 2	—	—
2 - 3	16	32
3 - 4	34	68
Not applicable	—	—
Total	50	100

Power Structure and Decision Making

An organisation is run by the defined role of the members. The defined roles fixes the rights and responsibilities within the organisational system. Within the limits of this system, the organisation conducts its affairs and takes decisions and implements the same. Therefore, an attempt was made here to examine and understand the power-structure and decision making process of the D.S.G.M.C. and the Sri Guru Singh Sabha.

It was gathered that the Delhi Sikh Gurdwara Management Committee consists of 55 members out of which 46 are elected from the various wards into which Delhi is divided and 9 members are co-opted by the members. The term of office of a member of the Committee is four years from the date on which the first meeting of the Committee was held.

It was also collected that the D.S.G.M.C. is elected to manage 16 shrines and other affairs but on the other side the Sri Guru Singh Sabha is elected to run ownly separate shrine. Consequently, the Sri Guru Singh Sabha consists of 21 members. The term of the office of a member is two years. The Executive Board of both the managing bodies consists five office-bearers and ten members and same method is adopted to take the decisions and implementation.

The office of both the managing bodies is managed by the Manager according to the rules and regulations of the Committee and Sabha and instructions issued by them from time to time through the Secretary. Both of the managing bodies are well knit and effective organisations and based on the well defined tenets of Sikhism.

It is observed that the general meeting of both the managing bodies is held every year and the meeting of the Executive Board in a month. Both of these organs observe such rules of procedure in regard to transaction of the business. About the mode of decision making in the Executive Board, the decisions on minor issues were generally taken unanimously and the decisions on major lapses or disputes such as new construction or expansion works, propagating and promotional activities or setting up new educational institutions, the were taken by a majority vote.

It has also been gathered that there were no major lapses or disputes in the managing body of Sri Guru Singh Sabha. Generally the democratic norms are regarded by the members of the Sri Guru Singh Sabha. But the study brought to light some dysfunctional aspects of the process of decision-making in the Delhi Sikh Gurdwara Management Committee (D.S.G.M.C.). The responses of the respondents are mentioned in the following table:

TABLE 6.14

Reactions of the Members of the Managing Bodies About the Present Decision-Making System

Reactions	*Respondents*	
	Rsponses	*Per cent*
Strongly satisfied	20	40
Mildly satisfied	10	20
Undecided	9	18
Dissatisfied	10	20
Strongly dissatisfied	1	2
Total	50	100

It is clear from the above table that 60 per cent majority of the members were either strongly satisfied or mildly satisfied against it 22 per cent of the members were dissatisfied or strongly dissatisfied. This majority told frankly that the democratic norms were not observed in the decision making system. Some members strongly complained that in some cases the higher authority took the decisions without consulting the Executive Board. These members also pointed out that a few elite class members dominated the decision making system. Mostly this majority of the respondents were associated with the D.S.G.M.C. Remaining 18 per cent were unable to deliver their consent.

It may be inferred from the data mentioned in the Table 6.14 that the democratic norms were observed in the mostly bodies of Sri Guru Singh Sabhas. On the contrary, those who dissatisfied with the present decision making alleged that some dysfunctional trends were crepted in the Delhi Sikh Gurdwara Management Committee.

V. ACTIVITIES OF THE MANAGING BODIES AND THE SHRINES

Discipline of active service or service to the humanity has

played a prominent role in the evolution of Sikh religion. According to the Sikhism, service should not be confined to fixed forms of sectarian charity but shall be freely varied according to the needs of those to whom it is rendered to serve this purpose the Sikh institutions were designed to abolish the invidous distinctions between man and man and to retain all who came into their orbit in the art of peace and service.

The Sikh shrines are the life and soul of the Sikh community. There very life is dependent upon the purity, emancipation and upon the freedom of these shrines from all corrupt practices. Mostly Sikh shrines are associated with the lives of the Gurus. These Sikh places of worship were from the time of Gurus and now their vary places are developed in the form of Historical prominent shrines and managed by the local managing bodies. The administration of these shrines is based mainly on the Delhi Sikh Gurdwara Act of 1971. Third part of this Act is totally laid down only philanthropic activities such as — to provide suitable accommodation for pilgrims, to maintain free Langars, to celebrate birth anniversaries, to open free dispensaries, to spread education and to render financial assistance to religious and educational institutions, societies and needy persons.

The Sikh Gurus laid so much stress on the philanthropic activities or relief to the needy and for helpless persons. They emphasised it as a part of daily routine to remove the differentiation between man and man.

The shrines are the main source of philanthropic activities. Consequently, they also lay great emphasis on the action oriented work and service (Sewa) and encourage the ideals of equality and brotherhood and also generate the disposition to set up charitable institutions. It was gathered that the shrines were working against the demoralising effect of social evils and ill customs. Therefore, an attempt was made to know the philanthropic activities rendering by the Managing

Bodies through shrines. A brief account of the activities may be classified under the following headings:

A. Religious Activities

An essential feature of the Sikh Shrines is the presence of the Guru. All the historical prominent shrines in Delhi are connected with the life of the Sikh Gurus. Those very places are not only sacred centres of the Sikhs but also cluster of some religious activities.

It was gathered that a variety of activities are performed by the Delhi Sikh Shrines, both prominent historical and those of Sri Guru Singh Sabha, to commemorate the days of their Guru's birth or martyrdom (Guru Purbs).

(i) Guru Purbs

The relevant data collected in this regard may be presented in the form of a list of some notable Guru purbs as below:

TABLE 6.15

The Month and Types of Guru Purbs

Month	*Namd of Guru Purbs*
May-June	Martyrdom of Guru Arjan-Universally commemorated.
July	Birthday of Guru Harkishan — celebrated only at Delhi.
November	Guru Nanak's birthday anniversary— Universally celebrated.
December	Birthday of Guru Gobind Singh — Universally celebrated.
December	Martyrdom day of Guru Tegbahadur — observed only at Delhi.

It was collected that three important anniversaries or Guru Purbs are celebrated universally and remaining celebrated where the real event was taken place. These three were the birth day of Guru Nanak, Guru Gobind Singh and the Martyrdom day of Guru Arjan Devji. In Delhi these festivals were celebrated by the shrines through their managing bodies. On this occasion, the Sikh Sangat take out colourful processions. The Sri Guru Granth Saheb placed in a decorated palanquin is carried upon a flower bedecked lorry, followed and preceded by enthusiastic and gaity-dressed devotees, singing parties and sword-stick performers, and escorted by horsemen, cycle or motorcycle contingents, and Panj Piyaras (five beloved ones) with drawn swords.

The main features of the Guru Purbs are also the Langar an Akhand Path, preparing the Karha Prasad (sweet pudding) and offering of the Prayer.

(ii) The Diwali

It was observed that the Diwali was also one of the most important festival of the Sikhs. It is celebrated by the Sikhs in the shrines with the zeal and zest. It falls in the last week of October or in the first — week of November. The number of visitors on this occasion run into massive figures. It takes the form of a big mela (fair) in the shrine's premises with the Punjabi life and culture.

(iii) The Baisakhi

Baisakhi (new year of the Vikaramiera) was also observed as most essential feature of the Sikhs. On this occasion various functions are made by the managing bodies of the shrines through a sub-committee constituted for the purpose. Attractive arrangements are also made for Langar and lodging. Round the clock free medical aid is available to the pilgrims in the premises of prominent historical shrines. The buildings of the shrines are illuminated with electric lights. Religious congregations are held jointly with the managing bodies. Special Ragi Jathas (experts in music) are obtained for Kirtan. Pilgrims and visitors participate in all religious activities with a great zeal. The recitation of Sri Guru Granth Saheb is carried out in the shrines and thousands of pilgrims and devotees come from far off places to pay homage and perform their worship.

B. Charitable Activities

The most beneficial and most effective means for the propagation of he religion are the charitable activities. The Fifth Guru, Arjun Devji, emphasised that every Sikh should share one-tenth part of his income for the charity. Since than it has been made a regular and essential feature in the Sikh Panth. Consequently, the income from it has also been registered under the Charitable Act.

The investigator has observed form the Annual Reports of the Delhi Sikh Gurdwara Management Committee, published every year, that the relief work of D.S.G.M.C., during Hindu-Sikh riots in Delhi in November 1984, has also been praiseworthy one. It has also been gathered from the records of D.S.G.M.C. that 1100 widows are registered under this committee in which 900 widows (victims of the riots) were getting Rs. 300 per month form D.S.G.M.C. During the riots in Delhi the role of this managing body had been most commendable one in rehabilitating the victims of the riots. It has also been noted that the D.S.G.M.C. had also established a "Relief Society" and distributed thousands of cotton, tericot and woollen cloths and woollen shawls in the riot's victims camps in the gurdwara premises.

It has also been observed that the Sri Guru Singh Sabhas have also played an important role at the time of Delhi riots in 1984. These Singh Sabhas had constituted a "Rehabilitation Committee" and rehabilitated the thousands of victims.

C. Educational Activities

Sikh institutions have played an important role in the field of education that it needs a complete volume for its explanation. But here we would make our attention to through light briefly on some aspects of educational institutions run by the managing bodies of the shrines. The concept of education in Sikh religion is religio-social as well as knowledge oriented. The shrines and their managing bodies have advocated for equality of opportunity including educational opportunity to all section of society specially to weaker sections and women. The establishment of Khalsa Schools and College was a bold and challenging step of the Sikh religion. These institutions have established an ideal in the field of idealism, naturalism and humanism. The educational programme of these institutions is distinctly considered as innovative and challenging in the light of the present trends towards adopting materialistic values and programme of education. The development of spirit of simplicity with distinctive nature in the students and following the gospel of religion and reliance are the outstanding achievements of these educational institutions. The specific outcome of these is to work and learn with dignity of manual labour. These institutions have produced more disciplined, more spirited, intellectually alert, morally stronger, physically equipped national minded and patriotic scholars than the scholars of usual types.

It was discovered that 3 P.G. Colleges (including one for women), 5 Senior Secondary Schools (including three for girls) and 7 Public Schools were managed by the governing body of the prominent historical shrines (D.S.G.M.C.) for the benefit of the public. It was also conveyed by the managing authority that many of them are aided by the government and the higher educational institutions are followed the complete syllabi as well as rules and regulations formed by the government. Now-a-days the contribution of these educational institutions cannot be denied in promoting the various opportunities to the masses and in imparting them the national, social, religious and cultural education.

The complete list of educational institutions run by the managing body of prominent historical shrines is given on next page:

TABLE 6.16

Educational Institutions in Delhi Under the Management of D.S.G.M.C.*

S. No.	*Name of the Institutions*	*Place*
1.	Shri Guru Tegbahadur Khalsa (P.G.) College	Delhi University Campus, Delhi.
2.	S.G.T.B. Khalsa College (Evening branch)	Dev Nagar (Karol Bagh), New Delhi
3.	Mata Sundari Girls' (P.G.) College.	Delhi University Campus
4.	S.G.T.B. Khalsa Boys' S.S. School	Dev Nagar (Karol Bagh), New Delhi.
5.	S.G.T.B. Khalsa Girls' S.S. School	— do —
6.	S.G.T.B. Khalsa Girls' S.S. School	Gurdwara Sis Ganj Campus Chandni Chowk, Delhi.
7.	S.G.T.B. Khalsa Girls' S.S. School	Gurdwara Bangla Saheb Campus Baba Khadag Singh-Marg, New Delhi.
8.	Sukho Khalsa S.S. School	Fateh Nagar, New Delhi.
9.	7 Guru Harkishan Public Schools	(i) India Gate, (ii) Vasant Vihar (iii) Karol Bagh, (iv) Punjabi Bagh, (v) Fateh Nagar, (vi) Loni Road (vii) Shahdara, Delhi
10.	Sri Guru Harkishan Boys' Primary School	Gurdwara Bangla Saheb Campus, New Delhi.
11.	Sri Guru Harkishan Girls' Primary School	Dev Nagar (Karol Bagh), New Delhi.
12.	One well organised library	Sri Guru Tegbahadur Niwas (Gurdwara Sis Ganj), Chandni Chowk, Delhi.
13.	Sri Guru Tegbahadur Institute of Electronics	Gurdwara Nanak Piyao Campus, G.T. Road, Rana Pratap Bag, New Delhi.

* Source: Administrative office of Delhi Sikh Gurdwara Management Committee, Campus of Gurdwara Sis Ganj, Chandni Chowk, Delhi.

Now to shift attention to educational activities of the Sri Guru Singh Sabha, it was discovered that the contribution of the Sri Guru Singh Sabhas can not be denied in promoting the basic educational opportunities. It was also observed that only have large size of Sri Guru Singh Sabhas such as—Punjabi Bagh Sri Guru Singh Sabha, Rajori Garden Sri Guru Singh Sabha, Tilak Nagar Sri Guru Singh Sabha, Lajpat Nagar Sri Guru Sabha, and so on one each prominent public school. These public schools were from class L.K.G. to Higher Secondary and were open to all classes of the society and have its own identity. However it may deserved to be mention here that there was hardly any significant contribution of these Sri Guru Singh Sabhas in the field of higher education.

Thus, it may be summed up form the above account that there is a great contribution of the Delhi Sikh Gurdwara Management Committee, which manages prominent historical shrines, in opening many basic and higher rich educational institutions throughout Delhi. But contrary to this, the contribution of Sri Guru Singh Sabhas, which manage independent shrine, was almost restricted to providing basic educational facilities.

D. Medical Activities

It was observed that the medical services are provided within the premises of the shrines by the managing bodies. The Delhi Sikh Gurdwara Management Committee and the large body of Sri Guru Singh Sabhas conduct various activities to cater the physical needs of the masses in general irrespective caste, creed, colour and nationality. These managing bodies serve the poor, need and sick coming from the different areas. In addition to the medical activities carried on by the managing bodies of the shrines, by way of their dispensaries, organise the charity eye camps, and free distribution of medicines among the needy and the poor.

It may be noted here that the Delhi Sikh Gurdwara

Management Committee (D.S.G.M.C.) and some prominent Sri Guru Singh Sabhas were found rendering the valuable services to the poor and the sick. The study also revealed that these managing bodies conducted charitable dispensaries consisting of Ayurvedic, Homoeopathic and Allopathic sections. Free Medical Relief Camps, Eye Camps and other Relief works have become a regular annual feature and provide a great service to poor patients in the locality and in the surrounding areas citing a prominent example of it is the Guru Harkishan Hospital which is run by the D.S.G.M.C. and known for their most skilled treatment and all possible care. This hospital is distinguished for skilled doctors and nurses. Another speciality of this hospital is that patients are treated with a faith in the healing power of the Guru's name and also touched by the kindness and gentleness. On the other hand it will also be relevant to add that one dispensary is run by each large Sri Guru Singh Sabha in each locality where the Sabha is situated. This dispensary was also rendering his valuable medical services to the needy and the poor. It was also discovered that in these medical centres, thousands of people took benefit of the medical services for treatment of the various diseases.

Thus, it is clear from the above discussion that the shrines and their managing bodies have always been pioneer in the different types of religious services and charitable activities in an organised form.

REFERENCES

1. The Delhi Sikh Gurdwaras Act, 1971 (No. 82 of 1971), Govt. of India Press, Minto Road, New Delhi.
2. "Registered Singh Sabha" means a Singh Sabha which is registered as a society under the Societies Registration Act, 1860, and controls a local gurdwara in Delhi.
3. Four Takhts: (i) Akal Takht, Amritsar, (ii) Takht Damdama Sahib, Anandpur, (iii) Takht Hajur Sahib, Nanded, (iv) Takht Keshgarh Sahib, Patna.

7

Religio-Cultural Beliefs and Practices

Having discussed the Mode of Management and Working of the Shrines, now an attempt has been made to examine and analyse the "Religio-cultural Beliefs and Practices of the Shrines. In this context to devote some space to explaining and comprehending the complete Belief system may only be relevant. At the outset, we may here attempt to explain the very concept of Religio-cultural Belief and Practice on which the attention has been focused in this chapter.

A religion is a more or less coherent system of beliefs and practices concerning a supernatural order of beings, forces, places or other entities. A religious belief is so universal, permanent and pervasive that unless we understand it thoroughly we shall fail to understand a society. The main function of the religious belief and practice is to affirm the moral superiority of the society over its individual members and thus to maintain the solidarity of the society. Every society whether primitive or civilised, has its own set of beliefs which mould the general conduct of human behaviour and also give a direction to behavioural patterns. When the religious beliefs are institutionalised in the society, they are supported by sanctions.[1] The beliefs and practices are also inseparable parts of culture and transmitted from generation to generation.

To elaborate it further religious belief is the cognitive aspect of religion; it attempts to explain the nature and origin of sacred things and implicitly assumes that they exist.[2] In this context we can say that the religious belief tells us also what the nature of sacred object is and how these objects relate to the super-empirical world.

Now to shift attention to another concept used in the investigation, religious ritual in the active side of religion. It is behaviour with reference to superempirical entities and sacred objects.[3] Like the belief itself, it comes to have a quality of sacredness attached to it. It is highly circumscribed as to time and place, expensive to the internal attitude and symbolic of the unseen powers. It can include any kind of behaviour known, such as the wearing of special clothing, recitation of special formulas, and immersion in certain rivers; it can also include singing, dancing, weeping, bowing, crawling, starving, feasting, and reading etc. On the same way religious practices (rituals) help to remind the individual of the holy realm, and also to revivify and strengthen his faith in this realm. It enables him to give expression his religious sentiments and thereby to achieve an emotional cathersis.

Both religio-cultural beliefs and practices must be comprehended if particular religious functioning is to be understood. Therefore, one of the focalpoint of the present investigation was to study the belief system of the shrines in Delhi. The following discussions will concentrate on empirical and non-empirical beliefs of the shrines. Empirical and non-empirical beliefs both are principal components of the belief system. According to Talcott Parsons, the cognitive ideology or orientation of the actor may necessarily be sub-divided in the category of empirical and non-empirical belief.[4] The distinction is simply that ideas or beliefs will be called empirical when, in terms of the major orientations of the cultural tradition of which they are a part, they concern processes which are defined as subject to understanding and maniputation in a pattern of practical rationality.[5] In other words, it can be said that the empirical beliefs are those which are within the reach of 'Logico-Meaningful Methodology.' On the contrary non-impirical beliefs are those which are defined beyond the reach of the scientific methodology of empirical science.

In this chapter, discussion on such points as empirical and non-empirical beliefs have been tested with 5-Point Scale.

I. Empirical Beliefs

As noted above that empirical beliefs are those which can be tested by dialectical approach. More specifically, an attempt has been made here to highlight the exact institutional process of the Sikh shrines. The responses in the form of empirical beliefs of the respondents are based on thirteen items on the basis of Five-Point Scaling Technique. The tables throw an ample light on these items.

(1) Beliefs of the Respondents Whether the Shrines are Mirror of the Sikh Ideals Where Every Sikh Get Real Peace

Table 7.1 suggests that 60 per cent respondents were strongly agreed, 30 per cent agreed and remaining were silent about the statement.

It may be concluded from the table that an overwhelming majority (90%) of the respondents were in favour of that the shrines are the clean mirrors of the Sikh ideals. It may also lead one to conclude that the Sikhs in general tend to identify themselves with the shrine legality. And in some cases it may be observed that the individual identity of a member gets submerged into the shrine identity. Therefore, it may further be concluded that in such cases the opinion norm or direction accepted by the shrine has a compelling force over its members to conform with the ways, procedures and usages held by the shrine which is symtomatic of the process of institutionalisation.

TABLE 7.1

Beliefs of the Head Priests Whether the Shrines Are Mirror of the Sikh Ideals

Belief	*Respondents*	
	No.	*Per cent*
Strongly agree	30	60
Agree	15	30
Uncertain	5	10
Disagree	—	—
Strongly disagree	—	—
Total	50	100

TABLE 7.2

Belief Whether the Shrines Are Following on the Ideals of the Gurus

Degree of Beliefs	*Respondents*	
	No.	*Per cent*
Strongly agree	25	50
Agree	15	30
Uncertain	4	8
Disagree	4	8
Strongly disagree	2	4
Total	50	100

(2) *Belief whether the Shrines Are Following out the Ideals of Ten Gurus*

Table 7.2 reflects that 50 per cent majority of the respondents were strongly agreed with 30 per cent agreed, 8 per cent uncertain, 8% disagreed and remaining 4 per cent were strongly disagreed.

It may be summed up form the data that the majority of the respondents (80%) were agreed about the right following of the shrines. Against this those disagreeing with it opined that the shrines had lost their previous status and sacred image due to the vested interests of the authority. The same inference and conclusion may be arrived at here as discussed above in the Table 7.1.

(3) *Belief Whether One and Uniform System of Management for the Prominent Shrines Should be Implemented*

The figures in Table 7.3 suggest that the highest 94 per cent of the resondents supported the statement and on the other hand a very nominal percentage (6%) were silent about the statements. It is interesting to note that nobody condemned the statement.

TABLE 7.3

Belief About the One Uniform System of Management for Prominent Shrines

Degree of Belief	*Respondents*	
	No.	*Per cent*
Strongly support	38	76
Mildly support	9	18
Indifferent	3	6
Mildly condemn	—	—
Strongly condemn	—	—
Total	50	100

In an ultimate analysis we can say that almost all the resondents supported with one voice that one and uniform system of management for prominent historical shrines should be implemented. It may well reflect that there is a trend of crystallisation and standardisation of the governing ways and of ruling procedures and norms.

(4) *Belief Whether the Shrines Are Being Used as a Mechanism to Maintain the Identity of the Sikhs*

An examination of the data shown in the Table 7.4 reveals

that 54 per cent respondents strongly agreed with 28 per cent agreed. Against it only 2 per cent strongly disagreed with 6 per cent disagreed and remaining 10 per cent of them could not decide about the statement.

TABLE 7.4

Empirical Belief Whether the shrines Are Being Used as a Mechanism to Maintain the Identity of the Sikhs

Degree of Beliefs	*Respondents*	
	No.	*Per cent*
Strongly agree	27	54
Agree	14	28
Undecided	5	10
Disagree	3	6
Strongly disagree	1	2
Total	*50*	*100*

It may be concluded that the majority of the respondents (82%) offered their approval and supported to the above statement. They also advocated that the shrines are the body and soul of the Sikh community and the identity of the Sikhs is based relatively upon the shrines. The trend emerging from the data is that in confusion and anxiety about maintaining a separate identity and entity these shrines are being increasingly relied upon for this purpose and whereby crystallised mechanism were being employed for the survival and solidarity of the Panth.

(5) *Belief Whether the Shrines Were Designed for Collective Mobilisation of the Sikhs*

In response to the question, "were the shrines designed for collective mobilisation of the Sikhs and of their resources?" 60 per cent majority of the respondents strongly supported whereas 30 per cent mildly supported. An analysis of remaining 10 per cent was not found significant.

TABLE 7.5

Empirical Belief Whether the Shrines Were Designed for Collective Mobilisation of the Sikhs

Degree of Belief	*Respondents*	
	No.	*Per cent*
Strongly Support	30	60
Mildly support	15	30
Undecided	4	8
Mildly condemn	1	2
Strongly condemn	—	—
Total	50	100

Our data here bear the evidence that there was an overwhelming volume of opinion in favour of designing the shrines for collective mobilisation of men and resources of the community, at large. Our observation here is that there was an increasing tendency of follower attending the frequent congregations taking place in these shrines. This went a long way in mobilising the men and materials in mass scale.

(6) Belief Whether the Shrines Are Offering Relentless Fight to Maintain Fundamental Tenets and Seminal Beliefs

It is evident form the Table 7.6 that 68 per cent respondents reacted favourably ranging from mild support to strong support. This may reflects that the trend of reverting to the fundamental tenets and seminal beliefs seems to be gaining momentum over the years. It may lead us to conclude that the Sikhs are, in for midable, numbers veering round the view that the revival of fundamental tenets is the only meaning and hope through which they can survive and later grow and develop in midst of other rival creeds and religions.

By way of conclusion, it may be said that the majority of the respondents agree with the statement and were of the opinion that the shrines are the pillars of the Sikh Panth and great efforts were made by the shrines to maintain their fundamental tenets and seminal beliefs.

TABLE 7.6

Empirical Belief Whether the Shrines Are Offering Relentless Fight to Maintain Their Fundamental Tenets

Degree of Belief	*Respondents*	
	No.	*Per cent*
Strongly agree	21	42
Agree	13	26
Undecided	12	24
Disagree	2	4
Strongly disagree	2	4
Total	50	100

(7) *Belief Whether the Present 'Dharam Yudh' Is Designed for Maintaining Individuality and Its Institutions*

The data presented in following Table 7.7 suggest that 66 per cent resondents accepted that the present Dharam-yudh is designed to preserve the pristine culture of the faith which was transmitted by the founders of the faith. Against it 34 per cent of the respondents, including those indifferent and those showing disapproval and strong disapproval, voiced their strong feeling averring that in the case of historical prominent Sikh shrines mostly the political pujaris were reported misusing their powers and misappropriating the resources of the shrines paying little regard for pristine culture and teaching of the Gurus.

To sum up, it can be said that the majority of the respondents accepted that the present 'Dharamyudh' is contrived to preserve the pristine culture of the Sikh Faith. Hence there was a growing consensus among the Sikh masses that the present Dharamyudh, launched through the shrines, is directed towards the preservation and integration of the pristine culture and the time-honoured beliefs and practices.

TABLE 7.7

Belief Whether the Present 'Dharam Yudh' Is Designed for Maintaining Individuality and Its Institutions

Degree of Belief	*Respondents*	
	No.	*Per cent*
Strongly accept	25	50
Accept	8	16
Indifference	9	18
Reject	6	12
Strongly reject	2	4
Total	50	100

(8) *Belief Whether the Sikh Community Is Showing Rigidity for a Separate Religion and Identity through the Shrines*

It is clear from the data that 56 per cent respondents strongly approved and 30 per cent approved of the respondents. This majority stated that the identity of the Sikh religion is strongly associated with the shrines. Consequently, in every circumstances, we have to preserve our separate recognition. On the contrary 8 per cent outrightly rejected. The majority of the resondents lent their support to the statement asserting that the community and the shrines were not free from the external political alienment and other sources dissuading them from being collected at a common ideology and common code of the rules and working.

It may be summed up from the data that an overwhelming majority (86%) of the Head priests approved that the Sikh community through the shrines is showing rigidity to protect the religion and their identity. Hence one may also conclude that a majority of cases, the Head priests, went in for the rigidity and the inflexibility of the approach.

TABLE 7.8

Belief Whether the Sikh Community Showing Rigidity for a Separate Religion and Identity

Degree of Belief	*Respondents*	
	No.	*Per cent*
Strongly approve	28	56
Approve	15	30
Undecided	3	6
Disapprove	4	8
Strongly disapprove	—	—
Total	50	100

(9) *Belief of the Head Priests Whether the New Values Are Proving a Bottle-Neck for the Smooth Functioning of the Shrines*

It is evident from the Table 7.9 that 40 per cent respondents strongly accepted the statement with 34 per çent mildly and stated that the new values are emerging day by day and proving a bottleneck for the smooth functioning of the shrines. They also acknowledged that during the recent years most of our shrines, particularly historical prominent ones, have become sources of a great deal of wealth in the shape of offerings. This has resulted in the bureaucratisation of the shrines and bitter feuds have appeared among management committee. Besides this, the growing industrialisation, urbanisation and advanced technology are also introducing new values which are directly responsible to hinder the smooth functioning of the shrines. Further, it is also evident from the said data that only 6 per cent of the respondents were not facing any problem to run the shrine due to the emerging new values. Remaining 20 per cent could not decide about their opinion.

In summing up, it may be concluded that approx. three-fourth majority of the respondents accepted that the new values are proving a bottle-neck in the smooth functioning of the shrines.

TABLE 7.9

Bead Priests and Their Belief About the Hindrance of New Values

Degree of Beliefs	*Respondents*	
	No.	*Per cent*
Strongly reject	1	2
Mildly reject	2	4
Undecided	10	20
Mildly accept	17	34
Strongly accept	20	40
Total	50	100

(10) Belief Whether the Shrines Is Powerful Agency for Promoting Both Individual and Social Righteousness

Table 7.10 suggests that 64 per cent respondents strongly approved of the statement with 30 per cent mildly approved advocating that the shrine gives an atmosphere to live and sit together. They also stated forcely that, in fact, the shrine is only that place which compels to individual to perform the righteous deeds.

TABLE 7.10

Belief Whether Only the Shrine is Powerful Media to Promote Individual

Degree of Belief	*Respondents*	
	No.	*Per cent*
Strongly approve	32	64
Mildly approve	15	30
Indifference	3	6
Mildly disapprove	—	—
Strongly disapprove	—	—
Total	50	100

By way of conclusion, it is interesting to note that almost entire majority of the Head priests (96%) approved that the shrine is the powerful media which guides and compels the individual to promote their rightout deeds. However here the researcher may venture to state that all was not right with this claim and pretension made by the Sikh priests. In this respect, as it is hardly any secret, that these time-honoured and hoary institutions were being used a clandestinely for promoting some sort of militancy, adventursm and chauvanism which does not sound well. It may amount to their achieving cultural goals without institutionalised norms and means for it and thus generating the forces of a-nomie.

(11) *Belief Whether an Attempt Should be Organised to Unite the Sikhs All Over the World into one Homogeneous Community*

It is clear from the Table 7.11 that a vast majority of the resondents (90%) reacted that a serious attempt should be organised to bring uniformity in the behaviour patterns and life-styles of the community. It is own observation that the Head priests of the shrines seemed more enthusiastic emphasising further they said that when our foreign-based and settled community faced some problem with the foreign government of that country, we demonstrated publicly against it and resorted to using the crystallised mechanism of a parallel culture in order to need the situation. A recent such occurrence took place in England when the Sikh community agitated against the compulsory use of Helmet for deriving vehicles and a snatched concession in this regard. Remaining 10 per cent respondents were indifferent.

It is interesting to conclude here that almost all the respondents were seen enthusiastic about the uniform mode of living, of praying, preaching and so on all over the world.

TABLE 7.11

Head Priests and Their Belief About an Organisation of the Sikhs into One Homogeneous Community

Degree of Belief	*Respondents*	
	No.	*Per cent*
Strongly approved	33	66
Mildly approved	12	24
Indifferent	5	10
Mildly disapproved	—	—
Strongly disapproved	—	—
Total	50	100

(12) *Belief Whether the Priests Are Also Pulling Their Weight Behind the Uniformity of Behaviour Patterns*

The data mentioned in the Table 7.12 suggest that 56 per cent respondents stated that the priests are the representative of the community and congregation and their responsibility is to revive and develop the pristine culture and identity of the Gurus. Therefore they were favouring strongly to bring the unformity of behaviour patterns of the community. Against it, approx. one-fourth majority of the respondents (24%) disfavoured it as they were found subserve it to the influence and authority of managing bodies and thus sometime were indifferent to the collective interest of the Sikh community, at large.

TABLE 7.12

Head Priests and Their Weight Behind the Uniformity of Behaviour Patterns

Degree of Beliefs	*Respondents*	
	No.	*Per cent*
Strongly favouring	15	30
Mildly favouring	13	26

Undecided	10	20
Mildly disfavouring	7	14
Strongly disfavouring	5	10
Total	50	100

It may be inferred from the data that majority of the respondents (56%) favoured with the view that he priests, through shrines, always raised their strong voice against the victimisation of the community and the shrines.

(13) *Belief Whether There Is Growing any Conflict Between the New Leadership of the Radical Priests and the Old Traditionalists*

It is clear from the data presented in the following Table 7.13 that 60 per cent respondents agreed with the statement viewing that our mandatory Five K's (Keshas, Kangha, Kara, Kachha and Kirpan) are being questioned by the younger generation. Further, it is also evident from the data that one. fifth majority of the respondents (20%) disagreed with it. Remaining 20 per cent were indifferent with the statement.

TABLE 7.13

Head Priests and Their Belief About Growing Conflict between the Radicals and the Traditional Ones

Degree of Beliefs	*Respondents*	
	No.	*Per cent*
Strongly agree	19	38
Mildly agree	11	22
Uncertain	10	20
Mildly disagree	6	12
Strongly disagree	4	8
Total	50	100

It may be summed from the data that 60 per cent majority of the Head priests were agreed that new leadership of radical priests did not want to live under the control of old priests of the shrines.

II. Non-Empirical Beliefs and Practices

Having analysed earlier in this chapter thirteen statements examining the empirical beliefs, now attention may be shifted to analysing and discussing the non-empirical beliefs. On this aspect, discussions on such points as belief in different dieties, belief in supernatural powers, authority of different scriptures and saints, and major religious practices have been undertaken.

(14) Non-empirical Belief of the Head Priests in Different Gods and Goddess

The responses and reactions to this question, "Do you believe and accept the authority of different Gods and Goddess?" were not presented in the tabulated form because mostly respondents regard to the different dieties. They accepted the authority of one God as Guru. They argued that different forms of God have one identity. They emphasised also that their Gods were their Gurus.

It may be concluded here that the Head priests of the shrines did not condemn the authority of different Gods and Goddess but believe only Ten Gurus with one entity.

Belief in Supernatural Powers

The main theme of this dimension, therefore, was to describe the respondents' belief on supernatural elements. More specifically an endeavour was made to know the reactions on eight items on the basis of five-point scale.

(15) The Existence of God

In Sikhism 'God is one, the only one,' the one without a second. It is certainly true to say that Guru Nanak believed in a personal God who is Omnipotent, an Omniscient Reality. Guru Nanak used Him in a variety of names as—Father, Lover, Master, and Great Giver. Guru Nanak and all his successors used both Hindu and Muslim nomeclature for God as, Ram, Govinda, Rab and Rahim, the attribute they usually ascribed to Him was that of the True Creator (Sat Kartar) or the True Name (Sat Nam Sri Vaha Guru). At the later stage in the evolution of Sikhism, Vahi Guru* Guru became the Sikh name for God.

In the above context, here an attempt was made to examine an analyse the responses of the Head priests on the existence of God as a non-empirical belief. The following table throws an ample light on the aspect.

It is clear from the data shows in the following Table 7.15 that the largest majority of the resondents (90%) hold the view that an existence of God is true. A meagre 10 per cent were unable to give a judgement on the aspect.

To sum up, it can be said that an overwheliming majority of the Head priests (90%) accepted the existence of God.

TABLE 7.15

Head Priest and the Belief in the Existence of God

Belief	*Respondents*	
	Frequency	*Per cent*
Absolutely	35	70
Partly True	10	20
Difficult to Judge	5	10
False	—	—
Absolutely False	—	—
Total	50	100

* Vahi Guru — Means 'Hail Guru' and this term is also very close to the Muslim 'Subhan Allah.' It has been suggested that this word is a combination of different Hindu names for God as : Vasudev, Hari, Govind and Ram.

(16) Belief in Existence of God as Formless of Embodied

There are two distinct schools of spiritual thought in the world in regard to God. One school accepts an authority of God as Formless (Nirankar) and other Embodied (Saakar). But in Sikhism the God is formless. Therefore, the responses of the Head priests on the Existence of God as Formless or Embodied are analysed. Table 7.16 throws an ample light on this aspect.

TABLE 7.16

Head Priests and Their Belief about God as Formless or Embodied

Belief	*Respondents*	
	Frequency	*Per cent*
Formless	35	70
Embodied	3	6
Both	2	4
Difficult to Judge	10	20
Total	50	100

This inference may be drawn from the table that approximately three-fourth majority of the Head priests (70%) had faith firmly in the formless existence of God.

(17) Belief that Whatever Happens in the Life of Man is Predetermined by God and it is also True abut the Events of the World

In this regard the data presented in the Table 7.17 suggest that 72 per cent majority of the respondents believe that whatever happens in the life of man is predetermined by God, whereas on the worldly level the percentage reduced to 54 per cent. Against it, 8 per cent and 10 per cent respectively were not prepared to recognise the fact. And remaining, 20 per cent at individual level and 30 per cent at worldly level, resondents were difficult to judge this fact.

TABLE 7.17

Belief of the Head Priests in the Theory of Determination at Individual and Worldly Level

Belief	*Respondents*			
	At Individual level		*At worldly level*	
	No.	Per cent	No.	Per cent
Absolutely True	20	40	14	28
Partly True	16	32	13	26
Difficult to Judge	10	20	18	36
False	3	6	3	6
Absolutely False	1	2	2	
Total	50	100	50	100

It may be summed up that slightly less than three-fourth majority of the respondents (72%) have greater faith with the fact that happens in the life of man is predetermined by God, whereas on the worldly level the percentage was reduced.

(18) Belief in the Theory of Karmas

The world Karam has many meanings: doing an act or work, also called Kriya; product, result, effect, motion, religious act of rite or conduct consequences of acts done in previous life. Commonly the meaning of Karma is good conduct which produces good results or fruit in the form of happiness with absence of pain.

In Sikhism, the doctrine of Karma according to which we reap what we so is not in exorable. The view of Guru Nanak is that so long as the ego (houme) is strong, the Lord allows the Law of Karma to operate the entire life. In this regard the data are presented in the Table 7.17.

To explore the responses on the doctrine of Karmas of the respondents the table given below indicates that 58 per cent majority of the respondents firmly believed in the doctrine of Karmas whereas 34 per cent had a mild faith in it. A meagre 4 per cent were not in favour of it. And remaining 4 per cent Head priests reacted that it was difficult to judge the statement.

TABLE 7.17

Belief of the Head Priests in the Doctrine of Karmas

Belief	*Respondents*	
	Frequency	*Per cent*
Absolutely True	29	58
Partly True	17	34
Difficult to Judge	2	4
False	1	2
Absolutely False	1	2
Total	50	100

The inference may be drawn that an overwhelming majority of the respondents (92%) had a greater faith in the Doctrine of Karmas. Here we may say that there is almost a similarity of views between Hindus and the Sikhs on the theory and the impact of Doctrine of Karmas.

(18A) Belief in the Swarga (Heaven) and Narak (Hell)

Heaven and Hell are states of mind and not geographical localities. They are symbolically represented by joy and sorrow, bliss and agony, light and fire. There is no such thing in Sikhism as eternal damnation or an everlasting pit of fire created by a revengeful God. God has given complete freedom and moral Choice to man to prefer hell to heaven and to prefer divine love to both hell and heaven. The Fifth Guru, Arjan Devji says that, "the sixty-eight places of pilgrimage are wherever the saints put their feet, heaven is wherever they utter the Nam (name of God).[6] Therefore, an attempt was made to explore the reactions of the Head priests regarding the belief in Swarga and Narak.

The data indicated in the Table 7.18 suggest that a vast majority of the Head priests (60%) firmly rejected that there is not any particular place in the space like Swarga and Narak. While they seemed to be fully convinced to the conception of Swarga and Narak given by the Sikh Gurus as, "Swarga (Heaven) is the state of being merged in the Absolute or the union with God and Narak (Hell) is isolation from the God." It is further clear from the said table that 20 per cent of the respondents reacted in affirmative about the concept. A meagre 20 per cent were unable to give the judgement about the concept.

TABLE 7.18

Belief of the Head Priest about the Swarga and Narak

Belief	*Respondents*	
	Frequency	*Per cent*
Absolutely True	6	12
Partly True	4	8
Difficult to Judge	10	20
False	9	18
Absolutely False	21	42
Total	50	100

In summing up, it may be said that 60 per cent majority of the Head priests had firm faith in the teachings of the Sikh Guru that Swarga and Narak are not any geographical localities but intimately related with the union and separation of God or Absolute.

(19) Belief in the Transmigration of Soul in the Eighty-Four Lacs Yonis

The doctrine of Karma is intimately related with the Theory of Rebirth. It is based on the conception of an intrinsic spiritual value in soul of men, which guarantees its everlasting existence. The relevant data here are presented in the following table.

It is clear from the data shown in the Table 7.19 that 44 per cent respondents showed their favourable view in the theory of transmigration. They believed that the good deeds or Karmas are the base of the transcedental life of man. If the man performs good deeds with remembrance of the Nam (name of God), he can not be transmigrated. This state is called as Final Liberation of Man.

Further, it is also evident from the table that 26 per cent of the resondents did not believe in the above theory. Rest 30 per cent felt difficulty to give their judgement.

TABLE 7.19

Belief in the Theory of Transmigration

Belief	*Respondents*	
	Frequency	*Per cent*
Absolutely True	12	24
Partly True	10	20
Difficult to Judge	15	30
False	10	20
Absolutely False	3	6
Total	50	100

It may be concluded that slightly less than fifty per cent Head priests (44%) believe in the theory of transmigration.

(20) Belief in the Final Liberation as an Ultimate Goal of Life

In Sikhism, the liberation of soul implies the realisation by the soul of its real nature and knowing the Reality beyond the phenomenal world. The state of liberation is the state of Jivan Mukti (free from the life-cycles of the birth) in Sikhism. An emphasis on Jivan Mukti has also bene given in the Sikh literatures as Gurmukh, i.e. the Guru oriented, and Manmukh, the man bound by lower passions of his mundane existence. The liberation or Jivan Mukti is obtained by meeting with the

Guru enjoying his grace and then adopting certain techniques. The most important of these is Nam Simran, meditation upon the name and nature of God.

The data presented in the Table 7.20 suggest that as many as 78 per cent Head priests asserted that the Moksha (Jivan Mukti) is the ultimate goal of their life, whereas 8 per cent of them accepted it true. They also acknowledged that it is an attainment of Union with God. It can occur only when the soul has reached the state of Saram khand (the realm of effort). It was also observed that, in the context of rational religious life, mostly Head priests seemed serious about the Final Liberation.

Further it is also clear from the said table that only a very marginal number of the respondents did not accept the Moksha as an ultimate goal of life. Remaining 8 per cent were not clear about this non-empirical belief.

TABLE 7.20

Head Priests and their Belief in the Final Liberation

Belief	*Respondents*	
	Frequency	*Per cent*
Absolutely True	39	78
Partly True	4	8
Difficult to Judge	4	8
False	2	4
Absolutely True	1	2
Total	50	100

It may be summed up that a good majority of the Head priests, like their counterparts in other religious (Hindus and Christians), accepted Moksha (Jivan Mukti) as an ultimate goal of life, practically they seemed serious about the good actions to achieve the Union with God or Final Liberation.

(21) Authority of Different Others Scriptures

Our concern here was to find out how the Head priests look upon the authority of other religious scriptures. It deserve to be mentioned that in the Sri Guru Granth Saheb the Gurus have asserted that the different sacred scriptures are authoritative which guide and direct to the human behaviour. Therefore in the light of the above an attempt has been made to high light the belief of the Head priest in the authority of different scriptures. Table 7.21 throws an ample light on this dimension.

Our data in the Table 7.21 suggest that 92 per cent Head priests accepted Vedas, 86 per cent Puranas and 90 per cent Smirities as an authority to guide and control of human behaviour. Only was a nominal number of the respondents were not aware of the authority of these sacred texts. As for their attitude towards Ramayana and Mahabharata, 16 per cent did not accept Ramayana as an authority, whereas 32 per cent did not accept Mahabharata as an authority showing their total ignorance about their contents. Deductively it may be said that the category of such priests was comparatively rigid with a closed mind on other religious scriptures.

The data presented in the Table 7.21 further reveal that 90 per cent majority of the respondents accepted that Upnishads are authoritative and only 10 per cent could not decide about it.

As regards the belief in the authority of Quoran and Bible, our data indicate that 60 per cent of the respondents accepted the authority of Quoran and 64 per cent of Bible. It may lead to observe and conclude that in comparative term Sikhism acknowledges and cherishes a religious affinity and similarity with the Islam and Christianity.

Table 7.21 may also clarify the exact position of belief in the authority of epics and the different scriptures.

TABLE 7.21

Head Priests and their Belief in the Authority of Different Scriptures

Different Scriptures	*Belief of the Respondents*											
	St. Accept		*Accept*		*Un-decided*		*Rejected*		*St. Reject*		*Total*	
	No.	P.C.	No.	P.C.	No.	P.C.	No.	P.C.	No.	P.C.	No.	P.C.
Vedas	40	80	6	12	4	8	—	—	—	—	50	100
Puranas	38	76	5	10	7	14	—	—	—	—	50	100
Smirities	39	78	6	12	5	10	—	—	—	—	50	100
Ramayana	15	30	27	54	3	6	5	10	—	—	50	100
Mahabharats	12	24	15	30	10	20	6	12	7	14	50	100
Upnishads	35	70	10	20	5	10	—	—	—	—	50	100
Quoran	14	28	16	32	20	40	—	—	—	—	50	100
Bible	18	36	14	28	18	36	—	—	—	—	50	100

III. Common Beliefs

In this frame of reference, it was also found of interest to discover whether the Head priests would like the priest of other religion with knowledge of Gurmukhi to take part in the religious activities of the shrines; whether they would like a layman with reading ability of Sri Guru Granth Saheb to perform ceremonial rites; whether they would like the Head priests of other religious to pay visits and render their services to the shrines? The replies to these questions may be presented and analysed in the relevant following tables.

(22) *Belief of the Head Priests What Place Will the Priest of Other Religion Knowing Gurmukhi Get in the Religious Activities of the Shrine*

It is clear from the Table 7.22 that per cent of the resondents accepted that the Gurmukhi knowing priest can only attend the congregational worship, 20 per cent allowed them to perform the Kirtan and Ardas and 10 per cent for reading the Sri Guru Granth Saheb with 4 per cent for following the ideals of Sikh religion.

TABLE 7.22

Head Priests and their Belief about the Priest of Other Religion

Participation of the Priest	*Respondents*	
	No.	*Per cent*
To attend the Congregation	29	58
To perform the Kirtan and Ardas	10	20
To read the Sri Guru Granth Saheb	5	10
To follow the ideals	2	4
No reply	4	8
Total	50	100

Hence, it may be concluded that the majority of the respondents reacted that Gurmukhi knowing priests of the other religions can only attend the congregation in the shrine.

(23) *Belief that Can any Layman with Reading Ability of Sri Guru Granth Saheb Performs the Ceremonial Rites in the Shrine*

It is clear from the data mentioned in the Table 7.23 that 84 per cent majority of the respondents stressed that the reading ability of the Sri Guru Granth Saheb is not the essential qualification to conduct the ceremonial rites in the shrine. Such respondents were opposed to a layman having ability to read the Sri Guru Granth Saheb to conduct the ceremonial rites in the shrine.

Contrarily it was observed that the practice of Initiation (Amrit Chhakna) is the major qualification to conduct the ceremonial rites in the shrine.

TABLE 7.23

Belief of the Head Priests that Can any Lay man Having Ability to Read the Sri Guru Granth Saheb Perform the Ceremonial Rites in the Shrine

Performance	*Respondents*	
	No.	*Per cent*
Never	42	84
Rarely	3	6
Occasionally	5	10
Daily	—	—
No reply	—	—
Total	50	100

(24) *Belief Whether the Religious Leaders and Head of the Various Denomination Can Exchange Visits and Services*

Our data here demonstrate that largest number of the Head priests (72%) were of the opinion that they were no exchange of visits or services by the religious preachers, leaders or intellectuals of other denominations. Remaining 28 per cent admitted that the religious leaders of other cults visit the shrine occasionally. Some of the respondents told frankly that for last three years the communal harmony between the Sikhs and the Hindus is affected. Consequently the exchange of the visits by them showed a declining trend.

TABLE 7.24

Head Priests and their Belief about the Exchange of Visits of the Preachers of other Denominations

Trend of Visit	*Respondents*	
	No.	*Per cent*
Once a day	—	—
Once a week	—	—
Once a month	5	10
Once a year	9	18
Never	36	72
Total	50	100

IV. Major Religious Practices

Religion becomes a cementery force only when belief is transformed into action. In fact, Prayer, meditation, and Kirtan are the most important parts of religion as they represent its real side. In Sikhism, a Sikh fellow or devotee can get the experience of intimate relation or union with the Guru or God through meditation and believe in one Timeless or Akal God.

Sikh Gurus laid a great emphasis upon the daily prayer and meditation. They also emphasised that a Sikh should rise-up in the early hours of the morn and practise the routine of Nam and the study of the scriptures and perform pious deeds. Therefore, an endeavour has been made here to observe the major religious practices adopted by the Head priests.

Our data mentioned in the following Table 7.25 clearly suggest that 94 per cent majority of the respondents strictly

TABLE 7.25

Belief of the Head Priests in the Major Sikh Religious Practices

Religious Practices	*Degree of Beliefs*											
	Strictly follow		*Follow*		*Undecided*		*Hardly follow*		*Never follow*		*Total*	
	No.	P.C.	No.	P.C.	No.	P.C.	No.	P.C.	No.	P.C.	No.	P.C.
To meditate only one God.	40	80	7	14	3	6	—	—	—	—	50	100
To offer three times prayer	42	84	6	12	—	—	2	4	—	—	50	100
To perform Kirtan	45	90	4	8	—	—	1	2	—	—	50	100
To perform Akhand Path	25	50	8	16	2	4	10	20	5	10	50	100
To perform Sahaj Path	25	50	10	20	5	10	8	16	2	4	50	100
Complete living according to the Guru's teaching	35	70	10	20	5	10	—	—	—	—	50	100

follow the mediatation with one God. 96 per cent offer three times prayer as was guided by the Ten Gurus, 98 per cent perform Kirtan, 66 per cent perform Akhand Path and remaining of the respondents either hardly followed or never followed of the practice of Akhand Path. 60 per cent followed the practice of Shahaj Path (interrupted reading of the Holy Book) and remaining respondents either hardly follow or did not follow this practice. On the other side, out of 50 Head priests 45 were seen passing their daily life according to the teachings of Gurus and 5 Head priests could not decide about the Sikh way of life.

The relevant conclusion drawn from the Table 7.25 is that the majority of the Head priests were following the ideals of Ten Gurus such as to meditate with one God and to offer three times prayer.

Further in this context it was also found interesting to investigate and discover whether the visits of the Head priests are limited to their own sacred places or do they visit the sacred places of the other communities also.

TABLE 7.26

The Comparative Visits of the Head Priests to their own Sacred Places and to those of other Religion

Visits	*Respondents*			
	Sacred places of the Sikhs		*Sacred places of other religion*	
	No.	P.C.	No.	P.C.
Never	—	—	45	90
Rarely	—	—	5	10
Frequently	35	70	—	—
Occasionally	15	30	—	—
Total	50	100	50	100

Our data in Table 7.26 indicate that largest majority of

the Head priests (90%) neve paid visits to the sacred places of other communities and only a marginal 10 per cent of the respondents told that they visited only rarely. Importantly enough this 10 per cent strength who paid visit to the sacred places of other religions belonged to the category of the converted ones showing some sort of emotional attachment to these places as a natural consequence. It was also gathered that the number of Head priests who visited their sacred places frequently stood at 35 (70%) whereas 15 (30%) visited occasionally.

By way of conclusion, it can be said that almost majority of the Head priests strongly believed in their own sacred places in comparison to the sacred places of the other religion.

REFERENCES

1. Johnson, H.M., *Sociology—A systematic Introduction*, p. 393.
2. Davis, Kingslay, *Human Society*, p. 533.
3. *Ibid.*, p. 534.
4. Parsons, Talcott, *The Social System*, p. 328.
5. *Ibid.*, pp. 328-329.
6. Cole, W.O. and P.S. Sambhi, *The Sikhs — Their Religious Beliefs and Practices*, p. 87.

8

Changing Patterns of Values

Having dealt with in foregoing chapters the descriptive and analytical account of the existing nature of the Sikh shrines in Delhi, it was deemed only appropriate to examine the process of social change and to try to present an integrated view on change in the Sikh shrines. It is attempted to analyse the social change both from within and without the social system or tradition. Taking a cue from the works of Redfield and Singer[1] (as quoted by Prof. Yogendra Singh in 'Modernisation of Indian Tradition,' *op. cit.*, pp. 25-26), the researcher has endeavoured to distinguish between the heterogenetic or exogenous and orthogenetic or endogenous forces of change. As for the direction of change the present analysis tries to deal with both traditionalisation and modernisation. And explaining how have the Sikh shrines moved or tended to move from traditionalisation towards modernisation. In the course of discussions here we have first taken up process of traditionalisation in the Sikh shrines whereas later part of discussion is mainly devoted to the process of modernisation in the Sikh shrines.

Before we shift attention to the main theme of discussion we have here devoted some space to explain the concept of values in popular parlance followed by the analysis and interpretation of changing patterns of values among the Sikh shrines as observed through the empirical data and its verification.

Values are the standards of desirability within a culture. They are the guidelines that we use to judge virtually everything we come into contact with a good or bad, beautiful and ugly, pleasant or unpleasant, appropriate or inappropriate. Values are also the standards that define our social situation and deal with the fundamental part of life. As with other elements of culture, values are both antecedents and consequences of social behaviour.[2]

Whether ancient or mdoern in origin, values have social significance in the present only if they actually influence the course of ongoing social behaviour. The structure of a society acquires stability through the existence of values. Unless values are shared, members of society would be unable to cooperate or even comprehend the behaviour of others.

It will not be out of place to mention here that the contemporary Indian society is passing through the transitional period. Developed communication, transportation, industrialisation and urbanisation etc. have influenced the social and institutional life of individuals. The old values are disappearing but the new values are not developing within an equal pace to replace them. And thus there is appearing a gap between the new values patterns and the old ones. In such situations the traditional behaviour of the Head priests and traditional atmosphere and image of the shrines have also been affected by the internal and external forces. Therefore, it was found essential to analyse and understand the changes in the value patterns of the shrines, priests, Sikh panth and their changing institutional aspects of behaviour brought about by the changing social situations and ecological trends. In this context, the relevant data are given in the following tables.

Attitudes Towards Sikh Shrines

Attitudes about Shrines' Influence over the Followers

There is no doubt that Sikh shrines have played a vital role in the Sikh history. Mostly Sikh shrines are associated with the lives or sacrifices of the Sikh Gurus. Consequently, the influence of the shrines cannot be denied even today. Hence, it was found of much interest to know that to what extent to these shrines excercise, influence over its followers in the contemporary social situations? The relevant data are given in the following table.

The data given in the Table 8.1 suggest that a largest majority of the respondents (74%) admitted that the influence was being maintained by the shrines over the followers. Against it 16 per cent respondents did not accept it. Remaining 10 per cent could not express their views on this aspect.

TABLE 8.1

Attitude of the Head Priests About Shrines Influence over the Followers

Attitudes	*Respondents*	
	No.	*Per cent*
Definitely maintained	26	52
Maintained	11	22
Undecided	5	10
Not maintained	5	10
Definitely not maintained	3	6
Total	50	100

It may be inferred from the above data that an overwhelming majority of the respondents (74%) endorsed the view that the shrines were still a force to reckon with in excercising its influence over the members. Hence, one may safely conclude that a vast majority of the Sikhs think highly of these shrines and attach emphatic belonging and attach great value, meaning and purpose to them.

Attitudes About the Measure of Sanctity of the Shrines

It is evident from the following Table 8.2 that 28 per cent of the Head priests acknowledge that the sanctity of the shrines was increased. They argued that mostly young generation of the Sikhs had surrendered their life to maintain the purity of the Sikh shrines. They also gave a significant and timely argument that the young Sikhs were being initiated increasingly while 24 per cent of them admitted that there was neither any appreciable increased nor decreased in the sanctity of the shrines and thus the position went almost unaltered. On the contrary, 28 per cent told frankly that the sanctity of the shrines, in the modern perspective, was being declined in comparison to previous times. And remaining 20 per cent neither showed their cold attitude nor enthusiastic one.

TABLE 8.2

Head Priests and the Measure of Sanctity of the Shrines

Attitudes	*Respondents*	
	No.	*Per cent*
Increased	14	28
Remained the same	12	24
Uncertain	10	20
Declined	9	18
Declined a lot	5	10
Total	50	100

From the analysis of above data it can hardly be convincingly argued that whether the sanctity of these shrines has increased or decreased. However, our own observation is that it has registered a rise as is evidence from ever increasing adherent claimed by these shrines.

Attitudes about the Shrines being Used as a Ladder for Political Ascendancy

According to the Sikh Shrines Act 1925 (Sections 106 to 111), the funds of the shrines and their bodies can be used only for religious, educational and charitable purposes. But, on the contrary, today no one makes any secret of this fact that the funds, personnel and the premises of the shrines are being used for political purposes. Therefore, an attempt was made here to probe whether the shrines are being used for political purposes or not.

TABLE 8.3

Attitudes of the Head Priests about Shrines as a Ladder for Political Ascendancy

Attitudes	*Respondents*	
	No.	*Per cent*
Often used	10	20
Used	8	16
Uncertain	13	26
Seldom used	8	16
Never used	11	22
Total	50	100

The relevant data in the Table 8.3 give a picture that a great many respondents hazard a claim that the Sikh shrines were not being used as a ladder for political power and pelt. However, the researcher may hold a different view based on his own field knowledge and experience. There was much in evidence to suggest that a good number of Head priests were influenced by political secular motivations and considerations making hardly any scruple about the unfair use of their office and position for political gains and objects.

Hence, it may be concluded that a trend of using the shrines for political ascendancy was gaining ground.

Attitudes about the Ongoing Terrorism and Violence

In fact, the shrine is that sacred training place were every Sikh gets the education of equality. The shrine is also a teacher which teaches the lesson of true humanity. It is believed that the shrine had ever given a lair of protection to the religious person and condemned the irreligious person. Therefore, an attempt was made here to know whether the shrines are engaged to condemn the irreligious activities of a person or not in the present circumstances.

The data on the above aspect, as presented in the Table 8.4, indicated that 46 per cent of the Head priests opined strongly that the shrines had ever condemned the irreligious activities while 28 per cent were mild about it. It was significant to note that there was some percentage however, small it may be, who dared into admitting that the pristine sanctity of these shrines was being lost gradually and further they reacted that the shrines should be freed from the bad politics otherwise their very survival will be at stake.

TABLE 8.4

Head Priests and the Condemnation of Ongoing Terrorism and Violence

Attitudes	*Respondents*	
	No.	*Per cent*
Strongly condemned	23	46
Mildly condemned	14	28
Undecided	7	14
Seldom condemned	4	8
Never condemned	2	4
Total	50	100

Attitudes Towards Sikh Panth for Community

The 'Sikh Panth' or religion is the youngest among the world religions not because of age, but because of rejection of many socio-religious things considered sacred by the Hindu Religion. It was conceived by Guru Nanak and multiplied and crystallised by the Nine Successors. They taught the lesson of human equality and provided the ideals and values to achieve the final goal of life and to remove the barriers between man and man.

The Sikh Panth is founded on the three pillars in the form of ideals and values. These were Kirt Karna, Nam Japna and Vand Chhakna. These may be translated as honest living hood, spiritual contemplation, and sharing of your earnings with others. However, it is important to remember that these ideals, produced by the Ten Gurus, can become functions only when institutionalised. The shrines have always given a practical shape to these ideals and enforced to the Sikh Panth to form an egalitarian society. The shrines can not be isolated from the Panth because panth is the principle of equality and the shrine is the practical demonstration of it. Therefore, an attempt was made here to examine the attitudes of the Head priests towards Sikh Panth itself. The following analysis of data throw an ample light on this aspect.

Attitudes about the Use of the Panth

The data mentioned in the Table 8.5 indicate that 54 per cent majority of the respondents were of opinion that the Sikh Panth was strong still and not being wrongly used by the adherents. They conceded that the Sikh Panth was developed into a cohesive and well marked order with social outlook. Consequently, there was no fear of loosing identity. On the other hand 28 per cent accept that, in fact, the Panth was being wrongly used by the interests motivated leaders. They argued that the Sikh Panth of today suffered a fear of identity. Remaining 18 per cent were uncertain.

The may be inferred from the data that the majority of the Head priests admitted that the Sikh Panth was not being wrongly used by the adherents. Hence it may be concluded that though the majority still favour this view that the Panth is being used mostly for the purpose for which came into existence. However, there were signs portending that some vested interests wanted these shrines to serve their ulterior motive and selfish trends.

TABLE 8.5

Head Priests and the Use of the Panth

Attitudes	*Respondents*	
	No.	*Per cent*
Absolute Wrong	20	40
Mild Wrong	7	14
Uncertain	9	18
Mild Correct	8	16
Absolute Correct	6	12
Total	50	100

Attitudes about Present Standing of the Panth

It is apparent from the following data mentioned in the Table 8.6 that 40 per cent of the respondents reported that the present standing of the panth progressively increased, whereas 22 per cent of them replied mildly about it. Such majority of the respondents estimated that the young generation of the Sikhs were being initiated more and more and did not want to hear any vulgar language or activity against the symbols and institutions of the Sikh community.

TABLE 8.6

Head Priests and the Present Standing of the Panth

Attitude	*Respondents*	
	No.	*Per cent*
Progressively increased	20	40
Mildly increased	11	22
Undecided	7	14
Mildly deceased	9	18
Negatively decreased	3	6
Total	50	100

The said table further indicates that 24 per cent of the respondents acknowledged that present standing of the Panth decreased. Remaining 14 per cent could not decide.

By way of inference it can be said that 62 per cent majority of the respondents admitted that present standing of the Panth was increased.

Present Age and the Reactions on the Present Standing of the Panth

TABLE 8.7

Age of the Head Priests and their Reactions on the Present Standing of the Panth

Present Age (in years)	*Respondents' Reactions*											
	Progressively Increased		*Increased*		*Undecided*		*Decreased*		*Negative Decreased*		*Total*	
	No.	P.C.	No.	P.C.	No.	P.C.	No.	P.C.	No.	P.C.	No.	P.C.
20-29	4	8	8	16	2	4	1	2	—	—	15	30
30-39	3	6	6	12	2	4	1	2	—	—	12	24
40-49	1	2	3	6	1	2	2	4	—	—	7	14
50-59	2	4	1	2	1	2	3	6	—	—	7	14
60 and above	1	2	2	4	1	2	4	8	1	2	9	18
Total	11	22	20	40	7	14	11	22	1	2	50	100

It is also evident from Table 8.7 that those respondents who wee in the age group 20 to 39 years, accepted that the present standing of the Panth increased. In this connection, it can be said that the young group of the Head priests supported but on the contrary the aged group of Head priests from 50 to 60 years and above opined that the present standing of the Panth decreased. Hence as it is true elsewhere so it is in the case of shrines. Our observation is that there is a divergence of views between the youngs supporting that the strength and popularity of the Panth has increased and the old aged decrying that the standing of the Panth has registered a decline.

Reactions about the Dress and Life Style

The Sikh community always attracted world wide attention because of his external identity. This identity was introduced and institutionalised by the last prophet, Guru Gobind Singh. The ideal of 'Saint Soldier' was also personified by him. The such symbols are visible manifestations of their commitment to a distinct religious philosophy and mental outlook. The Sikh Gurus emphasised on a particular way of life. They also guided how the Sikhs should live, think and act.

Here the investigator has endeavoured to examine the degree of reactions of the Head priests whether any disagreement is between young Sikhs and old ones.

TABLE 8.8

Head Priests and the Reactions about the Dress and Life Style

Reactions	*Respondents*	
	No.	*Per cent*
Clearly existing	22	44
Existing	9	18
Uncertain	6	12
Mildly existing	8	16
Non existing	5	10
Total	50	100

Our Table 8.8 shows that 44 per cent respondents stated that disagreement clearly exist on the question of dress and life-style between the young aged and the old aged Sikhs. 18 per cent held that it only exist. Whereas 16 per cent reacted that it exist mildly and 10 per cent stated that no disagreement exist.

It may be inferred that the wearing of traditionally prescribed dress and other belongings is being increasingly questioned. Support in this view our data (62%) indicate a growing a disagreement between the new extent and the old-timers on the question of dress and life-style. The consensus opinion was against any rigid prescription of dress rules and this is why Five K's have aroused some sort of controversy among the younger generation of the Sikhs who tended to defy the wearing of traditional Five K's.

Reactions Towards Hindu Religion

It is the patent fact of history that the philosophical foundations of the Sikh Panth was derived from the Hindu religious thought. Consequently, the separate identity of Sikhs can not be calculated without Hindus. It must be remembered here that the identity of the Sikhs and Hindus remained inter-linked and overlapped for four hundred years. Therefore, it was considered worthwhile to find out how the Hindu religion is viewed by the Head priests and how it has influenced their thinking and behaviour. The responses gathered in this regard are analysed in the following lines.

It is clear from the Table 8.9 that 58 per cent majority of respondents (36% showing strong regard and 22% mild regard) showed favourable attitude towards Hindu religion, whereas a nominal number of the respondents (12%) showed cold attitude. It may be noted here that the respondents of historical prominent shrines were found more rigid in their attitude and such respondents also showed cold attitude towards Hindu traditions.

Further data indicate that as many as 30 per cent were indifferent towards Hindu religion.

TABLE 8.9

Head Priests and the Hindu Religion

Reactions	*Respondents*	
	No.	*Per cent*
Strong regard	18	36
Regard	11	22

Indifferent	15	30
Disregard	3	6
Strong disregard	3	6
Total	50	100

It may be inferred from the data that 58 per cent majority of the Head priests showed favourable attitude towards Hindu religion.

Religious Education and the Attitudes Towards Hindu Religion

It was observed from the comparative data mentioned in the Table 8.10 that those respondents who had attended the Daire and Damdami Taksaal (Mr. Bhinderwale was the man of Taksaal) were found more fundamentalists towards Hindu religion in comparison to those who had taken the degree of Gyani course of essential religious education for performing the ceremonial rites in the shrine.

Attitude Towards Conversion

The Sikh religion is based on the philosophical thought of Ten Gurus. They established a reforming body with all the people embued with a zeal for reformed a spirit of selfless service could associate themselves. Basically, the Sikh Gurus were all Hindu Khatris by caste, but since its very beginnings the Sikh community contained a large proportion of Sikhs of the Jat caste.[4] The reason was that the khatris for centuries served as a teacher of the Jats. Hence it is mostly the Jats who were converted to Sikh Panth.

Here it is attempted to assess the attitudes and reactions of the Head priests towards the practice and institution of conversion, which contributed its own share to the origin and growth of the Sikh Panth.

The relevant data revealed that an overwhelming majority of the respondents (68%) supported conversion from other religion into Sikh religion either mildly or strongly. They

TABLE 8.10

Religious Education of the Head Priests and the Attitude Towards Hindu Religion

Religious Education	*Respondents' Attitude*											
	St regard		*Mild regard*		*Indi-fferent*		*Dis-regard*		*St disregard*		*Total*	
	No.	%	No.	%	No.	%	No.	%	No.	%	No.	%
Attending the Dairay	—	—	—	—	—	—	2	4	1	2	3	6
Attending the Damdami Taksaal	—	—	—	—	—	—	2	4	1	2	3	6
The Degree of Gyani Course	5	10	3	6	—	—	—	—	—	—	8	16
Receiving only religious education for performing the ceremonial rites	14	28	9	18	13	26	—	—	—	—	36	72
Total	*19*	*38*	*12*	*24*	*13*	*26*	*4*	*8*	*2*	*4*	*50*	*100*

emphasised that the process of conversion in our Panth was a revolutionary approach that provided social equality and moral sanctity for lower caste and sections of the society in their own right. The data in the Table 8.11 further reveal that a marginal number of the respondents (10%) were not in favour of the conversion. Remaining 22 per cent respondents did not comment on this aspect.

TABLE 8.11

Head Priests and the Lowest Person Joining the Panth, and Rejoining of the Converted (Patit's) in the Panth

Reactions	*Respondents' Reactions*			
	Reactions on lowest person joining the Panth		*Reactions on who got converted and later wanted to join the Panth*	
	No.	P.C.	No.	P.C.
Strong oppose	2	4	8	16
Mild oppose	3	6	5	10
Uncertain	11	22	11	22
Mild support	14	28	10	20
Strong support	20	40	16	32
Total	50	100	50	100

Further it has also been assessed that how did they react about the member or members who got converted to other religion and later wanted to join the Panth again.

Our data indicated that 26 per cent respondents reacted against the re-entry of such members showing strong opposition to mild opposition.

However comparatively a large percentage of respondents reacted favourably (ranging from strong degree to a mild degree) to the practice of conversion.

Attitudes Towards Shudras

The word 'Shudra' of Hindu social hierarchy of caste, which had been reffered to untouchables or low castes, has been replaced by Harijans (the people of God). Gandhiji also used this term for low caste and ever since this is being standardised

In Sikhism no caste hierarchy is maintained due to the reforming body of the society. This fact can easily be observed into the worship of the shrine and the service of langar (free mass meal). Prof. R.K. Mukherjee has remarked, "The institution of Langar or the community kitchen, where prince and peasant, rich and poor, Brahmin and Shudra, could mess together without social distinction fostered a spirit of charity on a large scale and also become a powerful binding force.[5]

In the present study it is attempted to find out what were the views of the Head priests towards Shudras making entry into the shrines, taking part into the ceremonial practices and other religio-cultural activities. The analysis of data is given in the following tables.

It is evident from the Table 8.12 that 72 per cent majority of the Head priests opposed (ranging from strong reactions 50 per cent and mild reactions 22%) about to interact and maintain social relations (such as friendly relations with marital relations too) with Shudras. Those who opposed to maintain the social relations with Shudras were into the age group of 20 to 49 years. It may be noted here that the young priests of the shrines did not want to maintain the social relations with Sudras. It is further clear from the data that 10 per cent of the respondents supported about it. They stressed that no caste hierarchical distance was maintained by our Gurus. Consequently they averred that if we are true devotees of the Gurus we must not maintain the social distance with the Shudras. Mostly this majority came from the age group of 50 to 69 years.

TABLE 8.12

Head Priests and in Integration with Shudras

Reactions	*Respondents*	
	No.	*Per cent*
Strongly opposed	25	50
Mildly opposed	11	22
Indifferent	9	18
Mildly support	3	6
Strongly support	2	4
Total	50	100

It may be inferred from the table that a largest majority of the Head priests opposed to maintain the social relations with the Shudras. This majority were young aged. On the contrary, the aged majority of the Head priests supported it.

Further, the position was also analysed about the entry of the Shudras in the shrines.

The relevant data indicate that 78 per cent majority of the Head priests favoured the statement and suggested that every person of the society could participate in the shrine's worship and in the service of Langar. But the ceremonial rites in the shrine can be performed only by an initiated Sikh or who adopted the Khalsa. The said data further indicate that 12 per cent respondents opposed to allowing a Shudra to perform the ceremonial rites or practices without first being initiated. In this regard they argued that every body was Sudra in our religion unless and until a person initiated. A meagre 10 per cent were unjudged.

It may be summed up that an overwhelming majority of the Head priests opined that the ceremonial practices (such as to sit on the dias just inside the Guru Granth Saheb and to perform the Katha and Akhand Path) can not be performed by the Shudras. Consequently the Shudras would not be allowed by the Head priests for taking part into the religious activities.

TABLE 8.13

Head Priests and their Reactions towards Allowing a Shudra Taking Part in the Shrine's Worship

Reactions	*Respondents*	
	No.	*Per cent*
Strongly oppose	4	8
Mildly oppose	2	4
Uncertain	5	10
Mildly favour	11	22
Strongly favour	28	56
Total	50	100

Attitudes Towards Women

Here the question was posed whether they would like giving woman higher status in the shrine.

Our data indicated that 26 per cent of the Head priests opposed strongly and 28 per cent mildly towards women for their not being given a higher status. They argued that the woman could not function as priests because of impurity. However, it was observed in the course of study no Sikh woman was found as priest.

However, 26 per cent of the respondents supported to the woman and confessed that the initiated woman may will be considered for having higher status in the shrine. And remaining 20 per cent did not give any comment. Hence it may be inferred that their attitude towards women having higher status in the shrine tends to become a bit liberal and democratic. But it leaves much viewed the situation differently reacting that to be desired.

TABLE 8.14

Head Priests and their Reactions towards Women Having Higher Status in the Shrine

Reactions	Respondents	
	No.	Per cent
Strongly support	8	16
Mildly support	5	10
Uncertain	10	20
Mildly oppose	14	28
Strongly oppose	13	26
Total	50	100

Attitudes Towards Inter-Community Marriage

To assess the nature of changes, the Head priests were asked, "Are you in favour of inter-caste or inter-community marriage?" The data reveal that 52 per cent majority of the Head priests were not in favour of inter-community marriage. This majority of the Head priests were not willing to settle the marriage of their children out of the Sikh community. Further 32 per cent were in favour of inter-community marriage but in that condition when the revolt was made by the children.

TABLE 8.15

Head Priests and their Attitudes towards Inter-Community Marriage

Attitudes	Respondents	
	No.	Per cent
Strongly Support	10	20
Mildly Support	6	12
Indifferent	8	16
Mildly Oppose	19	38
Strongly Oppose	7	14
Total	50	100

Further it is evident from the Table 8.15 that 16 per cent of the respondents showed indifferent attitude.

To sum up, it may be inferred that slightly more than fifty per cent majority of the respondents (52%) were not willing to give the hands of their sons and daughter to those outside the Sikh community. It may reflect that the idea of inter-community marriage was not thought of in favourable light evidencing that they were disposed towards isolation from other communities.

As for age as a factor in influencing the attitudes towards inter-community marriage, it was observed that comparatively the aged Head priests show inclination towards inter-community marriage, which may be due to their modern education. The following table may clear it.

To elaborate it, our data are regarding the impact of general secular education on the attitudes towards inter-community marriage.

The relevant data in the following Table 8.17 indicate that educated majority of the Head priests were more liberal to materialise the marriage of their children with non-Sikh community. On the contrary, those who were fundamentalists or who had taken only religious education were not in favour of the practice of inter-community marriage.

Attitudes Towards Modernisation

Modernisation is not an exclusive possession of any particular community or group. It should be remembered that once the forces of modernisation set in they effected all communities whether they are Hindus, Muslims or Sikhs though each community responded to modernisation in a different way.

Now-a-days there are a lot of changes being occurred in Indian society at different levels. Such changes have resulted

TABLE 8.16

Age and Attitudes towards Inter-Community Marriage

Age (in years)	*Respondents' Attitudes*											
	St. support		*Mild support*		*Indi-fferent*		*Mild oppose*		*St. oppose*		*Total*	
	No.	%	No.	%	No.	%	No.	%	No.	%	No.	%
20-29	4	8	5	10	3	6	—	—	—	—	12	24
30-39	3	6	1	2	2	4	—	—	—	—	6	12
40-49	1	2	1	2	1	2	—	—	—	—	3	6
50-59	—	—	1	2	2	4	10	20	7	14	20	40
60 and above	—	—	—	—	—	—	5	10	4	8	9	18

TABLE 8.17

General Education and the Attitudes towards Inter-Community Marriage

General Education	*Respondents' Attitudes*											
	St. support		*Mild support*		*Uncer-tain*		*Mild oppose*		*St. oppose*		*Total*	
	No.	%	No.	%	No.	%	No.	%	No.	%	No.	%
Illiterate	—	—	—	—	4	8	5	10	3	6	12	24
Literate	—	—	—	—	2	4	4	8	3	6	9	18
Below matric	—	—	—	—	1	2	6	12	2	4	9	18
Matric or equivalent	8	16	5	10	3	6	—	—	—	—	16	32
Graduate	2	4	—	—	—	—	—	—	—	—	2	4
Post-graduate	2	4	—	—	—	—	—	—	—	—	2	4
Total	*12*	*24*	*5*	*10*	*10*	*20*	*15*	*30*	*8*	*16*	*50*	*100*

from the powerful media of industrialisation and urbanisation. A new variety of norms and values emerged due to these factors.

Let us now turn to the Sikh shrines and the ways in which they have been influenced by the process of modernisation. The Sikh shrines are and have been repository of Sikh traditions. But the growing influence of modernisation also seems to have crept in these shrines in a varying degree modifying their thinking and behaviour. It is particularly about those shrines that have been Headed by the educated priests. As the investigator has already mentioned that the internal system of the shrines is maintained by the Head priest. The shrines are also directed by the genuine advice of these Head priests. It can be noticed here that these priests are the reference group for the congregation and what culture is assimilated by the Head priests was shared too by the followers.

In examining the attitudes of the Head priests towards modernisation our interest was to findout whether the Head priests of the shrines have shown any appreciation of modern conditions, modified way of living, accepted modern education, adopted modern custom and values and also towards general awareness of the country's issues.

Reactions Towards Modern Living

The data given in Table 8.18 reflect that 28 per cent of the Head priests replied totally in the negative opposing the modern way of living, while 50 per cent majority reacted with a mild favour. The view held by the respondents was no doubt liberal but without showing any strong liking towards modern living.

The said table further indicate that 14 per cent respondents expressed favourable view about it indicating that they were inclined to following this pattern of modern living after finishing their prescribed daily ceremonial job. On the basis of inspection and visits to the places of living of particularly the Head priests of prominent historical shrines, it can be noted that the residences were well furnished having modern amenities.

TABLE 8.18

Reactions of the Head Priests towards Modern Living

Reactions	*Respondents*	
	No.	*Per cent*
Strongly subscribed	4	8
Midly subscribe	3	6
Uncertain	4	8
Do not subscribe	25	50
Never subscribe	14	28
Total	50	100

It can be inferred from the data that the majority of the Head priests with their moorings in traditional past and in ordained life of the Panth were found opposed to modern way of living.

In this context it was also found fit to gather whether the Head priests liked the modern dishes in their intake. The study revealed that 60 per cent majority of the Head priests completely opposed it, while 24 per cent of the Head priests mildly subscribe to it. They acknowledged that the meaning of modern food was to drink the wine and to eat the meat. But they emphasised that though the Jhataka meat was prescribed by the Sikh Gurus but they did not touch even that.

Further, our data also indicated that only a negligible number (4%) of the Head priests subscribed towards modern food with 2 Head priests (out of 9) belonging to prominent historical shrines were found alcoholic. The data may be prescribed in the following table:

TABLE 8.19

Reactions towards Modern Food

Reactions	Respondents No.	Respondents Per cent
Never subscribe	30	60
Seldom subscribe	12	24
Uncertain	6	12
Mildly subscribe	1	2
Strongly subscribe	1	2
Total	50	100

Reactions Towards Modern Education

Education has been on of the most influential instrument of modernisation in India. It has led to the mobilisation of people's aspirations for nationalism, liberalism and freedom.[6] It alone has been responsible for the growth of an enlightened intellegentia which carried forward not only a movement for independence but also a relentless struggle for social and cultural reforms.

It is widely entertained that modern education encouraged the individual to develop his mental, physical, emotional and spiritual talents to the full.[7] It has provided an equality of opportunity for all members of society. In the same way the education has also created a lot of opportunities of job. It can be said here that there was a strong relationship between educational qualifications and occupational status. With this background, it was considered necessary to investigate and analyse the changes taken place in the attitudes of the Head priests towards modern education. The following analysis of data throw sufficient light on it.

The data shown in the Table 8.20 indicated that 46 per cent of the respondents strongly supported modern education. While 28 per cent supported mildly. Those who supported the modern education firmly believed that the differentiation between man and man is removed by the education. They also emphasised that there was a rich contribution of Guru Nanak. Public Schools are modern education in Delhi. Mostly these schools are functioning inside the gurdwara's premises.

Table 8.20 further reveals that a meagre 16 per cent opposed modern education. Such respondents criticised the system of modern education. The same table further shows that 10 per cent were found indifferent towards modern education.

It may be inferred from the data that an overwhelming majority of the respondents (74%) supported that modern education was essential for children to seek the job and for adjustment to the modern society.

TABLE 8.20

Head Priests and the Modern Education

Reactions	*Respondents*	
	No.	*Per cent*
Absolute support	23	46
Mild support	14	28
Uncertain	5	10
Mild oppose	5	10
Strong oppose	3	6
Total	50	100

Reactions towards Modern Norms and Values

Many sociologists maintain that shared norms and values are essential for the operation of human society. Unless norms and values are shared, members of the society would be unable to cooperate or even comprehend the behaviour of others. But with the impact of material values and secular motivations, our traditional values are now in eclipse. These changes in our norms and values are reflected in our changing mode of thinking and behaviour. In this condition, nobody can be isolated to himself. Therefore, an attempt was made here to discover whether the Head priests of the shrines have identified themselves with the modern norms and values or not.

It is evident from the Table 8.21 that 56 per cent Head priests never subscribed to the modern norms and values, whereas 26 per cent seldom subscribed. This majority of the Head priests argued that there was no value for emotional and human sentiments in the modern norms and values and hence they were disinclined towards them.

To shift our attention aside, our data also suggest a somewhat trend among 10 per cent of respondents who were found tend to adopt and to go in for the modern norms and values who were particularly the young aged.

TABLE 8.21

Head Priests and the Modern Norms and Values

Reactions	*Respondents*	
	No.	*Per cent*
Never subscribed	28	56
Seldom subscribed	13	26
Uncertain	4	8
Mild subscribed	3	6
Strong subscribed	2	4
Total	50	100

It may be summed up from the table that a largest majority of the Head priests (82%) were against towards modern norms and values.

Social Distance and the Head Priests

In the present investigation an attempt was also made by the investigator to observe the degree of social distance maintained by the Head priests with different groups and communities. To formulate a scale for this purpose, the researcher has taken an insight from the Bogardus Scale of Social Distance. However, in order to collect some more elaborate details we have devised and used a Nine-Point-Scale which was considered expedient and purposive for our study. In this scale 9 attributes were ordered as a continuum of social distance (from acceptability as a fellow worshipper to exclusion from the Panth).

The responses to various statements put to them are given in the following Table 8.22 and weighted scores are given in Table 8.23; which may exhibits the degree of Social Distance maintained by the Head priests of the shrines towards different groups and communities.

It is clear from the Table 8.22 that 80 per cent would allow Hindus as fellow worshipper (allowing to sit in the congregations). The Head priests not allowing to Hindus as their fellow worshipper were 20 per cent. It was observed that the Head priests of the prominent shrines did not want to be closed to Hindus. It appears to be the result of changed socio-cultural affiliations with the Hindus after the operation Blue Star (June-1984) and Sikhs-Hindus riots on November, 1984 (Delhi). Against it, the table further indicates that as many as 96 per cent and 92 per cent Head priests were found more liberal to admit Muslims and Christians respectively as their fellow worshipper in comparison to Hindus and Tribals.

As regards the reactions of the Head priests (24%) having Hindu as an employee in shrine were still more rigid in comparison to the other groups and communities shown in the Table 8.22. Contrarily speaking, the majority of the Head priests were more liberal having Muslims, Christians and Tribals as an employee in the shrine. It is clear from the foregoing lines that the majority of the Head priests of the shrines did not have that understanding reactions towards Hindus and Tribals; as it was observed in the case of Muslims and Christians meaning thereby that they comparatively showed affinity with Muslims and Christians.

However a different trend emerges in terms of their reactions towards Muslims having them as neighbours (Table 8.22, position 3). Our data interestingly revealed that 60 per cent majority of the Head priests reacted unfavourably towards allowing Muslims as their neighbours. It means that our previous finding regarding accepting Muslims as employees there was a positive correlation between Sikhs and the Muslims; while in the present finding there was a negative correlation between the Sikhs and the Muslims.

Viewing their reactions towards different communities taking food with them (position 4), the relevant data are presented in the Table 8.22. It is clear from it that mostly majority of the Head priests (92% for Hindus, 94% for Muslims, 90% for Christians, and 84% for Tribals) were pleased to take the food with all the groups and communities. It should be remembered here that the Langar (mass meal) still is an essential feature of the shrines and also all the Sikhs Gurus were in favour of this institution, and since than it was being crystallised. Hence we may come to conclude that the Sikh Community at large should belief and faith in the institution of Langar and broadly speaking they were found understanding and accommodating in allowing other groups and communities to take food with them.

To elaborate other positions on the continuum in the scale, we may now deal with our Table 8.22. Our data suggested (position 5) that 20 per cent of the respondents did not want to allow Hindus as a members of the community (Sikh Panth). Whereas those not allowing Muslims to become members of the community were 12 per cent; those not allowing Christians and Tribals were 24 per cent and 42 per cent respectively. Now what may be of significance here is their comparative reactions on this aspect between Hindus and Muslims, our data indicated that their social distance with the Hindus as somewhat increased as compare to Muslims. It may be worthy

TABLE 8.22

Reactions of 50 Head Priests to Four Groups and Communities by Percentages

Four Groups and Communities	*Positions*																	
	Position-1 would admit them as a fellow wor-shippers		*Position-2 would have them as an employee in the shrine*		*Position-3 would have them as a neighbour*		*Position-4 would take food with them*		*Position-5 would allow as a member of the co-mmunity*		*Position-6 would have close kin-ship by marriage*		*Position-7 would keep as a res-pective distance*		*Position-8 would treat as an alien to Panth*		*Position-9 would ex-clude them from the Panth*	
	No.	%	*No.*	%	*No.*	%	*No.*	%	*No.*	%	*No.*	%	*No.*	%	*No.*	%	*No.*	%
Muslims	48	96	44	88	30	60	47	94	44	88	39	78	36	72	15	30	50	100
Hindus	40	80	38	76	20	40	46	92	40	80	39	78	45	90	40	80	25	50
Christians	46	92	42	84	44	80	45	90	38	76	31	62	41	82	10	20	50	100
Tribals	32	64	28	56	31	62	42	84	29	58	25	50	28	56	46	92	20	40

* The above Social-Distance Scale is adapted from Emory S. Bogardus, 'Immigration and Race Attitudes,' (Boston: Heath, 1928), p. 25.

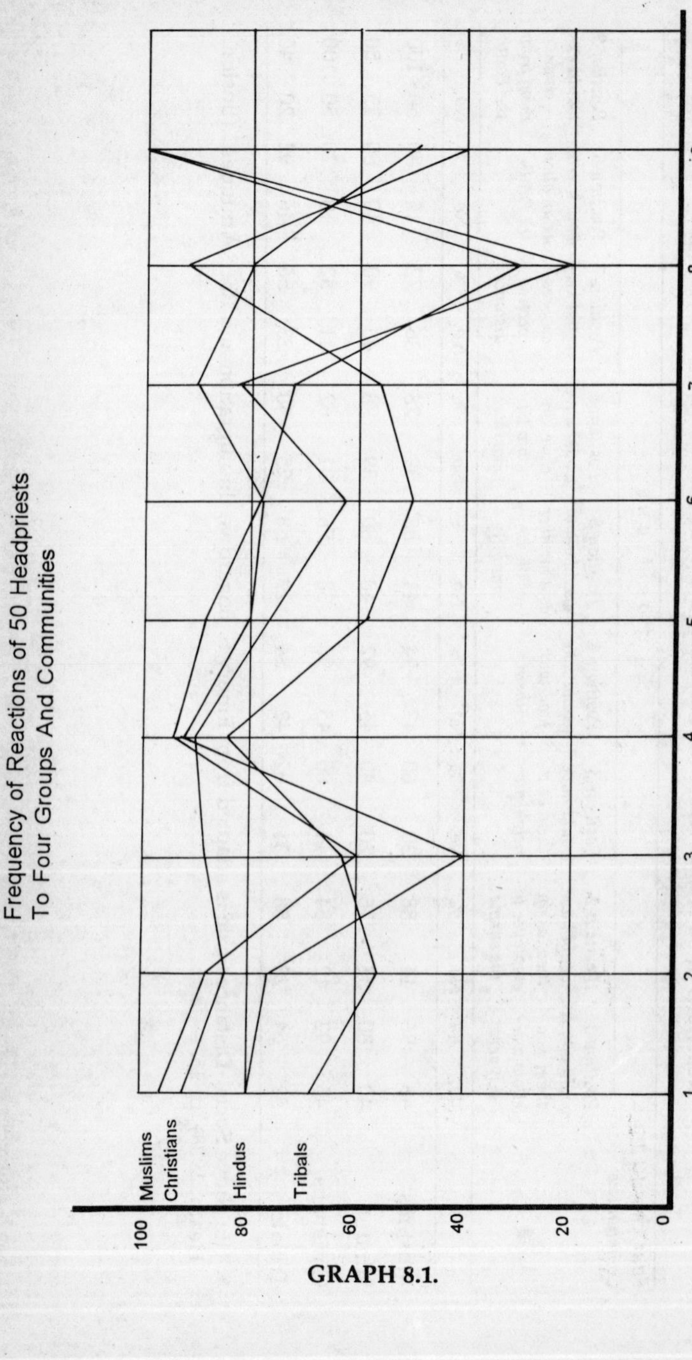
Frequency of Reactions of 50 Headpriests
To Four Groups And Communities
Muslims
Christians
Hindus
Tribals
100
80
60
40
20
0
1
2
3
4
5
6
7
8
9

GRAPH 8.1.

TABLE 8.23

Calculations of Weighted Social-Distance Scores* for Four Groups and Communities

Positions	*Groups and Communities*							
	Muslims		*Hindus*		*Christians*		*Tribals*	
	%	*Weighted scores*	%	*Weighted scores*	%	*Weighted scores*	%	*Weighted scores*
Position-1 Would admit them as a fellow worshipper	96	96	80	80	92	92	64	64
Position-2 Would have them as an employee in the shrine	88	176	76	152	84	168	56	112
Position-3 Would have them as a neighbour	60	180	40	120	88	264	62	186
Position-4 Would take food with them	94	376	92	368	90	360	84	336
Position-5 Would allow as a member of the community	88	440	80	400	76	380	58	290

Position-6								
Would have close kinship by marriage	78	468	78	468	62	372	50	300
Position-7								
Would keep as a respective distance	72	504	90	630	82	574	56	392
Position-8								
Would treat as an alien to Panth	30	240	80	640	20	160	92	736
Position-9								
Would exclude them from the Panth	100	900	50	450	100	900	40	360
Total Weighted Scores	—	*3380*	—	*3308*	—	*3270*	—	*2776*

* The weighted Social-Distance Scores are calculated from the multiplication of the per cent of group falling at each position by the value of that position.

Social-Distance Scores For Four Groups And Communities.

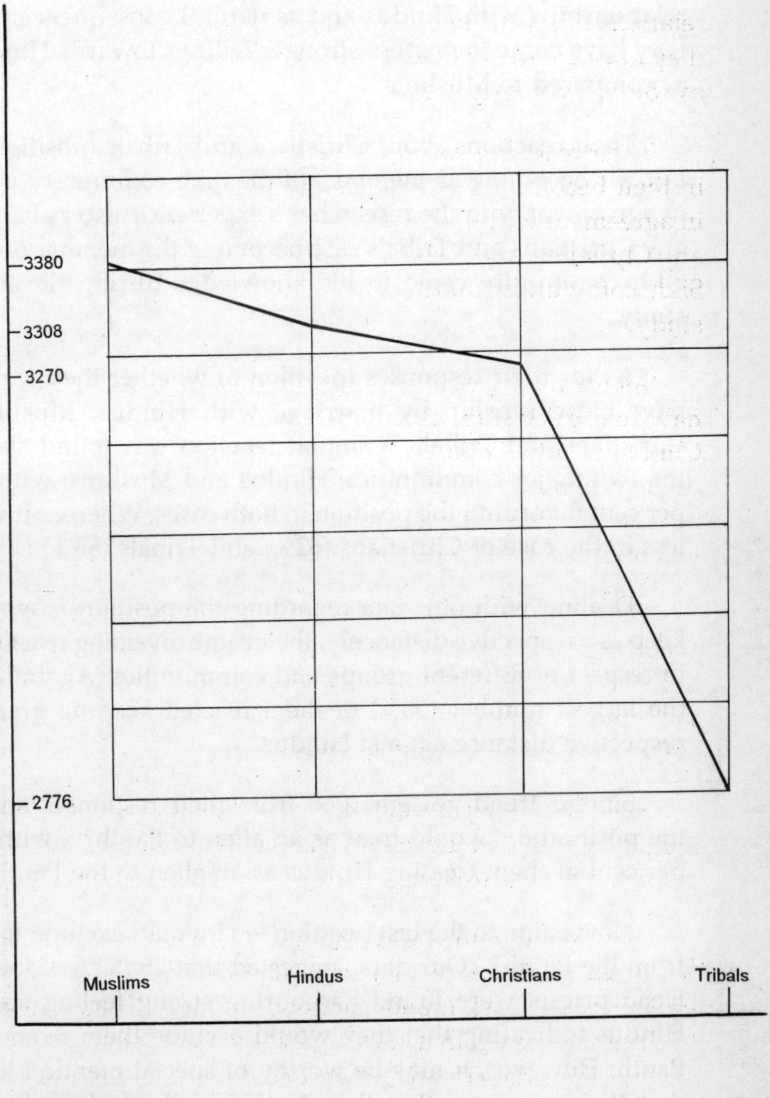

GRAPH 8.2.

of note here that the study was conducted in the year 1987, following the implications of Hindu-Sikh riots, 1984 in Delhi. Our observation here may be that the Sikhs got suspicious of Hindus as a result of the strains and stresses in their relationships with Hindus and as natural consequence of it they have come to possess stronger fellings towards Hindus as compared to Muslims.

Their reactions about Christians and Tribals (position 5) in their becoming as members of the Sikh community were in agreement with the researcher's experience also as hardly any Christians and Tribals case becoming the member of the Sikh community came to his knowledge during the field study.

As for their responses (position-6) whether they would have close kinship by marriage with Hindus, Muslims, Christians and Tribals, a similar reaction was found about the two major communities, Hindus and Muslims, with 78 per cent favouring the position in both cases. Whereas it was less in the case of Christians (62%) and Tribals (58%).

Dealing with our data regarding the position-7, would keep as a respective distance?", their came diversing reactions in respect of different groups and communities. Again here the largest number (90%) of them reacted keeping greater respective distance against Hindus.

Similar trend got emerged from their responses about the position 8, "would treat as an alien to Panth?", with 80 per cent of them treating Hindus as an alien to the Panth.

Now come to the last position 9, "I would exclude them from the Panth?" Our data suggested that 25 (50% of them) Head priests were found harbouring strong feeling about Hindus indicating that they would exclude them from the Panth. However, it may be worthy of special mention here that their reactions that they in their full number (100%)

were of the view that they would outright exclude Muslims and Christians from the Panth. It may reflect that if we go back to their history and traditions of recent times the Sikh Panth hardly chose Muslims and Christians for being converted to Panth. Hence, it may stand to reason to believe that they, over the years, have come to entertain reactions that they would exclude Muslims and Christians from the Panth with one voice. Therefore, it was Hindus in general and their lower sections, Harijans or Shudras, and others in particular got converted to Sikh Panth and embraced Sikhism. Prominent among other factors leading them to this conversion might have the excesses and other acts of operation and persecution perpetrated against these lower people involving both the minority and sometimes the majority as well. It is also clear from our data that 50 per cent of the respondents went to length of the saying that they would exclude them from the Panth may reflect a lack of affinity and nearness with Hindus in the present times.

REFERENCES

1.(i) Redfield, Robert: "The Social Organisation of Tradition", *Far Eastern Quarterly*, Vol. 15, 1955-56, pp. 13-21.

(ii) Singer, Milton: "The Cultural Pattern of Indian Civilisation: A Preliminary Report of Methodological Field Study", *Far Eastern Quarterly*, Vol. 15, 1955-56, pp. 23-36.

2. Ritzer, George and others: *Sociology-Experiencing—A Changing Society*, p. 52.

3. Bates, A.P. and Julian, J.: *Sociology—Understanding Social Behaviour*, p. 30.

4. Dr. Kapoor, *Rajiv Alochan:* op. cit., p. 5.

5. Mukherjee, R.K., *The Culture and Art of India*, p. 348.

6. Singh Yogendra: Cultural Integration and Changing Values (A study of value-system of Educated youth), *Socio-logical Bulletin*, Vol. XIII, Sep. 1964.

7. Harlambos, M.: *Sociology—Themes and Perspective*, p. 179.

9

Findings and Generalisation

The present study is undertaken to probe the extent and magnitude of institutionalisation in the Sikh shrines of Delhi Territory. It may be noted here that, at the time when the study was conducted roughly 12000 (including those in Delhi) Sikh shrines were found working throughout the country, 100 crore of rupees were channelled and having more than 25,000 employees.

The institution of Gurdwara was initiated by the First Prophet, Guru Nanak in the fifteenth century in the form of Dharamsal or Dharamsala to teach, preach and flourish the basic tenets of the faith. After Guru Nanak, the institution of Dharamsal was extended by later Sikh Gurus. These Dharamsals began to be called Gurdwaras in the Guruship of the Sixth Prophet, Guru Hargobind in the early seventeenth century. The Dharamsals eventually became the Gurdwaras, literally, the Guru's door or house. The term and institution of Gurdwara, which now-a-days is used today for Sikh places of worship, came into general use after the Sikh Scripture, Sri Guru Granth Saheb, was proclaimed as Guru by the Tenth and Last Prophet, Guru Gobind Singh in the late seventeenth century.

From the very beginnings, the Sikh shrines remained the platform of the Panth and played a vital role to inspire and organise the Sikh faith. They were designed mainly to remove the hierarchical order from the society. In due course of time, these shrines came to have a supra-national identity. Their main goal was directed to crystallise the religious fundamentalism in preference to removing the social inequalities.

It has been observed that these Sikh shrines and their congregations have become restricted and limited to the members of their own faith serving the purpose of an umbrella and shield for them.

Another notable observation is that this Gurdwara system is made as an estate of the Sikhs and becoming a rallying point in the present circumstances. There is no doubt that this Gurdwara system with its platform, income, administration jurisdiction, stock of opinions and powers, has the capacity to sustain the long-drawn struggle for a separate state. It will not be out of place to mention here that the present Dharamyudh is merely launched by the Sikhs to bind all the shrines with their income and property under one system of management and also to revive and crystallise the classical traditions and culture.

As stressed in the foregoing paragraphs and with no fear of contradiction in terms, the researcher would aver that the present study deals with the historico-empirical analysis pertaining to the Process of Institutionalisation of Sikh Shrines—with special reference to prominent Sikh shrines in Delhi Territory. It is a prominent sacred and religious place of the Sikhs having a fine array of Sikh shrines — the historical Sikh shrines and the shrines of Sri Guru Singh Sabha, representing the same orders but slightly different in their system of management. In order to examine the hypothetical propositions, the present study is classified in terms of following postulates: preliminary remarks abut the concept of institutionalisation and how it is evidence in the case of Sikh shrines, socio-historical origin of Sikhism and the Sikh shrines, social structure of the Sikh shrines, economic structure of the Sikh shrines, mode of management and working of the Sikh shrines, religio-cultural beliefs and practices of the Sikh shrines, and changing patterns of values of the shrines. All these dimensions were taken into account to judge the internal merits of structural and patterns of the Sikh shrines, at micro level, in the substantive context of institutionalisation.

On the basis of materials collected and analysed in the preceding chapters, a few significant findings have been obtained under some categorised dimensions:

(I) In the first postulate the researcher has briefly touched upon the rudimentry and the seminal idea behind the process of institutionalisation in general and particularly and more importantly in relation to the Sikh shrines.

We may look at the Process of Institutionalisation as a continuous crystallisation of different types of norms, organisation and frame-work, directing and controlling the process of exchange of different commodities. It is also a process of innovation of various appropriate institutional norms and organisational frame-works, as well as a process of setting up new types of structural frame-works. To explain further, we may mean by institutionalisation the standardisation of behaviour patterns and behavioural expectations in a collectivity.

In the light of the above remarks, now to shift to the main theme as discussed in this postulate, it deserves to be emphasised that the Process of Institutionalisation of Sikh Shrines here is mainly concerned with the religious conservatism, doctrinnaire principles, dogmatic beliefs and the fundamental values for whose perpetuation, preservation and persistence, the Sikh shrines are out to wage a grim and relentless fight. It may remained us of a long standing demand of the Sikhs to bind all the historic shrines in the country under one system of management to ensure uniformity of religious practices, goals and activities in all the religious places of the Sikhs. It was observed that this process of institutionalisation is gradually and quietly creeping into the Sikh shrines who are using it as a mechanism and means for self-preservation, identity and separate entity. The study reveals that the ongoing institutionalisation of Sikh shrines is consciously or unconsciously creating a climate conducive to a collective mobilisation of the Sikhs and in-gathering of the faithful and is emerging as a tremendous force to reckon with in the present times. This process may further be reflected among the Sikhs in their showing structural-functional rigidity for a separate identity, purity of faith and separate symbols. In this context, we may conclude here that the institutionalisation of Sikh shrines is being used primarily to revive the fundamental tenets, seminal beliefs and cultural practices hoping thereby that this process will bring self-preservation and identity of their faith.

Now to devote attention to where the study was carried on, from whom the data were gathered and what was the size of sample and so on. The researcher would like to add that due to the wide — ranging and extensive nature of the problem of the present study was restricted to Delhi. This study was conducted on 50 Sikh shrines located in proper Delhi making a random stratified sample selected from a total of 236 Sikh shrines. This sample of, approximately, 21 per cent was considered adequate and properly represented to supply valid informations and produce reliable results. Our method here has been mainly the structural-functional perspective using interview-schedule and some case-study data. We have preferred the statistical Model as compared to ethno-historical one to facilitate the measurement and replication.

(II) To come to the second postulate it may be noted that it is divided into A and B parts. The brief summary of growth and development of Sikhism and the conclusions derived from it are discussed in the A part and the socio-historical background of the Sikh Shrines of Delhi in brief is summarised in the B part.

(A) As for the 'Origin of Sikhism,' it may be concluded that the Sikhism, comparatively a young and distinct religion, is based on the teachings of Guru Nanak and his Nine Successors. It was observed that the history of Sikh religion is 519 years old (from 1469 A.D. upto date) but the total span, in which it shaped, of the fundamental growth and development of Sikh faith is only 239 years old (from 1469 A.D. to 1708 A.D.). This period can be divided into two parts (from the birth of Guru Nanak in 1469 A.D. until the death of Guru Govind Singh, 1708 A.D.). In the first part of one hundred thirty nine years (from the first Guru, Nanak Devji upto fifth Guru, Arjan Devji), the first Five Gurus pronounced the ideals of a new social order and the second part of the remaining hundred years (from the sixth Guru, Hargovindji upto last, Guru Govind Singh) witnessed the development of traditions and institutions which supplemented the social order.

From the preceding analysis of growth and development of Sikhism (as discussed broadly in Chapter no. 3) it may be inferred conclusively that Guru Nanak organised and shaped the Sikh society on separate ideological patterns establishing the Dharamsalas, which later became Gurdwaras, where his followers could meet together to practise the Dharam of his concept and spread his message to others. Guru Nanak exhorted Guru Angad, and others not to devote wholly to only meditation but to devote efforts and energies to the shaping of the Panth. The growth of the Gurumukhi script, invented by Guru Angad and of the Sikh scriptures, mainly Sri Guru Granth Saheb, compiled by Fifth Guru, Arjan Devji, were instrumental in estabilishing of the separate identity of the Sikhs. Added further, the militarisation of the Sikh movement (giving a birth of Khalsa in 1699 A.D. by Guru Govind Singh) gave a new dimension to the growth of Sikhs and gave rise to a separate organisational identity known as the Sikh Panth practising their universal humanism.

In this frame of reference the researcher would like to confine himself to a few major findings which have emerged form the present study in so far as it pertains to the growth and development of Sikhism.

In the first place, it may be concluded that there was no substantive and distinct existence of Sikhs as a single authonomous religious community in the sense of shared set of traditions, cultural meanings and social practices and even as late as the second half of nineteenth century the boundary separating Sikhs from Hindus was not pronounced.

In the second place the researcher would like to conclude that the Sikh faith was born out of the decline of Brahaminical influence. Consequently, all the Sikhs movements went a long way in the purging of Hindu customs and Brahaminical influences and brought about the institutionalisation of Sikh traditions and rituals.

In the third place, it may be inferred that the Sikh faith, though, owes its beginning to a Khatri Hindu , Guru Nanak and the following Nine Khatri Gurus. Its main body was constituted of Jats who were at the top of caste hierarchy among the Sikhs. It was in the time of Guru Govind Singh when Jats were baptised in large numbers who later stabilised their position maintaining upward mobility and becoming chief instrument of the Sikhs rise to power.

In the fourth place, it may be observed that, from the very beginning of Sikhs and until the Tenth Guru Govind Singh and even today, the Sikh identity has been, in the process of crystallisation, isolating itself from Hindu identity. A sharp memory and knowledge of their history provides a fillep to Sikh identity and the historic places (shrines) have been instrumental in the spread of this knowledge far and wide. Similarly, their history is remembered and celebrated at festivals, fairs, congregational gatherings and at other important events in the Sikhs history.

(B) Now to discover the 'Socio-historical origin of the Sikh shrines in Delhi,' the data were collected from published and unpublished sources. On the basis of Sikh literature and archaeological sources collected from National Archieves and Delhi Archieves, Delhi and analysed, the researcher may conclude that, after Punjab, the Delhi Territory has a long and outstanding tradition of Sikh shrines and also remained thereby a powerful centre of cultural transmission. Hence, our finding here is that, as a natural consequence of it, almost all the Sikh Gurus visited the place and left indelible impact on the Indian culture as well as on the culture of the people of Delhi. In the course of time, these vary places got transformed into the historical pilgrimage centres (Karam-sthals). Now these places are known as the most sacred and historical prominent centres* of the Sikhs.

It was also gathered that the historical prominent places or shrines of the Sikhs of Delhi have a long history of bitter struggle. The archaeological evidence reveal that these places were established in the form of Dharamsaal and came into existence as Gurdwaras after death of Guru Gobind Singh in 1708 A.D. when Baghel Singh (a sincere and true devotee of Sri Guru Govind Singh) captured Delhi in 1790 A.D. and secured promise from Shah Alam II to restore all the historical places connected with the lives of Gurus of the Sikhs. Accordingly he followed up to locate the existing historical places of the Sikhs in the late eighteenth century. Further, it was also discovered that these historical places were demolished many times in the Moughel Period and mosques

---

* The findings and conclusions thereon are based on 16 historical (including 6 transferred to Delhi Sikh Gurdwara Management Committee by disputed Sri Guru Singh Sabha) plus 34 other shrines managed by Sri Guru Singh Sabha.

were established. Finally, the beautiful and imposing buildings of historical Sikhs shrines in Delhi (such as — Gurdwara Sis Ganj, Bangla Saheb Rakab Ganj, Majnu Tilla, Bala Saheb, Mata Sundari, Damdama Saheb, Nanak Piayo, Moti Bagh and Gurdwara Banda Singh Bahadur etc.) were designed and constructed in 1925 and later. At present these historical or prominent shrines are managed by Delhi Sikh Gurdwara Management Committee (D.S.G.M.C.) and are instrumental in meeting the religio-sectarian expectations and aspirations of the followers of the faith.

Now to discuss the Sikh shrines of the second category being run by Sri Guru Singh Sabha, hence, the observations and findings made in their respect may claim to break new grounds. The researcher faced many problems in collecting the relevant sufficient data because the available literature and other authoritative sources were almost silent about this category of shrines. The researcher was not in knowledge of any systematic study made so far about them. The observation ground here, the researcher mainly relied on the field data, experiences personal interviews, personal visits to the religious places using it as the primary sources of data.

To sum up some major findings here, it may be pointed out that these shrines called Local Shrines* and came into existence when a large number of Sikhs came from Western Punjab and settled in far-flung areas of Delhi, particularly, after the partition of the country in 1947. Our observation is that prior to the partition of the country, there was no existence of these shrines as such those followers of the faith, living a bit away from the main stream of Delhi, used to be accommodated by the historical shrines in their religio-cultural congregations, meets and other ritualistic observances. However, as later developments, these migrants, followers of the faith, felt increasingly inconvenienced in joining the

---

* These shrines are taken to mean those that are managed by Sri Guru Singh Sabha.

congregational worship in the historical shrines. Hence, a great need arosed among the migrant followers for having their own separate places of worship. The stimulus for it was provided by those who wanted to gain religious popularity. Consequently, the initiated Sikhs formed an independent body of Sri Guru Singh Sabha and the management of the shrines, thus established particularly, after the partition of the country, was handed over to this elected body. As revealed by the study that these shrines, though of a lesser standing and strature, came to have their their own well defined tenets, ideals and religious functioning similar to historical prominent ones. With the passage of time, these shrines too have developed their own system of management, identity and emotional unity. The relevant field data suggest that these local shrines claim the greatest strength (93.2%) but the history of these shrines is not more than fifty years old. On the other hand the historical prominent shrines have a too meagre strength (6.8%) but their standing may be traced to the period of two to three centuries earlier.

It was told during the investigations that the shrines belonging to the Sri Guru Singh Sabha and those to Delhi Sikh Gurdwara Management Committee were not found pulling together and rather they bore signs of mutual rivalry. However the researcher would like to react that there was a little evidence to suggest that these two categories of Sikh shrines were visibly indirect clash and or confrontation.

III. To understand the 'structural core of the Sikh shrines' the basic social data were collected regarding the age of the Head priests, caste, general and religious education, occupational background, nature of local dialects, marital status and nature of habitation, life-style, succession practice, role-expectations, orienting factors and attitudes of the Head priests. To find out the intimate and in-depth knowledge of standing and working of some major Sikh shrines, the researcher has made some case studies also. There were four case studies relating to Gurdwara Sis Ganj, Gurdwara Rakab Ganj, Gurdwara Bangla Saheb run by D.S.G.M.C. and Gurdwara Punjabi Bagh managed by Sri Guru Singh Sabha.

To come to the 'age of the Head priests,' the majority of them belonged to the young age-group from 30 years to 40 years. The statistical analysis reveal that the average age came 41.5 years. Hence, it may be easily inferred that the Head priest is appointed when the person is in active and energetic period of life. As for the caste background, it was gathered that before initiation the majority of the Head priests (65%) belonged to the Jats and Harijan. It may suggest here that the Jats and Harijan were remained main constituent parts of the Khalsa till the death of Guru Govind Singh in 1708 A.D.

As regards the 'general education,' it was arrived at that the majority of the Head priests (60%) obtained average education. As for the religious education, it was observed that the majority of the Head priests (72%) acquired only essential religious education like as —reading the Sri Guru Granth Saheb and performing the Katha and Kirtan. It may broadly be inferred here that the level of general and religious education among the Head priests did not receive any thrust. It was also observed during interview with the religious Heads and leaders that the religious authorities were found more conscious of opening religious academies cattering to the needs of good religious education.

The data regarding the, 'occupational background of the Head priests' revealed that the majority of the respondents belonged to the farmer families having largely a rural background. It may be inferred here that the farming occupation was predominent as such an overwhelming number of the Head priests had fewer opportunities of their exposure to modern education.

As for the 'local dialects combination,' it was found

interesting to note that a largest majority (60%) of the Head priests use the combination of Gurmukhi and Hindi dialects. It may be suggested here that the Sikh Gurus also adopted and patronised the Gurmukhi and Hindi dialects. It may be mentioned here that the Gurmukhi of the language of Sikh scriptures had its roots in Hindi and Sanskrit and the same dialects still commanded its preponderence over other dialects.

The data on 'marital status' showed that the percentage of married respondents was highest and the practice of desertion and divorce was almost non existent. It may be inferred here that their orientation towards family was fairly strong.

The data regarding the 'nature of habitation' showed that an overwhelming majority (84%) of the Head priests were migrant. It was also gathered that the majority of the respondents were migrated from Pakistan, Rajasthan and Kashmir. It may be mentioned here that these places were the centres where the Sikh Gurus lived and preached and the Sikh tenets were embraced by the majority of the other faiths.

One of the focal point of the present study was to find out the life-style and succession practice of the Head priests. In the dimension of life-style, we have taken into consideration as the age of being initiate, the age of being Head priests, orienting factors, nature of attachment, tenure, age of retirement, term and nature of job, Grade's structure and main eligibility critaria of the Head priests and following conclusions were drawn.

As regards the "age of being initiate of the Head priests', it was gathered that the majority of the Head priests (62%) took their initiation at the age of 10 to 19. It may be noted here that the young children were also initiated at Anandpur (Punjab) where Sri Guru Govind Singh founded the Khalsa. It was observed that this practice held it won even now. Hence, it may be generalised that the age practice once introduced by Sri Guru Gobind Singh has come to be crystallised as a tenet and doctrine of Sikh religion which is still being religiously stuck to revealed that the majority of the respondents (40%) took over as Head priest at the age of 40 to 49 years. The statistical analysis indicated that the average age of being Head priest was 45.9 years. The researcher would like to make comment that the responsibilities of Head priests require the maturity of age. Consequently the statistical analysis here was found significant. As regards the orienting factors, it was gathered that the majority of the respondents (36%) identified themselves with this profession drawing encouragement from their fore fathers engaged in the service of these shrines. It may be inferred from it that the shrines are job-oriented and consequently the qualified children of the Head priests are accomodated in the shrines.

As regards the nature of attachment of the Head priests, it was concluded that the majority of the respondents (72%) entered the profession for propagation of the ideals set by the Ten Sikh Gurus. It may support the proposition that they hold religious values dear to their heart and are alive to their commitment to the promotion of their Panth.

In relation to the 'tenure of office of the Head priests' it was observed that approx. One-third majority of them, who were associated with the prominent historical shrines, were holding their permanent office and the tenure for the rest of 66 per cent was found temporary in nature. The permanent Head priests were belonging to D.S.G.M.C. and getting service benefits whereas those temporary who mostly belonging to Sri Guru Singh Sabha and were deprived of service benefits.

As for the 'age of retirement of the Head priests' the study revealed that this was 60 years among the Head priests of the prominent historical shrines (34%) whereas in the case of Head priests of Sri Guru Singh Sabha (66%) it was not fixed. Hence, an obvious inference can be drawn form it that there was a protection of service among the Head priests of

Delhi Sikh Gurdwara Management Committee and contarily the Head priests of Sri Guru Singh Sabha did not enjoy such protection. Consequently, the impression left was that in comparative terms the Head priests of Sri Guru Singh Sabha were not found that enthusiastic and among themselves too there was a ranking claiming a varying degree of prestige and standing.

As regards the 'terms and nature of job,' it was gathered that 34 per cent respondents were holding a transferable job from one shrine to another and rest of the 66 per cent respondents were holding a non-transferable job. To add to it, it may be said that those Head priests whose job was transferable were attached with the prominent historical shrines, and whose job was non-transferable were associated with the shrines of Sri Guru Singh Sabha.

As for the 'eligibility criteria for appointment of the Head priests,' it was collected that among 44 per cent of them the possession of spiritual knowledge and experience figured up prominently as compared to other bases. Further, it was also observed that 78 per cent Head priests attained their status by promotion from the lower position of Sewadar and priest which may reflect a trend of their going traditional instead of being open in an assigning status to the Head priests.

Regarding the 'attitude towards kinship relations in the staffing of these shrines,' it was gathered that a large number of the Head priests (68%) supported the kinship relations in the staffing of the shrines. It may also be noted here that the majority of the Head priests, who supported their view, have claimed a strong voice in the managing body and were found more powerful to gain favours from the authority of the managing body for their simply subscribing to the interests of the body. Therefore the authority did not mind the Head priests having their way in selecting the success or of their choice. This practice however was limited to the prominent shrines. This may reflect that in the matter of staffing personal consideration are given precedence.

As for the attitude of the Head priests towards 'principles of governing of the shrine,' it was inferred that an overwhelming majority of the Head priests (88%) were fund humanist and democratic in their dealings towards the congregations and the lay public. However, a notable observation here is that, in actual practice, it was found that in the present state of affairs in the country their rituals, observances and other religious ceremonies largely attracted and rather allowed the members of their own faith to join and take part in the deliberations and business discussions.

As regards their attitude towards their 'position of power and authority' the study revealed that the majority of the Head priests (associated with the prominent historical shrines) showed a sense of religious pride and privilege in adorning such an important seat of Head priest. But an opposite picture emerged that the Head priests of the small shrines of Sri Guru Singh Sabha were somewhat uncomfortable and afraid about the very survival of the concerned shrine for their having no dependable and tangible economic support and other patronage.

So far as the 'Uniform Civil Code for the Community' is concerned, it was observed that almost all the Head priests supported the Uniform Civil Code with one voice considering it essential for the welfare of the community. The study further revealed that almost all the respondents were found much conscious about the uniformity in behaviour patterns, religious, beliefs, values, goals and activities which reflects a clear trend of ongoing process of institutionalisation in their religio-cultural ideology.

As regards the reactions of the Head priests about what they entertained 'regarding Sikh Separateness,' the study revealed that a large number of the respondents reacted that the Sikhs belonged to a separate people having a separate identity in their behaviour and symbols established by their Ten Gurus. It may reflect that they held crystalisation of their religious beliefs, norms and values in esteem.

Coming to the aspect of 'Khalsa Raj,' we may conclude that the majority of the Head priests asserted that the meaning of Khalsa Raj was a spirit of internal solidarity and consciousness among the Sikhs which should not be allowed to merge with other creeds and communities. This reflects a trend of crystallisation and internalisation of their norms and values.

IV. As regards the 'economic structure,' it can be said that it provides solid base for the smooth and constructive working of an organisation. Hence speaking from economic point of view the Sikh shrines not only fulfil the religio-sectarian demand of the followers of the faith but also economic one. It was gathered that the economic system of the Sikh shrines was based on the religious offerings and endowments. It may also be noted here that the net work of the shrines was spread throughout the country as an estate expanding with 12000 shrines and 100 crore of rupees. In view of the importance of economic structure, we have collected the data from official and unofficial accounts of the managing bodies of the shrines and a few significant conclusions about their income and expenditure were drawn as follows:

Regarding the 'sources and amount of income of the shrines,' it was gathered that the shrines employed different methods to raise their income. But all these methods of income were based completely on charity. The various sources of income of the prominent historical shrines may conveniently be divided as: (i) Ritualistic offerings such as — Charat, Prasad, Langar and Paths, (ii) Rent and property, (iii) Charitable and miscellaneous donations.

The analysis of the sources of the income of the shrines showed that the prominent historical shrines, received an enormous amount of money from the massive support of the

Sikh community. The Budget of the managing body of prominent historical shrines was estimated at Rs. 3.79 crores in which 90 per cent income (approx. 3.4 crores) was derived from prominent historical shrines. The study indicated that, between 1956-57 and 1986-87, the income of prominent historical shrines in Delhi increased from Rs. 8.49 lacs to tabout Rs. 3.79 crores. This increase in income was due to liberal donations by the Sikhs, an increase into the Sikh popualtion of Delhi following the disturbances in Punjab and the significant increase in the number of Sikh institutions.

A stocktaking of the budgetary figures of the last thirty years (from 1956-57 to 1986-87) may speak well of the fact that the income of the prominent historical shrines increased after the outbreak of the Hindu-Sikh riots in November 1984 in Delhi. The reason for it may be a sudden wave of enthusiasm and a spurt in religious sentiments and activities. To add further we may say that the members of Sikh community got enthused with the feelings of their rites and obligations and thus we may here conclude that the general reactions of the Sikh masses and particularly those of the Sikh religious leaders incuding Head priests were that they the obligation to protect their group or community was deeply internalised and was taken very seriously.

Regarding the 'sources of income of the shrines of Sri Guru Singh Sabha' (which manages an independent shrine), it may be inferred that the large shrines of Sri Guru Singh Sabha, such as — the shrine of Punjabi Bagh Singh Sabha, Tilak Nagar's, Lajpat Nagar's, Greater Kailash's etc., raised their income through two types of offerings, one common offering and another Shabad offering, and charities. On the contrary, those shrines of Sri Guru Singh Sabha which were small in structure, followers and devotees were fighting still for their economic existence. It may lead us to conclude that in the case of large shrines there was a better normative economic pattern as compared to small ones. Members of both the category of shrines responded differently to the expectations showing a varying degree of performance and conformity to the economic needs of the Sikh shrines.

As regards the 'expenditure side,' it was gathered that outlay of the managing body of prominent historical shrines (D.S.G.M.C.) can broadly be categorised into — (i) Customary expenditure including daily religio-cultural services, Langar and Gurupurbs celebrations, etc. and (ii) present day expenditure occasioned by daily and modern requirements, such as construction and maintenance of gurdwara property, salaries of gurdwara employees and education and welfare activities.

As for the amount of expenditure incurred on various items in relative terms, we may say that the maximum amount of expenditure was being spent on Dharam Prachar or institutional expenses. In this context, it may be noted that between 1957 to 1987 the expenditure on this item increased from rupees 24.69 lacs to Rs. 1.19 crores while total budget of 1986-87 was estimated at approx 3.23 crores. It may clearly show that in comparative terms the norms of religious profession, practice and promotion predominently guided the Sikhs at large and particularly the Head priests mainly charged with this. Therefore, it may safely be concluded here that the norms of religious propagation and promotion by means of Dharam Prachar were widely accepted in the entire community and they were seem deeply inculcated in the personalities of the Head priests. In the respect of expenditure on various items another notable observation is that there was however no uniformity of opinion and reactions among the members. They rather showed varying degree of conformity to the normative pattern of expenditure. It may bring out the fact the social positions as occupied by the members mainly guided their varied reactions to this aspect.

V. One of the focal point of the present study was also to examine and analyse the 'Mode of Management and Working of the shrines.' In this postulate the investigator has studied the internal and eternal management and working of the shrines. The internal management was structured with adequate staff of Head priests, priests, pathi, kirtan Jatha, Jathedar and Sweadar. On the contrary, the external management was consisted of executives, representatives and their officials. Now first to analyse the internal management. Some of the inferences arrived at in this area may be listed hereunder.

As regard the 'rights vested in the office of Head priests,' it was observed that the majority of the Head priests (50%) had the supervisory rights covering the daily working of the shrines, taking an order with the daily services and monitoring other routine matters.

Regarding the 'main functions of the Head priests' in the shrine, it was observed that in majority of cases the Head priests were concerned with the function of keeping the organisation healthy and strong. And for it they devised new ways and mechanism considered expedient to the demand of the situation and requirement of time. It may reflect that their mode of functioning tends to get oriented to the process of institutionalisation.

Now to come to discuss the 'mode of awarding punishment by the Head priests to those erring persons in the shrine,' it was found that a sizable majority (80%) of the Head priests were confined themselves to issuing warnings to the erring persons. However a few (20%) Head priests who were in truck with the members of the managing body exercise their right of terminating the erring members. Though exact data could not be collected about it but the reports were of two-three such cases who were terminated. It may show that in order to ensure social control in the shrine more and more emphasis was given to the conformity to norms, whereas the cases reported about the violation of these norms showing social deviation were penalised particularly by those

Head priests who wilded power and influence with the members of the managing body. This may also bare evidence to the ongoing process of institutionalisation of these shrines.

Regarding the 'Daily Routine of Shrines,' it was observed that there was strict enforcement of the code of conduct for the daily life in the prominent historical shrines. Secondly, it was found that the daily routine of the shrines was institutionalised with the strict following of sub-institutions such as — Vak, Kirtan, Ardas, Karha Prasad, Akhand Path and the Langar etc. Thirdly, it was gathered that the religious institution of the Sangat was rooted in their history and philosophy claiming a general and wide acceptance among the devotees and other fellow brethren. The study further revealed that every Sikh who joins the congregation in the shrine also shares the service of the shrine which reflects a character of internalisation of norms and standardisation of behaviour patterns. Lastly, it was also discovered that the daily routine of the shrines is getting oriented day by day to the protection of the community. And thus the concept of universal quality and brotherhood as long as enshrined in the Sikh panth tends to decline or to take a backsheet.

As regards the external management of the shrines, the investigator has covered 50 members of the executive body of the shrines, who figured as President or Secretary and also some were the members of various committees. Some of the inference arrived at in this field may be listed on the following.

As for the 'aims of objectives of the managing body of the shrines,' it was observed that two objectives which had received greater attention from the members of the managing body of the prominent historical shrines and the shrines of Sri Guru Singh Sabha were the progagation of Sikh religion (66%) and the ensuring of safe custody of funds and property (20%) of the shrines. In order to collect more and more funds for religious propaganda and for the spread of religious knowledge they have institutionalised the parting away of one-tenth of their income to the maintenance and development of the shrines. This norm of gifting away some part of their income for the cause of their religion and welfare of the shrine was found internalised among the members. It expressed itself on the occasions of mobilisation of economic resources needed for the rennovation, enrichment of embellishment of the shrine and its belongings.

As regards the 'political mobilisation and voting behaviour of the members of the managing bodies,' our observation is that in the election of managing bodies an overwhelming majority (80%) of the members pledged their unreveserved support to the candidate having close links with the shrines. For it the Head priests and other office-bearers impress them with the tenets and doctrines of their religion and thus were seen taking recourse to some sort of indoctrination. In consequence of this the freedom of voting right gets somewhat impeded. When it comes the question of general civic elections in Delhi and around almost similar was the observation in the case of general civic elections of local bodies, state or of the central when feelings of the creed, faith and other ethnic considerations when played up in order to influence the Sikh voters at large.

As for the 'eligibility base for candidate seeking the highest status in the management committee,' it was found that 76 per cent of the members gave the first priority to religious affiliation. In this connection, through our data may not sufficiently bare out the fact, the researcher, on the basis of his own experience and his inside knowledge, may conclude that the party support (i.e. mainly concerning Shromani Akali Dal and Master Tara Singh Group) and money power also appeared a factor in influencing the election politics. Hence an inference may be drawn again here that there was in evidence of their using subtle and tacit religio-political and economic devices and mechanism for larger political gain which may be seen as a part of the global view of the process of institutionalisation of these shrines.

As regards the working of the managing bodies, it was gathered that the working of the Delhi Sikh Gurdwara Management Committee and the body of Sri Guru Singh Sabha is carried out through various committees constituted by the Executive Board. Generally the committees of the D.S.G.M.C. and S.G.S.S. comprise 10 or 15 members and 2 and 3 members respectively. The office of both the managing bodies is managed by the Manager according to rules and bylaws of the body and instructions issued by it from time to time through its Secretary. Under this major dimension some other sub-dimensions were also taken into account. The relevant conclusions are given on the following.

To analyse the 'pattern of leadership of the managing bodies,' it was observed that 52 per cent members of both the managing bodies were in favour of the democratic pattern and remaining 34 per cent and 14 per cent were in favour of the power and money-oriented and self-oriented respectively.

As for the reactions of the members about the 'present set up the managing bodies' it was observed that the majority of the respondents were not satisfied with the existing set up of the managing bodies.

As regards the 'factors of organisational weakness,' it was collected that the 70 per cent respondents accepted that the organisational weakness was in evidence due to the lack of unity and greedy leadership.

As for the 'affairs of the managing bodies,' it was found that the affairs of the Delhi Sikh Gurdwara Management Committee were not in sound health and this needed proper handling. On the contrary the shrines belonging to the Sri Guru Singh Sabha gave somewhat a better picture.

Regarding the 'groupism and factionalism in the managing bodies,' it may be concluded that the Sikh shrines affiliated to the Sri Guru Singh Sabha were not affected much by groupism and factionalism. Contrarily, the groupism and factionalism was existed in the body of prominent historical shrines on the basis of personal loyality to the leaders and similar to the economic interests.

So far as the 'power structure and decision making of the managing bodies' is concerned the study revealed that both of the managing bodies are well knit and effective organisations and based on the well defined tenets of Sikhism. It was gathered that the D.S.G.M.C. (managing body of prominent historical shrines) was consisted of 55 members out of which 46 were elected from the various wards of Delhi and 9 members were coopted. Contrarily, the managing body of Sri Guru Singh Sabha was consisted of 21 elected members. The Executive Board of both the managing bodies was consisted five office-bearers and ten members and same method is adopted to take the decisions and implementation. The decisions on minor issues were generally taken unanimously and decisions on major lapses or disputes such as new construction or expansion works, propagational and promotional activities or setting up new institutions, were taken by a majority vote.

The present study further indicated that there were no major lapses or disputes in the managing body of Sri Guru Singh Sabha. Generally the democratic norms were regarded by the members. But the study brought to light some dysfunctional aspects of the process of decision-making system in the Delhi Sikh Gurdwara Management Committee.

Coming to the aspect of 'activities of the shrines and their managing bodies' the study makes it evident that the shrines are the main source of philanthropic activities. Consequently, they also lay great emphasis on the action-oriented work and services and encourage the ideals of quality and brotherhood. It was also gathered that variety of activities were performed by both the managing bodies of the shrines, such as-religious charitable, educational and medical activities.

It may deserve to be mentioned here that these socio-cultural activities are directly associated with the institutionalised patterns and cultural goals which constitute the structural core of the Sikh panth. This institutionalised structural core of the Sikh faith clearly reflects a trend of institutionalisation in the Sikh panth and their symbols.

VI. The focus of the present study was also to examine and analyse the Religio-cultural beliefs and practices of the shrines. Under the postulate we have studied the complete belief system of the shrines. The following conclusions and generalisations were arrived at which concentrated on empirical and non-empirical beliefs as a principal components of the belief system. The distinction in between is simply that the empirical beliefs, in Parsonian terminology, are those which are within the reach of Logico-Meaningful Methodology and, contrarily, the non-empirical beliefs are those which are defined beyond the reach of the scientific methodology of empirical science. Hence, the following conclusions of empirically beliefs were arrived at after using Five-point Lickert Scale.

Regarding the empirical belief whether the shrines were mirror of the Sikh ideals where every Sikh gets real peace and solace, it was concluded that an overwhelmingly 90- per cent of the Head priests were in favour of it. Hence, it was also concluded that the opinion norm or direction accepted by the shrine to the ways, procedures and usages which is symptomatic of the process in institutionalisation.

As for the belief whether the shrines were being used as a mechanism to maintain the identity of the Sikhs, it was inferred that 82 per cent Head priests offered their approval and advocated that the shrines remained always the symbols of self-preservation, identity and separate entity. The trend emerging from the data is that in confusion and anxiety about maintaining a separate identity the prominent historical shrines were being increasingly relied upon for this purpose and whereby crystallised mechanism was also being employed for the survival and solidarity of the Panth.

As regards the belief whether the shrines were designed for collective mobilisation of the Sikhs and of their resources, it was collected that there was an overwhelming (90%) volume of opinion in favour of it. Our observation here was that there was an increasing tendency of followers attending the frequent congregations taking place in these shrines. This went a long way in mobilising the Sikhs and the symbols.

Coming to the belief about the shrines whether they were offering relentless fight to maintain fundamental tenets and seminal beliefs, it may be concluded that the majority of the Head priests (68%) reacted favourably to it. It may reflect that the trend of reverting to the fundamental tenets and seminal beliefs seems to be over the years gaining momentum. It may also lead us to conclude that the Sikhs are veering round the view that the revival of fundamental tenets is the only meaning and hope through which they can survive and later grow and develop in midst of other rival creeds and religions.

Regarding the belief whether the present Dharamyudh is designed for maintaining individuality and its institutions, it was gathered that the majority of the respondents (66%) accepted with this view that the present 'Dharamyudh' is contrived to preserve the pristine culture of the Sikh faith. Hence there was a growing consensus among the Sikh masses that the present fight for rightous cause of Dharam is directed towards the preservation and integration of the pristine culture and the time-honoured beliefs and practices. Hence it may lead us to conclude that the values and norms of protecting and preserving their pristine nature of their creed and cult found great acceptance among the Sikh masses.

As regards the belief whether the Sikh community is showing rigidity for a separate religion and identity through the shrines, the study highlighted that a majority of cases (86%) went in for the rigidity, and the inflexibility of the approach. The trend emanating from this finding may be referred as the case of institutionalised norms stiffening the approach and attitude of the Head priests and their followers towards the separate entity and identity of their religion and culture which may bear the elements of institutionalisation.

The data regarding the belief 'whether an attempt should be organised to unite the Sikhs all over the world into one homogeneous community,' showed that a sizable (90%) majority of the respondents were in favour of the belief. Our observation here is that mostly Head priests seemed more serious emphasising the view that when our foreign based community faced any problem with the government of that country, we demonstrated against it and resorted the crystallised mechanism of the parallel culture. Our generalised view also here is that almost majority of all over the world were seen enthusiastic about the uniform mode of living, thinking, preaching and acting. It evidences the multiplication and diversification of our norms and social institutions which may be looked upon as a part of the general phenomena of institutionalisation.

Our study also revealed that 56 per cent respondents favoured the view that the priests, through their seats of power and possession, have always raised their strong voice against the victimisation of Sikh Panth, community and the shrines. It demonstrates the fact that the norm of providing full safety, security and protection to the members of the community at large was deeply ingrained in the personalities of the Head priests and other members around.

Having concluded and generalised the empirical beliefs of the shrines, now an attention may be shifted on the non-empirical beliefs. On this dimension the findings on such points as belief in different dieties, supernatural powers, authority of different scriptures and saints and major religions practices, may be mentioned on the following:

Regarding the belief about 'existence of God and the God as Formless or Embodied,' the study revealed that 90 per cent respondents accepted the existence of God. As regards their belief in God as Formless or Embodied, the study further highlighted the fact that approx three-fourths majority of the respondents had faith firmly in the formless existence of God. It may also lead us to conclude here that the Guru Nanak and his successors were worshipped the Nirakar God. Consequently the same pattern of worship as Nirakar Guru was still being followed by Sikhs.

As for the belief in the 'theory of determination,' it was gathered that the majority of the Head priests (72%) had greater faith in the theory of determination at individual level, whereas on worldly level the percentage was reduced (54%).

As regards the belief in the 'theory of Karmas,' our inference here is that 92 per cent respondents had a greater faith in it. Here, it can be said that there is almost a similarity of views between Hindus and the Sikhs on the theory and the impact of doctrine of Karmas.

Regarding the belief in 'Swarga and Narak,' it may be concluded that 60 per cent majority of the Head priests had firm faith in the teachings of the Sikh Gurus that Swarga and Narak are not any geographical localities but intimately related with the union and separation of God or Absolute.

As for the belief in the 'Transmigration of soul in the eighty four lacs yonis,' it was concluded that 44 per cent respondents showed their favourable view believing it that the good deeds are the base of the transeendental life off man. It may also be inferred here that the spiritual structure of the Sikh Panth is based on the remembrance of Nam (Name of God). Consequently they emphasised the repetition of Nam not to be transmigrated in the world.

The findings under the belief in the 'Final Liberation as an ultimate goal of life' proved that 86 per cent majority of the respondents like their counter parts as Hindus and Christians accepted Moksha (Jivan Mukti) as an ultimate goal of life.

In the present investigation, our concern was also to analyse how the Head priests look upon the authority of other religious scriptures. In this regard, it was concluded that 92 per cent Head priests accepted Vedas, 86 per cent Puranas and 90 per cent Smirities as an authority to guide and control of human behaviour. Regarding their attitude towards Ramayana and Mahabharata 16 per cent did not accept as an authority, whereas 32 per cent did not know even the contents of Mahabharata. Here it may be inferred that the category of such Head priests was comparatively rigid with a closed mind and narrow outlook on the other religious scriptures and were found reserved to their sacred scripture Sri Guru Granth Saheb. In this context, it may be generalised that the rigidness of the Sikhs about their own sacred scriptures is their sanctioned situation directed by the internalised norm. And in that situation, the majority of the members are expected to be guided by the accepted norm. This may reflect a trend of crystallised system of the Sikh Panth.

The study further highlighted that 60 per cent and 64 per cent Head priests accepted the authority of Quoran and Bible respectively. It may lead us to conclude that comparatively the Sikh Panth feels a religious affinity and similarity with the Islam and Christianity demonstrating thereby that there is comparatively a conformability to christianity and Islam as demonstrated graphically earlier in the preceding Chapter.

While putting question 'what place will the priest of other religion knowing Gurmukhi get in the religious activities of the shrine,' the study suggested that majority of the Head priests (58%) reacted that Gurmukhi knowing priests of other religions can only attend the congregations in the shrines. They would be allowed to perform the Kirtan, Ardas and reading of the Sri Guru Granth Saheb.

Regarding an another common belief that 'can any layman with reading ability of Sri Guru Granth Saheb performs the ceremonial rites in the shrine,' it may be inferred that an overwhelmingly 84 per cent opposed the layman having ability to read the Sri Guru Granth Saheb to conduct the ceremonial rites in the shrine. They stressed that the practice of initiation (Amrit Pahul) is the major qualification to conduct the ceremonial rites in the shrine. It may suggest the trend that a majority of cases they were seen believing in a close system approach and showing blind loyality to their own language, rituals and procedures.

Coming to the last Common belief whether the 'religious leaders and Head of the various denominations specially of Hindus can exchange visits and services,' it was gathered that 72 per cent number of the respondents were of the opinion that last five years the affinity between the Hindus and the Sikhs was affected. Consequently, the frequent exchange of visits by the Heads of the various a Hindus religious orders and denominations showed a declining trend.

An analysis regarding major religious practices indicated that 94 per cent Head priests strictly follow the practice of meditation with one God, whereas 96 per cent offer three times institutionalised prayer as was guided and directed by the ten Sikh Gurus. 98 per cent and 66 per cent Head priests perform Kirtan and Akhand Path respectively as major religious practices. The study further revealed that 60 per cent follow the practice of Shahaj Path. Here it is interesting to note that almost all the Head priests were spending their life following the teachers of the Gurus. In the light of our observation and finding we may safely conclude that comparatively the practices in the Sikh Panth were found more institutionalised with internalisation of norms and values in a collectivity. It may largely bear a semblance to the process of institutionalisation.

VIII. Under this postulate, it was conceived that, due to the scientific advancement and spread of material civilisation, the old values are disappearing but the new values are not developing with an equal pace to replace. Consequently, there is appearing a gap between the new value patterns and the old ones. In such situations marked by secular motivational considerations the traditional behaviour of the Head priests and the traditional ethos of the shrines have also been affected by the orthogenetic and heterogenetic forces. Therefore, in this context, the changes in values patterns of the shrines, priests, Sikh Panth and their changing institutional aspects of behaviour, were studied and some broad conclusions and generalisations were drawn as follows.

The data regarding the attitudes towards shrines' influence over the people showed that an overwhelming majority of the Head priests (74%) endorsed the view that the shrines were still a force to reckon with in exercising its influence over the members. Our inference here is that a vast majority of the Sikhs think highly of these shrine and feel an emphatic attachment with great values, meaning and purpose to them. It may clearly show that their value to the aspects of religious influence and authority of the shrine and of the Head priests tended to become internalise and thus deeply ingrained.

Regarding attitudes towards the shrines being used as a ladder for political ascendency, the study revealed that a great many respondents made a claim that the shrines were not being used as ladder for political ascendency. However, the researcher on the basis of his field observation may hold a different view that the good number of Head priests of prominent historical shrines were influenced by political considerations making hardly any scruple about the unfair use of their office and position for political gains and objects. It may be inferred to as a case of insturmental values with an element of expediency. Though it is certainly not a majority view, however, it cannot be ruled out that in the case of a few individual Head priests the tendency of their using the office and authority for secular considerations seems to have become general expected standard of behavour.

As for the attitudes about 'ongoing terrorism and violence,' the study bore out that 74 per cent Head priests opined that the shrines have always condemned the irrelegious activities. It was significant to mention here that there was some small percentage who dared into admitting that the pristine sanctity of the shrines was being lost gradually and also reacted that the shrines should be freed from bad politics otherwise their future will be at stake. Hence, it may be inferred that there is a near consensus about values aiming towards the sanctity and dignity of the shrines. It amounts to a harmony between the rights of the Sikhs in general and the obligations of the priests towards them.

The data regarding the attitudes towards the 'use of the Sikh Panth' showed that through the majority had the positive view. However, there were signs portending that some vested interests wanted these shrines to serve their ulterior motive and selfish trends. Further the data regarding the attitudes towards present standing of the Panth showed that 62 per cent respondents admitted that the present standing of the Panth has increased estimating the view that the young generation of the Sikhs of today were being initiated and who were intolerant and touchy about the use of vulgar language against the symbols and the institutions.

An analysis of the 'present age of the Head priests and the reactions on the present standing of the Panth' showed that there was a divergence of views between the youngs supporting that the strength and popularity of the Panth has increased whereas old and the aged were found decrying that the standing of the Panth has registered a decline. Hence it may be cited as a case of the divergence of values between the young and the old about the influence and standing of the shrine and it may go some way explain why the young people, are, by and large, getting enthused and provoked to get themselves initiated.

As regards the attitudes towards 'dress and life-style' it was inferred that the wearing of traditionally prescribed dress and other belongings is being increasingly questioned. 62 per cent data support the view indicating a growing disagreement between the new entrants and the old timers on the question of dress and life-style. Hence, there are conflicting ideas between these two social aggregates about the life-style and dress. As all values imply a cognitive element it is a question of deciding between what is desirable and what is not.

As for the attitudes towards 'Hindu religion,' the study indicated that the Head priests of the prominent historical shrines were found more rigid in their attitude towards Hindu religion. Here it was also gathered that those respondents who has taken religious knowledge and learning (such as to attend the Daire and Damdami Taksaal) were found more fundamentalists towards Hindu religion in comparison to those who has taken the essential religious education (such as the Gyani course) for performing the ceremonial rites in the shrine. Hence it may be inferred here that the values, acquired by those instructed through Damdami Taksaal and other such hard core bodies, gave rise to the fundamental norms being internalised vis-a-vis Hindus and other communities. On the contrary, values acquired by those who were instructed through Gyani course or the like did not give rise to any such behaviour pattern.

To deal with the 'process of conversion and the Sikh Panth,' it may be said that the majority of the respondents (68%), supported conversion from other religion into Sikh religion. Further the data indicated that some percentage of the members of the prominent historical shrines reacted against the re-entry into the Sikh Panth of those who were once alleged to have descended to the level of a Patit. Hence, it may lead us to conclude that the norms of a Patit joining the Sikh fold again did not receive any acceptance among them.

Regarding the attitudes towards 'Shudras,' the study highlighted that the largest (72%) majority of the Head priests opposed to maintain the social relations (such as friendly relations with marital relations too) with the Shudras. An analysis of data further indicated that the young Head priests were found more rigid in maintaining the social relation with Shudras whereas the aged Head priests supported it.

As regards the attitudes towards 'Shudras taking part in the shrine's worship,' the study revealed that the opinion of the majority was that the ceremonial rites in the shrine are performed by an initiated Sikh priest. Consequently, the Shudra can only participate in the worship as a common devotee not as a performer of the religious activities. Hence Shudras in their community are not regarded having an eligibility criteria for performing the religious rites and ceremonies.

Regarding the attitudes towards women, the inference was that the strength of Head priests (54%) were not in favour of the women as giving higher status in the shrine because of impurity. However, it was observed in the course of the study that no Sikh women was found as priest. Hence, their cultural values and regulative norms go at variance with woman as well as Shudras rising to any position of authority in the management of the shrine as they have typical system of social interaction preventing them from assuming any office of authority in religious matters.

Regarding the attitudes of the Head priests towards 'modernisation,' our interest here was to find out whether the Head priests have shown any appreciation towards modified way of living, modern education, modern customs and values etc.

As for the reactions towards 'modern living,' the study endorsed the view that the majority of the respondents with their moorings in traditional past and the ordained life of the Panth were found opposed towards modern way of living. Further, the data regarding the 'liking of the Head priests towards modern food' showed that 60 per cent majority of the Head priests opposed it. They told that the meaning of modern food was to drink the wine and to eat the non-vegetarian food. The data further showed that the taste of adopting the modern food was found in a meagre number of the Head priests of the prominent historical shrines. Hence their social structure is marked by cultural patterns of such evaluation and overt action that may not be normative in general sense but still become standardised and stable to contribute to specific patterns of conduct and behaving. And so appears to be the case of their having dislike, hostility or even rejection of modern way of living and food.

The data regrading the 'modern education' showed that 74 per cent respondents supported the modern education viewing that the modern education is essential for children to seek the job and for adjustment to the modern society. The study also revealed that there was a healthy contribution of Guru Nanak Public Schools in modern education. Contrary to their reactions towards modern way of living and modern food, the trend emerged from their attitudes towards the modern education suggests their growing acceptance and liking for the modern education. And which tended to guide them in making a choice for type of education in appropriate circumstances.

The analysis regarding the attitudes towards modern 'norms and values' indicated that 82 per cent strength of the respondents were found against towards it supporting the view that there is no place for emotional and human sentiments in the modern norms and values. However, our analysis about the position of young ones indicated that they held different modes of thinking attaching appropriate significance to the modern values and norms. It shows that the acceptance and more so the internalisation of the norms may vary among the individuals as we find it in the case of attitudes towards modern education among young ones on the one hand and aged on the other.

Also in the context, an attempt was made to measure and examine the varying grades and degrees of understanding and intimacy characterising the social relations of Head priests towards various ethnic types of communities, social classes and minorities viz., Hindus, Muslims, Christians and Tribals. To measure the social distance, an insight was taken from the Bogardes Social Distance Scales. The Modified Social Distance Scale used for the purpose had a attributes which are ordered as a continuum of social distance (from acceptability as a fellow worshipper to exclusion from the Panth).

The relevant data (vide Tables 8.22 and 8.23 indicated rather unusual and unexpected developments indicative of their observing greater social distance from first to Hindus and second to Tribals as compared to Muslims and Christians. The researcher's view is that it may be attributable to the charged socio-cultural affinity with the Hindus resulting from 1984's Operation Blue, in Golden Temple in Amritsar aggravated further by Hindu-Sikh riots in November 1984 in Delhi. As for the distance from the ethnic minority of Tribals here the investigator may react that it is due to their cultural pattern of thinking and behaviour and allowing no social interaction with the Tribals worth the name.

Testing of the Hypotheses

It may be pointed out that the present study is explorative and descriptive. Hence, no well defined hypotheses were formulated to test its validity and reliability. However, some specific hypotheses were formulated to establish the relationship between historicity and sociality responsible for the unique developments in the shrines resulting from the process of institutionalisation. Our Chapter II deals with these hypotheses covering the different aspects and dimensions of the study. Here what concerns us is the logic requiring the acceptance or rejection of the hypothesis on the basis of the resulting data enabling us to arrive at some logic conclusions. Now to test these hypotheses one by one.

A. The hypothesis stands supported that the Sikh shrines striving for uniformity of religious beliefs and practices. A majority of Head priests were found enthusiastic about it. To cite a recent example of it we may here refer to the demonstration and agitation staged by the Head priests with other Sikh religious Heads and followers using crystallised mechanisms when they pulled their weight behind the foreign based and settled community in their violating against the compulsory use of 'Helmet' while driving on the roads. Also to cite another similar cases in the demand of 'All India Sikh Gurdwaras Management — System, for sometime passed which further proves this hypothesis.

(B) The hypothesis is also proved that there is insistance on standardisation of behaviour patterns and conformability to rigid rules of conduct. It was observed that the behavioural aspect of almost all the shrines was being standardised gradually and the members were forced to follow the rigid rules of conduct.

(C) Our third hypothesis was that the mostly Sikh shrines specially prominent historical ones were working for their cultural identity and separate entity. Our relevant data lend full support to this hypothetical proposition. Actually it needs hardly any emphasis that the Sikh shrines constituting body and soul of the Sikh community are determinent of maintaining the separate entity and identity of the Sikh community. As a natural consequence of this, the shrines were found mobilising the Sikh masses providing motivation to them to show conformity in their behaviour patterns.

(D) Our conclusion is that the process of balkanisation, polarisation and crystallisation of religious forces marked by the regeneration and revival of fundamental values is touching a new high. Hence, in an ultimate analysis we may say that mostly the Sikhs were found veering round the view that the revival of fundamental values is the only meaning and hope through which they can survive and later grow in the midst of rival groups and communities.

(E) Our fifth major hypothesis runs that the role and functioning of the shrines is tradition bound making their credibility and respectability questionable. In this regard our investigation revealed that in the present times their rituals, observances and religious ceremonies largely attracted and rather allowed the members of their own faith to join and take part in the deliverations and serious discussions. It may reflect the trend that some sort of chilliness and rigidness towards other community and classes seem to have entered in the consequent working of the shrines guided by them. In consequence of this, the concept of universal equality and brotherhood is declining gradually, which supports our hypothesis.

(F) Our Sixth major hypothesis is that the hoary shrines tend to become oblivious of their time — honoured roles and functions stands get almost rejected. Here drawing upon our relevant data we may react that the hoary and time — honoured Sikh shrines were still of force exercising influence over its members to conform their ways of thinking, doing and living to the prescribe normative pattern of behaviour, usages and procedures, beliefs and practices, and so on. However we may here take an exercise in excoursion by observing that through these time honoured shrines have, as may be feared, not become oblivious of their long cherised goals, at the same time there were reports that they were being used clandestinely for promoting some sort of militancy and chauvanism in lieu of their secular and democratic image reflecting some sort of anomic conditions. It may sound to us as a situation of conflicting norms and role conflicts.

(G) In the seventh place, our hypothetical formulation that the priestly roles in modern perspective were not in proper shape stands proved. Our data here indicated that the Head priests of prominent historical shrines were found involved in capturing and maintaining a powerful hold in running the shrines. Our making a notable observation here, we may say that the Head priests so contrived as to secure favours from the members of the managing body by providing the temptation to them that they will serve their electoral ends.

(H) Lastly, our hypothesis that the loyality towards the shrines was on a declining side due to the mutual discord and dissensions of the members of the managing body stands borne out. Our argument here is that the lust for power and possession among the members of the managing body (particularly belonging to the prominent historical shrines) have involved them in financial intrigues and personal rivalaries which amounts to an offence against their proclaimed, loyality and commitment towards the shrines. It reflected the trend that the norms of self-aggrandizement and self-acquisitiveness became operative in the social system of members of the managing body occupying particular social position. And as such they took these norms so seriously and in psychological terms had sufficient internalised the same. Thus the members in their turn were expected to be guided by these norms as the situation called for.

A Plan for Future Role of the Sikh Shrines

The institution of Gurdwara or shrine was initiated by

the Guru Nanak in the form of Dharamsal with the aim of combating religio-cultural disparities among the masses. These Dharamsals were not confined only to the particular faith, groups and communities. In the course of time, these Dharamsalas eventually became the Gurdwaras and taught the lesson of universal equality and brotherhood. Thus, it is not difficult to understand that these shrines provided a great inspiration in the past, left deeper impact on Indian mind and contributed to the religio-cultural history of India. But due to the emergence of new religious and cultural values, they have come to formulate and perpetuate their own codes of conduct, beliefs and practices, norms and values demanding its adherence strictly having separate identity and entity. These later developments have led them to have their own vast resources for the propagation and promotion of the faith and now they came to be reckoned as an active force of the Sikh society.

In the light of the above theoretical formulations, it can be said that the Sikh shrines have played a vital role in the past and formed egalitarian norms and values. To take of the present times the study brought out the fact that several managing bodies of the shrines were rendering valuable services but their efforts were found political motivated. On the other hand the managing body of prominent historical shrines having huge resources did not seem much concerned with the vital questions facing out country today. Therefore if in the present time they do not play the role which the society expects of them in the changing social situations they will gradually loose their image and importance. On the basis of present study we can say that these shrines will have a bright future if they redefine their objectives in order to justify their relevance to the modern society. In the present anomical circumstances there is an essential need to integrate and reconstruct the Indian society. The Sikh shrines having their vast resources form an integral part of Indian society can contribute great share to meeting these challenging situations of today by assuming new roles and responsibilities as were guided and directed by the Sikh Gurus. Hence it may be suggested here that a concerted and sustained effort by the community through shrines should be organised to curb disintegrating forces and fissiparous tendencies.

Bibliography

SOURCES OF INFORMATION

(I) Sikh Sources

Anand, Balwant Singh. 1983 *'The Sikhs and Sikhism'*. New Delhi: Delhi Sikh Gurdwara Management Committee.

Archer, John Clark. 1946. *Sikhs in Relation to Hindus, Muslims, Christians and Ahmadiyas: A Study in Comparative Religion:* Princeton: University Press.

Ashta, Dharam Pal. 1967. *Sikhism and Indian Society*. Simla: Indian Institute of Advanced Study.

_____. 1959. *Poetry of the Dasam Granth*. Delhi: Arun Prakashan.

Banerjee, I.B. 1947. *Evolution of the Khalsa*. 2 Vols. Calcutta: Mukherjee and Co.

Barrier, N. Gerald. 1970. *The Sikhs and Their Literature*. Delhi: Manohar Book Service.

Barrier, N.G. and Harbans Singh. 1976. *Punjab Past and Present: Essay in Honour of Dr. Ganda Singh*. Patiala: Punjabi University.

Chaddah, Mehar Singh. 1982. *Are Sikhs A Nation*, Delhi: Delhi Sikh Gurdwara Management Committee.

Cole, W. Owen and Sambhi, Piyara Singh. 1978. *The Sikhs: Their Religious Beliefs and Practices*. New Delhi: Vikas Publishing House.

Cunningham, J.A. 1972. *History of the Sikhs*. Delhi: S. Chand and Company.

Dardi, Gopal Singh. 1979. *History of the Sikh People.* New Delhi: Sikh University Press.

Dilgeer, Harjinder Singh. 1980. *The Akal Takht.* Jullandar: Punjabi Book Company.

Field, Dorothy. 1979. *Religion of the Sikhs.* Patiala: Punjabi University.

Fox, Richard. 1985. *Lions of the Punjab: Culture in the Making.* Berkeley, Los Angeles: University of California Press.

Gandhi, Surjeet Singh. 1980. *Struggle for the Sikhs for Sovereignty.* Delhi: Gurdas Kapur and Sons.

Gill, Pritam Singh. 1978. *Heritage of Sikh Culture.* Jullandar: New Academic Publishing Company.

_____. 1978. *History of Sikh Nation.* Jullandar: New Academic Publishing Company.

Gulati, K.C. 1974. *The Akalis: Past and Present.* New Delhi: Ashajanak Publications.

Gupta, Hari Ram. 1978. *History of the Sikhs.* New Delhi: Munshi Ram Manohar Lal.

Hershman, Pail. 1981. *Punjabi Kinship and Marriage.* Delhi: Hindustan Publishing House.

Ibbetson, D.C.. 1916. *Punjab Castes.* Lahore: Govt. Printing Press.

Izmirlian, Harry, Jr. 1979. *The Politics of Passion: Structure and Strategy in Sikh Society.* New Delhi: Manohar for South Asia Books.

Jain, N.K. 1981. *Contribution of the Sikh Gurus to Indian Spirituality* in *Sikh Gurus a and the Indian Spiritual Thought* (edited by Taran Singh). Patiala: Punjabi University.

Jalandhary, Surjeet. 1985. *Bhindranwale Sant.* Jullandhar: Punjab Pocket Books.

Josh, Sohan Singh. 1974. *Akali Morcha Ka Itihas.* Delhi: Peoples Publishing House.

Joshi, Chand. 1984. *Bhindranwala: Myth and Reality.* New Delhi: Vikas Publishing House.

Juergensmeyer, Mark Jan.-June, 1988. "The Logic of Religions Violence: The case of the Punjab" in *Contribution to Indian Sociology.* Delhi: Sage.

Kapoor, Rajiv Alochan. 1987. *The Sikhs Separatism: The Politics of the Faith.* Delhi: Vikas Publishing House.

Kaur, Amarjit. 1984. *The Punjab Story.* New Delhi: Roli Books International.

Kaur, Jitinder. 1986. *The Politics of Sikhs: A Study of Delhi Sikh Gurdwara Management Committee.* New Delhi: National Book Organisation.

Kaur, Madanjit. 1983. *The Golden Temple: Past and Present.* Amritsar: Guru Nanak Dev University.

Kaur, Ravinder. July-Dec., 1986. "Jat Sikhs: A Question of Identity." In *Contribution to Indian Sociology.* Delhi: Sage.

Kohli, S.S. 1975. *Sikh Ethics.* New Delhi: Munshi Ram Manohar Lal.

Macaulifee, Maxs Arthus. 1909. *The Sikh Religion: Its Gurus, Sacred Writings and Authors.* Oxford: Oxford University Press.

Malhotra, Avtar Singh. 1984. *The Punjab Crisis and the Way Out.* New Delhi: Communist Party of India.

Mann, Jaswant Singh. *Some Documents on the Demand for a Sikh Homeland.* Chandigarh: Manjit Printing and Publishing Company.

Marenco, Ethene. 1976. *The Transformation of Sikh Society.* New Delhi: Heritage Publications.

McLeod, W.H. 1975. *The Evolution of the Sikh Community: Five Essays.* New Delhi: Oxford University Press.

Mukherjee, Partha, N. 1986. "Akalis and Violence" in Amrik Singh (ed.) *Punjab in Indian Politics: Issues and Trends.* Delhi: Ajanta Books International.

Narang, Gokal Chand. 1960. *Transformation of Sikhism.* New Delhi: New Book Society of India.

Nayar, Kuldip and Khushwant Singh, 1984. *Tragedy of Punjab: Operation Blue Star and After.* Delhi: Vision Books.

Pramod Kumar, *et. al.* 1984. *Punjab Crisis: Context and Trends.* Chandigarh: Centre for Research in Rural and Industrial Development.

Roy, Naharranjan. 1970 *The Sikh Gurus and the Sikh Society.* Patiala: Punjabi University.

Sethi, G.R. 1927. *Sikh Struggle for Gurdwara Reform.* Amritsar: Union Press.

Shourie, Arun. May 12, 1982. "The Politics of Pandering: The Trouble in Punjab." *Indian Express.* New Delhi.

"Sikhs in the Main Stream of National Life." New Delhi: DAVP. Ministry of I&B, Govt. of India.

Singh, Amrik (ed.) 1986. *Punjab in Indian Politics: Issues and Trends.* Delhi: Ajanta Books International.

Singh, Avtar. 1970. *Ethics of the Sikhs.* Patiala: Punjabi University.

Singh, Dalip. 1979. *Sikhism: A Modern and Psychological Perspective.* New Delhi: Bahri Publication.

Singh, Gobinder. 1986. *Religion and Politics in the Punjab.* Delhi: Deep and Deep Publications.

Singh, Gopal. 1979. *A History of Sikh People, 1469-1978.* New Delhi: World Sikh University Press.

_____. Feb., 1987. "Are We Promoting the Sikh Ethos." in *Indian Express.* New Delhi.

_____. 1971. *Religion of the Sikhs.* Bombay: Asia Publishing House.

Singh, Gurbachan. 1976. *Guru Tegbahadur: Background and the Supreme Sacrifice* (edited). Patiala: Punjabi University.

Singh, Harbans. 1983. *Heritage of the Sikhs*. Delhi: Manohar Publications.

_____. 1970. *Guru Nanak and the Origin of the Sikh Faith*. Bombay: Asia.

Singh, Jagdish. 1982. *The Founders of Sikh Religion*. Delhi: Guru Nanak Foundation.

Singh, Jagjit. 1981. *The Sikh Revolution: A Perspective View*. Delhi: Kendriya Singh Sabha.

Singh, Kahan. 1931. *Gurshabad Ratnakar Mahankosh: Encyclopaedia of Sikh Literature*. Patiala: State Govt.

Singh, Khushwant. May, 1982. "Divided by A Common Heritage." in *Weekend Review:* A Times of India Publication. Delhi.

_____. 1953. *The Sikhs*. London: George Allen and Unwin.

_____. 1977. *A History of the Sikhs*. Vol. I and II. Bombay: Oxford University Press.

_____. Feb. 19, 1987. "Longowal Chalo." in *Indian Express*. Delhi.

Singh, Mehar. 1975. *Sikh Shrines in India*. Publication Division. Ministry of I&B.

Singh, Mohinder. 1978. *The Akali Movement*. New Delhi: Macmillan Company of India Limited.

Singh, Taran. 1981. *Sikh Gurus and the Indian Spiritual Thought* (edited). Patiala: Punjabi University.

Singh, Teja. 1984. *The Gurdwara Reform Movement and the Sikh Awakening*. Amritsar: S.G.P.C.

Singh, Teja and Singh Ganda. 1950. *Short History of the Sikhs*. Bombay: Orient Longmans.

Tully, Mark and Satish Jacob. 1986. *Amritsar: Mrs. Gandhi's Last Battle*. Delhi: Rupa and Co.

Upretty, P.R. 1980. *Religion and Politics in Punjab in the 1920's*. Delhi: Sterling Publishers.

(II) Sociological Sources

Abraham, M.F. 1982. *Modern Sociological Theory*. Delhi: Oxford University Press.

Aggarwal, P.C. 1971a. *Caste, Religion and Power: An Indian Case-Study*. New Delhi: Shri Ram Centre for Industrial Relations.

Aron, Raymond. 1967. *The Industrial Society: Three Essays on Ideology and Development*. London: Weindenfield and Nicolson.

Bates, A.P. and Julian, J. 1975. *Sociology: Understanding and Behaviour*. Houghton: Mifflin Company Boston.

Batteille, Andre. 1965. *'Caste, Class and Power*. Berkely: University of California Press.

Bottomore, T.B. 1985. *Sociology: A Guide to Problem and Literature*, Bombay: Blackie and Sons.

Chandra, Bipan. 1984. *Communalism in Modern India*. Delhi: Vikas Publishing House.

Chaudhary, K.C. 1978. *Role of Religion in Indian Politics*. Delhi: Sundeep Prakashan.

Damle, Y.B. 1982. *Caste, Religion and Politics in India*. New Delhi: Oxford and IBH.

Davis, Kingslay. 1981. *Human Society*. Delhi: Surjeet Publications.

Desai, A.R. 1973. *Recent Trends in Indian Nationalism*. Bombay: Popular Prakashan.

_____. 1976. *Social Background in Indian Nationalism*. Bombay: Popular Prakashan.

Downie, N.M. and Heath, R.W., 1970. *Basic Statistical Methods*. New York: Harper and Row.

Dubey, S.C. 1975. *Social Mobility Among Professions*. Bombay: Popular Prakashan.

Dumont, Louis. 1988. *Homo Hierarchicus: The Caste System and Its Implications.* New Delhi: Oxford University Press.

Durkheim, Emile. 1954. *The Elementary Forms of Religious Life.* (translated by Joseph Ward Swain). Illinois: The Free Press Glenoce.

Edward, Allen L. 1957. *Techniques of Attitude Scale Construction.* New York: Appleton Century Crafts.

Etzioni, Amitai. 1961. *Complex Organisations: A Sociological Reader.* New York: Holt.

_____. 1965. *Modern Organisations.* New Delhi: Prentice Hall of India Limited.

Farguhar, J.N. 1967. *Modern Religious Movement in India.* Delhi: Munshi Lal Manohar Lal.

Gisbert, P. 1973. *Fundamentals of Sociology.* New Delhi: Orient Longmans.

Ghosh, S.N. 1987. *Criminal Riots in India.* New Delhi: Uppal Publishers.

Ghurye, G.S. 1953. *Indian Sadhus.* Bombay: Popular Prakashan.

_____. 1965. *Religious Consciousness.* Bombay: Popular.

_____. 1969. *Caste and Races in India.* Bombay: Popular.

Goode, W.J. and Hatt, P.K. 1981. *'Methods in Social Research.'* New Delhi: McGraw-Hill Book Company.

Gupta, V.K. 1979. *'Teachers' Attitude Towards Abortion.'* Unpublished Masters dissertation submitted to the Rohilkhand University, Bareilly.

Gupta, V.K. and J.K. Misra, Jan. 8, 1989. 'Identity Crisis in Contemporary India: In the Context of the Sikh Religion and Institutionalisation of the Sikh Shrines'. Research Paper submitted in 10th U.P. Sociological Conference in Kashi Vidyapeeth, Varansi.

Hansraj. 1980. *Social Research in Theory and Practice.* Delhi: Surjeet Publications.

Hoult, T.F. 1968. *The Sociology of Religion.* New York: The Dryden Press, Inc.

Hutton, J.G. 1983. *Caste in India.* Delhi: Oxford University Press.

I.C.S.S.R. 1974. *A Survey of Research in Sociology and Social Anthropology.* Vol. 1. Bombay: Popular Prakashan.

Jahoda Marie, Morton Deutsch, and Stuart W., Cook. 1959. *Research Methods in Social Relations.* New York: Holt, Rinehart and Winston, Inc.

Jonson, H.M. 1986. *Sociology: A Systematic Introduction.* New Delhi: Allied Publishers.

Kapadia, K.M. 1968. *Marriage and Family in India.* New Delhi: Oxford University Press.

Kothari, Rajni. 1970. *Politics in India.* Delhi: Orient Longmans.

_____. 1970. *Caste and Politics in India.* Delhi: Orient Longmans.

_____. 1986-87. "This India." *Hindustan Times,* Delhi.

_____. March 6-13, 1988. "Ethnicity". Article Published in *Illustrated Weekly,* Times of India Publication, Bombay.

Kuppuswamy, B. 1979. *Social Change in India.* New Delhi: Vikas.

_____. 1983. *Elements of Social Psychology.* New Delhi; Vikas Publishing House.

Kuthiala, S.K. 1973. *From Tradition to Modernity.* New Delhi: Abhinav Publications.

Maciver, R.M. and C.H. Page, 1985. *Society.* Delhi: Macmillan.

Merton, R.K. 1968. *Social Theory and Social Structure.* Delhi: Amrind.

Mills, C. Wright. 1977. *The Sociological Imagination.* London: Oxford University Press.

Mishra, J.K. 1976. *Socio-Economic Conditions of Sadhu Organisation in Pilgrimage Centre in U.P.* under publication. (Allied). Ph.D. Thesis submitted in Agra University, Agra.

Mishra J.K. and Singh, S.D. 1978. *Vagyanic Samajik Anusandhan Aur Survekshan*. Indore: Kamal Prakashan.

Mitra, Chandan. Jan. 26, 1988. "Punjab: Three years have passed but they continue to Defy." *Times of India*. Delhi.

Mitchell, G.D. 1970. *A Dictionary of Sociology*. London: Routdlege and Kegan Paul.

Mukherjee, R.K. 1949. *Structure of Social Values*. London: Macmillan and Co.

Mukherjee, D.P. 1958. *Diversities*. Delhi: Peoples Publishing House.

Nayar, P.K.B. 1982. *Sociology in India*. New Delhi: B.R. Publishing House.

Oommen, T.K. and Mukherjee, Partha, N. 1986. *Indian Sociology: Reflections and Introspections*. Bombay: Popular Prakashan.

Oommen, T.K. 1977a. "Sociological Issues in the Analysis of Social Movements in Independent India." in *Sociological Bulletin*. (26 (I): 14-37.

_____. March, 1984. *Punjab: Sociological Factors*. Article published in the '*Week*'. Malyala Press, Kottayam.

_____. Jan. 26, 1988. "Communalism: Its Various Dimension", '*Hindustan Times*,' Delhi.

Pant, V.K. 1979. *Urban Growth and Social Change in Eastern U.P.* Gorakhpur: Nirdoshista Publishers.

Parsons, T. 1952. *The Social System*. Illinois: The Free Press.

_____. 1964. *Evolution of Societies*. New Jersy: Prentice Hall.

Parsons, T. and Edward Shils (eds.). 1951. *Towards General Theory of Action*. Harward: University Press.

Prabhu, P.H. 1979. *Hindu Social Organisation: A Study in Socio-Psychological and Ideological Foundations*. Bombay: Popular Prakashan.

Raj Gopal, P.R. 1987. *Communal Violence in India.* Delhi: Uppal Publishers.

_____. 1987. *Social Change and Violence: The Indian Experience.* Delhi: Uppal Publishers.

Rao, M.S.A. (ed.). 1978. *Social Movements in India.* Vol. I. New Delhi: Manohar.

_____. 1979a. *Social Movements in India.* Vol. II. New Delhi: Manohar.

Redfield, Robert. 1955-56. "The Social Organisation of Tradition." Vol. 15. *Far Eastern Quarterly.*

Rex, John. 1961. *Key Problems of Sociological Theory.* London: Routledge and Kegan Paul.

Ritzer, George and Others. 1979. *Sociology—Experiencing A Changing Society.* Boston: Allyn and Becon.

Saberwal, S. (ed.). 1978. *Process and Institutions in Urban India.* New Delhi: Vikas.

Sayles, Leonard and Strauss, George. 1977. *Managing Human Resources.* New Jersey: Prentice Hall Inc. Englewood Cliffs.

Saberwal, S. 1981. "Elements of Communalism." *Mainstream,* March 21 and 28: 27-30 and 15-19.

Sharma, K.L. 1980. *Essays on Social Stratification.* Jaipur: Rawat.

Singer, Milton (ed.). 1959. *Traditional India: Structure and Change.* Chicago: Aldine.

Singh, Yogendra. 1986. 'Modernisation of Indian Tradition: A Systematic Study of Social Change.' Jaipur: Rawat.

_____. 1977. *Social Stratification and Change in India.* New Delhi: Manohar.

_____. 1983. *The Image of Man: Ideology and Theory in Indian Sociology.* Delhi: Chanakya Publications.

_____. 1986. *Indian Sociology: Social Conditioning and Emerging Concerns*. New Delhi: Vistaar.

Sriniwas, M.N. 1966. *Social Change in Modern India*. Berkeley: California University Press.

_____. 1986. *India: Social Structure*. Delhi: Hindustan Publishing Corporation.

Thapar, Romes (ed.). 1977. *Tribe, Caste and Religion in India*. Delhi: Macmillan.

Tripathi, B.D. *Sadhu of India: The Sociological View*. Bombay: Popular.

Weber, Max. 1958. *The Protestant Ethic and the Spirit of Capitalism*, Tr. by Parsons. New York: Charles Scribner's Sons.

_____. 1964. *The Theory of Social and Economic Organisation* (edited by T. Parsons). New York: The Free Press.

(III) Documentary Sources

(i) Journals

1. *Contributions to Indian Sociology*. Vol. 19 to Vol. 22. From Jul.-Dec. 1985 to Jan.-June, 1988. New Delhi: Sage.
2. *International Journal of Sociology of Family* (Selected Volumes). Delhi: Vikas.
3. *Work Employment and Society*. Published by British Sociological Association.
4. *Sociological Bulletin*. Published by Indian Sociological Society. (Selected Volumes).
5. *The Social Science Review*. Published by Indian Social Science Association.
6. *Social Change*. Published by Council for Social Development, Delhi.
7. *Studies in Sociology and Social Anthropology*. Published by Hindustan Publishing Corporation, Delhi.

8. *Sociological Abstracts.* Published by International Sociological Association, Madrid. Spain.
9. *Studies in Sikhism and Comparative Religion.* Vol. I to Vol. VII. from 1982 to 1988. Guru Nanak Foundation. New Delhi.
10. *Sikh Review* (Monthly). Karnani Mansion. Calcutta.
11. *Sis Ganj* (Gurmukhi Monthly). Pub. by D.S.G.M.C. Delhi.
12. *Singh Sabha Patrika (Gurmukhi Monthly).* Published by Sri Guru Singh Sabha. Sector 28. Chandigarh.

(ii) Periodicals

1. *Caravan* (Fortnightly English). Delhi: Delhi Press Bhawan.
2. *Dharamyug* (Hindi Weekly). Bombay: Times of India Press.
3. *India Today* (Hindi and English Fortnightly). Delhi. Living Media Pvt. Ltd.
4. *Saptahik Hindustan* (Hindi Weekly). New Delhi. Hindustan Times House.
5. *The Illustrated Weekly of India.* Bombay: The Times of India Publication. Delhi.
6. *The Indian Observer Weekly.* April 15, 1983. Delhi: 26F. Cannaught Place.
7. *The Week.* March, 84. Kattayam: Malayala Manorama Co. Ltd.
8. *The Week and Review.* Delhi: Hindustan Times Publication.

(iii) Reports

1. *Imperial Gazetteer of India* (Provincial Series, Punjab), Vol. I, Superintendent of Govt. Printing, Calcutta, 1908.
2. *Punjab District Gazetteer,* Vol. 13, Delhi District, 1912-13.

3. *Census of India,* 1951, 1961, 1971, 1981, Govt. of India Press.
4. *Gazetteer of India* (Delhi), April, 1976, Delhi Administration, Delhi.
5. *Delhi Census Handbook Series,* 27.
6. *Gazetteer of Delhi District,* 1983-84, Compiled and Published under the Authority of Punjab Govt.
7. Cunningham's *Archaeological Reports* I, IV and XVI.
8. *Asiatic Society's Journals* Supplementary number of Vol. XXXIII, 1864, 1870.
9. *Archaeological Survey of India,* Four Reports, 1862, 1863, 1864, 1865, Vol. I, Govt. Central Place, Shimla, 1871.
10. Final Report on the Settlement of Land Revenue in the Delhi District, 1872-77, Victory Press of Lahore.
11. *The Delhi Sikh Gurdwaras Act, 1971,* Published by Govt. of India, Ministry of Law and Justice.
12. Delhi Sikh Gurdwara Management Committee, *Annual Budget,* Delhi, 1956-1986.
13. Gurdwara Prabandhak Committee, Bye-Laws and Rules of the Gurdwara Prabandhak Committee, Delhi Province, Delhi, 1942.

(iv) Newspapers

1. *Hindustan Times,* Hindustan Times House, Kasturba Gandhi Marg, New Delhi.
2. *Indian Express,* Express Building, Bahadur Shah Zafar Marg, New Delhi.
3. *Jan Satta,* Express Building, Bahadur Shah Zafar Marg, New Delhi.
4. *The Sunday Observer,* Jaico Press Pvt. Ltd., at Veer Arjun, Bahadur Shah Zafar Marg, New Delhi.

(v) Personal Sources

1. Prof. Harbans Singh, Editor-in-Chief, *Encyclopaedia of Sikhism,* Punjabi University, Patiala.

2. Dr. Mohinder Singh, Director, Guru Nanak Foundation, Near Qutab Hotel, New Delhi.
3. Shri Khushwant Singh, Freelance Journalist, 49E, Sujan Singh Park, New Delhi.
4. Dr. Jitinder Kaur, Lecturer Dept. of Political Science, Khalsa College, Delhi University Campus, Delhi.
5. Prof. Devendra Swaroop, Retd. Professor of History, D.A.V. College, Delhi.

(vi) Encyclopaedia

1. *International Encyclopaedia of Social Sciences,* The Macmillian Company, New York, 1972.
2. *Encyclopaedia of Religion and Ethics:* Editors—Hastings, J. and others, 38, George Street, New York (Selected Volumes).
3. *Encyclopaedia of Sikhism,* Editor-in-Chief, Prof. Harbans Singh, Punjabi University, Patiala.

The General Table Showing the Universe of the Study in the Delhi Territory.

I. The Shrines managed by Delhi Sikh Gurdwara Management Committee:

(A) *The Prominent Historical Sikh Shrines and their Site*

1. Gurdwara Sis Ganj (Chandni Chowk)
2. Gurdwara Rakab Ganj (Opposite Central Secretariat)
3. Gurdwara Bangla Saheb (Connaught Place, Near Gole Post Office)
4. Gurdwara Moti Bagh (Outer Ring Road)
5. Gurdwara Damdama Saheb (Nizamuddin, Behind Humayun's Tomb)
6. Gurdwara Mata Sundari Ji (Mata Sundari Lane, Behind J.P. Hospital)

7. Gurdwara Nanak Piyao (G.T. Road, Near Rana Pratap Bagh)
8. Gurdwara Bala Saheb (Outer Ring Road, Near Ashram)
9. Gurdwara Majnu-kă-Tilla (Outer Ring Road, Near Khyber Pass)
10. Gurdwara Banda Singh Bahadur (Meharauli, Near Post Office)

(B) *The Shrines surrendered by Disputed Sri Guru Singh Sabha their Site*

(1) Gurdwara Karol Bagh (Near Ajmal Khan Market)
2. Gurdwara Darya Ganj (Opposite Golcha Talkies)
3. Gurdwara Pipal Mahadev (Near Hauz Qazi Police Station)
4. Gurdwara Badarpur (Faridabad Road)
5. Gurdwara Dhaka Dhirpur (Nirankari Colony)
6. Gurdwara Pahari Dheeraj (Sadar Bazar, Old Delhi)

II. The Shrines Managed by Sri Guru Singh Sabha and their Site (each shrine is managed by separate body of Sri Guru Singh Sabha).

1. Gurdwara Sri Guru Singh Sabha, I-E/214, Lajpat Nagar, *New Delhi.*

2. Gurdwara Sri Guru Singh Sabha, Moti Nagar, *New Delhi.*

3. Gurdwara Sri Guru Singh Sabha, Lawrence Road, *New Delhi.*

4. Gurdwara Sri Guru Singh Sabha, Kirti Nagar, *New Delhi.*

5. Gurdwara Refugee Singh Sabha, Original Road, Karol Bagh, *New Delhi.*

6. Gurdwara Sri Guru Singh Sabha, Tilak Nagar, *New Delhi.*

7. Gurdwara Sri Guru Singh Sabha, DDA Colony, Kalkaji, *New Delhi.*

8. Gurdwara Sri Guru Singh Sabha, E-242, C, Greater Kailash, Part-I, *New Delhi.*

9. Gurdwara Sri Guru Singh Sabha, Malviya Nagar, *New Delhi.*

10. Gurdwara Sri Guru Singh Sabha, D Block, Janakpuri, *New Delhi.*

11. Gurdwara Sri Guru Singh Sabha, 'A' Pocket, Shalimar Bagh, *New Delhi.*

12. Gurdwara Sri Guru Singh Sabha, A-1/23, Paschimpuri, *New Delhi.*

13. Gurdwara Sri Guru Singh Sabha, 'C' Block, Janakpuri, *New Delhi.*

14. Gurdwara Sri Guru Singh Sabha, Nauroji Nagar, *New Delhi.*

15. Gurdwara Punjabi Satsang, Multani Dhanda, Gali No. 3, Pahar Ganj, *New Delhi.*

16. Gurdwara Sri Guru Singh Sabha, New Moti Nagar, 11/4, Punjabi Bagh, *New Delhi.*

17. Gurdwara Sri Guru Singh Sabha, Malviya Nagar Extension, *New Delhi.*